Football and Popular Culture

Football is ubiquitous and a permanent fixture of modern life. More than a sport, it frequently manifests in broader popular culture. This book examines the significance of football for, and in, popular culture across a wide range of forms, including music, film, and social media.

Football and Popular Culture plots a new path in Football Studies, drawing on original research in countries including England, Brazil, Germany, Canada, and Yugoslavia. The book includes both historical and contemporary perspectives, exploring some of the most important themes in the study of sport and culture, including identity, nationalism, fandom, and protest. It presents diverse case studies ranging from sonic violence among Brazilian *torcidas organizadas* to fan-led commemoration of the Munich air disaster, which together help us to better understand the intersection of sport, society, and popular culture.

This is fascinating reading for any student or researcher working in sport studies, cultural studies, media studies, sociology, or contemporary history.

Stephen R. Millar is Leverhulme Early Career Fellow in Ethnomusicology at Cardiff University, UK.

Martin J. Power is Senior Lecturer in Sociology at the University of Limerick, Republic of Ireland.

Paul Widdop is Senior Lecturer in Sport Business Management, Leeds Beckett University, UK.

Daniel Parnell is Senior Lecturer in Sport Business at the University of Liverpool, UK.

James Carr is Lecturer in Sociology at the University of Limerick, Republic of Ireland.

Critical Research in Football

Series Editors:

Pete Millward, Liverpool John Moores University, UK
Jamie Cleland, University of Southern Australia
Dan Parnell, University of Liverpool, UK
Stacey Pope, Durham University, UK
Paul Widdop, Leeds Beckett University, UK

The *Critical Research in Football* book series was launched in 2017 to showcase the inter- and multi-disciplinary breadth of debate relating to 'football'. The series defines 'football' as broader than association football, with research on rugby, Gaelic, and gridiron codes also featured. Including monographs, edited collections, short books, and textbooks, books in the series are written and/or edited by leading experts in the field whilst consciously also affording space to emerging voices in the area, and are designed to appeal to students and scholars who are interested in the range of disciplines in which critical research in football connects. The series is published in association with the *Football Collective*, www.footballcollective.org.uk.

Available in this series:

Politics, Ideology and Football Fandom
The Transformation of Modern Poland
Radosław Kossakowski, Przemysław Nosal and Wojciech Woźniak

The Development of Women's Soccer
Legacies, Participation and Popularity in Germany
Henk Erik Meier

Russia and the 2018 FIFA World Cup
Edited by Richard Arnold

Football and Popular Culture
Singing Out from the Stands
Edited by Stephen R. Millar, Martin J. Power, Paul Widdop, Daniel Parnell and James Carr

Football and Discrimination
Antisemitism and Beyond
Edited by Pavel Brunssen and Stefanie Schüler-Springorum

Football, Politics and Identity
James Carr, Daniel Parnell, Paul Widdop, Martin J. Power and Stephen R. Millar

https://www.routledge.com/sport/series/CFSFC

Football and Popular Culture

Singing Out from the Stands

Edited by
Stephen R. Millar, Martin J. Power,
Paul Widdop, Daniel Parnell and
James Carr

Routledge
Taylor & Francis Group
LONDON AND NEW YORK

First published 2021
by Routledge
2 Park Square, Milton Park, Abingdon, Oxon OX14 4RN

and by Routledge
52 Vanderbilt Avenue, New York, NY 10017

Routledge is an imprint of the Taylor & Francis Group, an informa business

British Library Cataloguing-in-Publication Data
A catalogue record for this book is available from the British Library

Library of Congress Cataloging-in-Publication Data
Names: Millar, Stephen R., editor. | Power, Martin J., editor. | Widdop, Paul, editor. | Parnell, Daniel, editor. | Carr, James, editor.
Title: Football and popular culture : singing out from the stands / edited by Stephen R. Millar, Martin J. Power, Paul Widdop, Daniel Parnell, and James Carr.
Subjects: LCSH: Soccer--Social aspects--Cross-cultural studies.
Classification: LCC GV943.9.S64 F647 2021 | DDC 796.334--dc23
LC record available at https://lccn.loc.gov/2020054013

ISBN: 978-0-367-43350-5 (hbk)
ISBN: 978-1-032-00648-2 (pbk)
ISBN: 978-1-003-00260-4 (ebk)

Typeset in Goudy
by SPi Global, India

Contents

List of Contributors vii
Preface ix

Introduction: Football and popular culture 1
STEPHEN R. MILLAR, MARTIN J. POWER, DANIEL PARNELL, PAUL WIDDOP AND JAMES CARR

PART I
Sound and violence in football culture **9**

1 Kicking metaphors of the body around in the mediation of self and other: conceptual metaphor in the *multimodal* construction of football songs and chants 11
SIMON MCKERRELL

2 'You call this democracy?': FC Saint Pauli supporters, football chants, and the police 25
MAX JACK

3 Sound, violence and gender performances in Brazilian football 39
PEDRO SILVA MARRA

4 Capital culture, political performance: listening to football in Ottawa 2014–2015 51
JORDAN ZALIS

PART II
Football and screen **69**

5 Kicking, not screaming: an examination of football (soccer) and female footballers in Australian screen-based narratives 71
FREYA WRIGHT-BROUGH AND LEE MCGOWAN

6 European cinema and the football film: 'Play for the people who've accepted you' 87
SEÁN CROSSON

7 Football, fantasy, film: cinema and the cultural politics of fans' imaginative investments in football stars 108
MARCUS FREE

PART III
Football and/as cultural identity **123**

8 Yugoslav football and British popular culture 1975–1991: from Petar Borota to 'Sexton's Lions' 125
DEJAN ZEC AND MILOŠ PAUNOVIĆ

9 Unwrapped: football fans and *The Anfield Wrap* 140
CIARÁN RYAN

10 The resuscitation of a babe: interrogating the fan-led virtual dedicatory practices of Duncan Edwards 154
GAYLE ROGERS

11 'What's he know about the Premier League?': football media and the perpetuated archetypes of 'Englishness' 170
JONATHAN CABLE

Index 186

Contributors

Jonathan Cable is Lecturer in Sport Journalism at the University of Gloucestershire, UK. His research interests lie in football culture, protest, and sport media.

Seán Crosson is Director of Graduate Research and Teaching in the Huston School of Film & Digital Media, Leader of the Sport & Exercise Research Group, and Co-Director of the MA Sports Journalism and Communication programme at NUI Galway, Ireland.

Marcus Free is Lecturer in Media and Communication Studies at Mary Immaculate College, University of Limerick, Ireland. His research interests include the interrelationships between sport, national identity, gender and race in film, print, and broadcast media.

Max Jack acquired his PhD in Ethnomusicology from the University of California, Santa Barbara, USA and is Visiting Lecturer in Social/Cultural Anthropology at Humboldt University of Berlin, Germany. Funded by the German Academic Exchange Service (DAAD), he conducted close to three years of field research in Ireland and Germany on hardcore football fans called ultras.

Pedro Silva Marra is Professor in the Communications and Media Department at Federal University of Espírito Santo (UFES), Brazil, where he teaches sound production on journalism and cinema in undergraduate courses. He leads the research group Ateliê de Sonoridades Urbanas (Urban Sonorities Atelier). His work on popular music, sound in urban cultures, sounds of football, sound and violence, and sound and political demonstrations can be found at: https://sonoridadesurbanas.com/.

Simon McKerrell is a Reader in Music and Society at the International Centre for Music Studies at Newcastle University, UK. He is Chair of the British Forum for Ethnomusicology as well as an expert performer of Highland-, Border- and Uilleann-pipes and has toured, taught, and performed throughout the world, and recorded 12 commercial albums. He is interested in the social impact of music and how this relates to policy.

Lee McGowan is a researcher, writer, and teacher. His primary research interests are in Football Studies, creative writing, and digital narratives. He is Senior Lecturer in Creative Writing at the University of the Sunshine Coast, Australia.

Miloš Paunović is Associate Researcher at CPES (Belgrade) and also teaches history in a private high school in Belgrade, Serbia. His main research interests cover the impact of British foreign policy and British culture on the former Yugoslav lands during the twentieth century. He is also interested in the relations between ex-Yugoslav/Balkan nations in the 1990s. He was one of the co-founders of the Centre for Sports Heritage (Belgrade).

Gayle Rogers works as a visual artist and manager of the Workers Gallery in the South Wales Valleys, UK, where she advocates for artist-led regeneration. Gayle's academic research considers the commemoration of her ancestor Duncan Edwards.

Ciarán Ryan is a member of the Department of Creative Arts, Media and Music at Dundalk Institute of Technology, Ireland.

Freya Wright-Brough is a researcher, teacher, and screen practitioner. She is a research assistant at both Queensland University of Technology and the University of the Sunshine Coast, Australia, and she lectures and tutors in screen at QUT. Her research focuses on ethical encounter in arts-based collaboration and screen practice. Freya has worked as a screenwriter for the Motion Picture Company in Sydney, Australia, and her digital narrative works such as the 24 Hour Writing Project and the 365 Day Challenge have been showcased at the National Young Writers Festival, Unleashed, TEDxQUT and more.

Jordan Zalis is a PhD candidate in ethnomusicology at Memorial University of Newfoundland. Recipient of the Helmut Kallmann Scholarship in Canadian Music (2016) and currently a doctoral fellow of the Social Sciences and Humanities Research Council of Canada, Jordan's research sits at the intersection of sound, music, sport, and society. Together with writing and performing experimental music (instrumental, ambient, noise-pop, punk rock, and rock n' roll), Jordan works in early American music, songbird jazz, and the cold blues. Jordan's ongoing doctoral project investigates the relationships between hip hop, basketball, and community building in Toronto.

Dejan Zec is a research assistant at Kedge Business School in Bordeaux, France, and Sustainability Research Institute at the University of Leeds, UK. The focus of his research is on social history and everyday life, especially history of sports, physical activity, and leisure. In more recent years he developed interest in researching history of healthcare and well-being, social dynamics, and trust in the field of healthcare, as well as concepts of sustainability and social responsibility. He is member of the editorial board of *The International Journal of the History of Sport*.

Preface

In February 2016, a group of scholars working across a range of disciplines founded the Football Collective.[1] Responding to real and tangible issues in academia, such as social isolation, limited departmental support, and increasing demands in relation to teaching and learning and research, the Collective established a network to support those working on football-related research. The Football Collective held its inaugural conference at FC United of Manchester's Broadhurst Park in November 2016. Here, ideas were shared, friendships formed, and collaborations kicked off, which included securing the host for the 2017 conference in Ireland.

The Football Collective's second annual conference was hosted by the Popular Music and Popular Culture Research Cluster, at the University of Limerick, and focused on the overarching theme of *Football, Politics, and Popular Culture*. The conference organisers James Carr, Martin Power, and Stephen Millar hosted a global cohort of guests in November 2017. The meeting was memorable both for the quality and scope of research presented and, crucially, for the development of important social and academic connections. Conversations between strangers grew into collaborations with colleagues and, ultimately, led to the formulation of this book and its stablemate, *Football, Politics, and Identity*.

In 2017, the Football Collective launched the *Critical Research in Football* book series to showcase the inter- and multidisciplinary breadth of debate relating to 'football'. Thus far, the series has attracted considerable interest from global football scholars. The range of topics is vast, including fandom, consumption, fiction, history, migration, medicine, legacy, politics, activism, and events. Indeed, the series is steadily becoming a go-to place for football scholars to publish their research. Books in the series are written and/or edited by leading experts in the field, while consciously also affording space to emerging voices in the area. They are designed to appeal to students and scholars interested in the range of disciplines in which critical research in football connects.

1 The Football Collective's founding members were John Hayton, Peter Millward, Jamie Cleland, Joel Rookwood, Mark Doidge, Danny Fitzpatrick, Anthony May, John Hughson, Paul Widdop, and Daniel Parnell. For more information about the Football Collective, visit https://footballcollective.org.uk.

Introduction

Football and popular culture

Stephen R. Millar, Martin J. Power, Daniel Parnell, Paul Widdop and James Carr

In the past three decades, the academic study of football has grown exponentially. From its origins in sociology and criminology, Football Studies has emerged as a confident, self-reflexive, and multidisciplinary field in its own right. Seminal studies on hooliganism (Taylor 1971; Ingham et al. 1978; Dunning et al. 1988; Armstrong and Harris 1991; Giulianotti et al. 1994; Giulianotti 1995; Armstrong 1999), subcultural aesthetics (Redhead 1993), and nationalism (Bairner 2001), have been joined by important contributions on globalisation (Sandvoss 2003; Giulianotti and Robertson 2009), regional identity (Gehrmann 1997; Armstrong and Mitchell 2008), fandom (Dixon 2016; Brooks 2019; Irak 2019; Hodges 2020; Kossakowski et al. 2020), and the promotion of health and well-being (Ekblom 1994; Krustrup and Parnell 2019), as well as those continuing the field's initial focus on social disorder and violence (Dunning et al. 2002; Sugden 2006; Testa and Armstrong 2010; Pearson 2012; Spaaij and Testa 2017; Newson et al. 2018, Newson 2019). And despite an initial focus on Europe and South America, important ethnographic work has now been carried out across the globe. Yet, while the two are deeply connected, football's connection to popular culture remains underexplored.

Putting football and popular culture in context

Although cultures differ considerably, they all have common components, norms, values, symbols, and language, which 'characterize a society or social groups within that society' (Marsh and Keating 2006: 20). Indeed, culture and society are said to be so closely interwoven that Giddens argues, somewhat paradoxically, that 'no cultures could exist without societies. But equally, no societies could exist without culture' (1997: 18). Many sociologists see the culture of modern societies as being 'differentiated and fragmented', while others argue that contemporary societies still possess a core/hegemonic (and increasingly global) 'culture or "ideology"' which is generally accepted by everyone within that society (Marsh and Keating 2006: 20).

The specific activities which we traditionally associate with 'culture' include classical music, literature, painting, and sculpture. Yet this limited view of 'culture', which 'concentrates on the intellectual aspects of a civilization', has facilitated an understanding which creates a clear distinction between what is perceived to be 'high culture with enduring aesthetic merit' and popular culture, which is understood as a mere 'commercial product with little aesthetic merit' (Ibid.). Indeed, in their work on the culture industry, Theodore Adorno and Max Horkheimer argued that capitalist production methods deliberately produced an artificial division between 'high' and 'low' culture because it masked the transactional relationship between the two (Adorno and Horkheimer 1997: 135).

However, many in the academy and beyond use the term 'popular culture' to 'designate cultural patterns that are widespread among a society's population' (Macionis 2018: 100). Popular culture enables diverse masses of people to 'identify collectively'. Moreover, it provides people with a chance to modify the 'prevailing sentiments and norms of behaviour' (Delaney 2007). Indeed, the British cultural theorist Stuart Hall (2009: 122–123) argued that popular culture was a mechanism where 'collective social understandings are created' and where the 'politics of signification' are deployed to influence how individuals see the world.

For decades, disciplines across the arts, humanities, and social sciences have advanced their shared interest in the critical analysis of popular culture and the elucidation of its social meaning, significance, and material impact. Theoretically, this body of work has interrogated the potential of popular culture to promote and foreclose alternative or hegemonic frameworks of understanding within the public consciousness, analysing creative processes and outputs in terms of the social, political, and historical moment in which popular culture is produced and disseminated – particularly within critical reception theory frameworks and fandom studies – as a means of appreciating consumption as a form of prosumption and creation. In essence, this vast body of work has broadened discussions of the role that popular culture plays in shaping and (re)defining our understandings of how societies operate (see Storey 2015 for an excellent overview of these ideas).

Within his conception of the culture industry, Adorno focused on the status of popular music(s) in particular. He stated that pop music was 'important as a socially communicative object and dialectic product', but because pop was seen as a "'low' cultural form it lacked philosophical and academic examination' (Brett 2011: 172). He could just as easily have been making that very same argument about football. If one accepts Raymond Williams's definition of popular culture as 'a particular way of life' (1985: 91), one could say that football *is* popular culture. And just as it is necessary to demonstrate the 'dialectic links between the social production of music and its aesthetic qualities' (Adorno 1989: 426, cited in Brett 2011: 172), we argue that it is necessary to do likewise with football and popular culture.

While versions of football have been played across the world since ancient times,[1] both football and popular culture as we know it today were shaped by important sociocultural and political processes during the British Industrial Revolution, which saw the creation of a new working class with its own rituals, rites, and traditions. The period saw working-class men fight for, and gain, the right to vote, panicking some social commentators who feared their newfound position would have corrosive effects on the sociocultural makeup of Britain. This was perhaps best illustrated by Matthew Arnold's 1869 *Culture and Anarchy* (2006), which attempted to distinguish between a 'high culture' associated with social elites and popular culture consumed by the masses. Yet football had a foot in both camps.

Football had a long history and association with the English peasantry, who played a rough version of the game we know now (Andrews 2013: 12). The moral panics associated with modern 'hooliganism' had their historical equivalents and both the British crown and Parliament legislated against football on the grounds that it was a violent and corruptive practice. Yet this working-class game was taken up by English public schools in the nineteenth century, who would in turn popularise the game throughout the world by taking it to Britain's colonies across the globe. Here, football, among other sports, served both as a means to entertain those stationed in far-flung imperial outposts and in the projection of British soft power, which helped inculcate notions of British 'fair play' (Besnier et al. 2018: 55). Yet, as important as the empire was in helping to spread football throughout Britain's colonies, trade connections and educational networks played an even greater role in the global spread of football, from Scottish artisans in Sweden, to English schools in Germany and British sailors operating in Italy and Brazil (Giulianotti 2000: 8).

The chapters in this book concern themselves with football and/as/in popular culture. Although such themes have been considered in relation to particular teams (see, for example, Bradley 2004; Esplin and Walker 2007), *Football and Popular Culture* is the first volume to explore the multifaceted nature of football and/is/in popular culture through multiple case sites across the world.

Structure, content, and themes

Drawing on perspectives from film studies to sociology, and from psychoanalysis to ethnomusicology, *Football and Popular Culture* presents case studies from across Europe, the Americas, and Australia written by a range of academics, artists, and activists from a wide variety of countries. The chapters encompass a range of topics in both established areas of study as well as emerging areas of scholarship and will appeal to a wide range of disciplines. This interdisciplinary collection of essays extends across and beyond the social sciences, with each author offering new theoretical and applied contributions to the growing critical literature in Football Studies.

The book is divided into three sections exploring football's connection to sound, screen, and cultural identity. Building on work carried out in the UK, Germany, Brazil, and Canada, Part I focuses on the role of football songs and chants in constructing social distance and the role of sound in the reproduction of football-related violence more broadly.

Simon McKerrell kicks things off with his chapter on conceptual metaphor in the multimodal construction of football songs and chants. McKerrell sees football and music as deeply embodied practices that share a similar orientation within the academy, not least because of their principal focus on the non-textual. He argues for greater attention to the metaphorical and somatic discourse of songs, chants, and tunes about football as a way reveal the agency of our bodies. McKerrell maintains that everyday cultural expressions of Self and Other should be at the centre of disciplinary understandings of society, gender, race, and politics because of both their ubiquity and what they communicate about our socially constructed embodied lives.

From the UK, we turn to Germany, where Max Jack's chapter focuses on the hardcore fan group, Ultras Saint Pauli (USP), and the role crowd performance plays as a form of collective communication. Drawing on fieldwork carried out alongside USP ultras, Jack explores USP's sonic and visual displays, highlighting the cyclical relationship between these ultras and the German police, arguing that violence forms a mutually beneficial and consensually antagonistic relationship between the two.

Pedro Marra's chapter on the power of violent football chants in Brazil builds upon Jack's German case study as well as similar ethnomusicological work carried out by Herrera (2018) in Argentina. Marra shows how, when sung collectively, football chants contribute to the formation of particular masculinities, encouraging homophobia and physical violence that would be unacceptable in other contexts. Marra's self-reflexivity in relation to the performance of homophobic chants is particularly interesting and speaks to criticisms of seminal studies of football subcultures that have omitted such awkward realities (Hughson 1998: 49).

The final chapter in this section focuses on the invention of a new musical tradition in Ottawa, Canada. Drawing on fieldwork conducted with two supporters' groups of Ottawa Fury FC, Jordan Zalis explores how the Stony Monday Riot and the Bytown Boys Supporters Club successfully lobbied the club's owners to cease broadcasting pre-recorded music and allow fans to develop new sonic traditions. In so doing, Zalis explores the intersections of tradition, position, and place in Ottawa's football stadium and the plurality of experience and meaning that accompanies this negotiation of space.

Part II explores the politics of representation in football films and television shows. The section begins with a chapter on the representation of female footballers on screen in Australia, in which Freya Wright-Brough and Lee McGowan contextualise contemporary Australian football shows within a framework that has, historically, been hostile towards women. Using case studies drawn from three female-focused football television programmes, Wright-Brough and McGowan discuss changing themes and aesthetics among female football fiction and how these have developed and matured over time.

This chapter is followed by Seán Crosson's excellent exploration of football in European cinema. Here Crosson highlights the comparative gap in depictions of sport cinema in Europe, as compared to the United States, before excavating the subgenre of European football films. In responding to larger developments, both within specific European countries and the continent more broadly, Crosson argues that football films have served as a barometer of changing cultural values and concerns since the early twentieth century.

Deploying concepts from object relations psychoanalysis, Marcus Free's chapter critically examines films that portray football fans' psychic investments in two individual players – Diego Maradona and Eric Cantona. Here, Free explores the tensions between the status of the player as a potentially de-contextualised, narcissistic extension of the self and a potential symbol of collective identity, solidarity, and political resistance.

The final part of the book turns towards football and/as cultural identity. Although important work has already been carried out in area of popular culture (see Brown 1998; Armstrong and Giulianotti 1999), this section adds new contributions in the areas of subcultural production, digital fan media, online heritage, and debates around Englishness. Dejan Zec and Miloš Paunović's chapter begins by sketching out western cultural influence in Eastern Europe during the early twentieth century, before focusing on the consumption of British football culture in the Socialist Federal Republic of Yugoslavia. Here, the authors provide a fascinating insight into how subcultures operating in Yugoslavia used football as a means to resist against the prevailing power structures that frustrated political organisation via more traditional routes.

Ciarán Ryan's chapter focuses on issues pertaining to long-distance fandom, exploring how social media has assumed the role once occupied by fanzines in connecting supporters and clubs. Centring on the Liverpool FC-focused *The Anfield Wrap* (TAW), Ryan examines how this podcast and its website negotiate the boundaries between fandom and commerce, exploring notions of authenticity in relation to LFC fandom and how this inflects listeners linguistically, through international audiences' adoption of Liverpool vernacular.

The penultimate chapter expands the theme of long-distance fandom to incorporate the long-deceased. Focusing on those killed in the 1958 Munich air disaster, Gayle Rogers explores fan-led dedicatory practices, both online and offline, through the prism of Manchester United and England legend Duncan Edwards. Through interviews with fan curators, Rogers, herself a relative of Edwards, examines the commemorative practices used by fans both to curate the legacy of Edwards and the Busby Babes, as well as to legitimise their own role in the process.

The book closes by revisiting notions of Englishness in football. However, where earlier studies focused on the changing composition of England's national team (see for example Back et al. 2001), Jonathan Cable directs his focus on more recent attacks on the management of English Premier League clubs as symbolic of their role as cultural custodians, which he connects to nostalgia for an earlier form of myth-based nationalism.

***

Football is more than a sport and frequently manifests in broader popular culture. From the sonic construction of atmosphere to cinematic explorations of the cultural politics of football, football is ubiquitous and a permanent fixture of modern life. Taken together, *Football and Popular Culture* plots a new path in Football Studies, while paying homage to important work that has led us to this point.

That said, it is important to acknowledge those aspects of football and popular culture not included in the book. *Football and Popular Culture* does not contain any discussion of football-related videogames, trading cards, or gambling, each of which has its own (sub)cultures, codes, and traditions (see, for example, Crawford 2006; Reershemius 2019; Owonikoko 2020). Nevertheless, by drawing together voices from across the academy and beyond, we feel *Football and Popular Culture* succeeds in marshalling important discussions from a range of disciplinary perspectives across the world to further the growing field of Football Studies.

Note

1 For an excellent overview of football's origins, see Giulianotti (2000).

Bibliography

Adorno, T. 1989. *Introduction to the Sociology of Music*, trans. E. B. Ashton. New York: Continuum.

Adorno, T. and M. Horkheimer. 1997. *Dialectic of Enlightenment*, trans. John Cumming. New York: Continuum.

Andrews, I.S. 2013. 'It's a Man's Game: English Football and Socio-Cultural Change'. Unpublished PhD thesis, London School of Economics and Political Science.

Armstrong, G. 1999. *Football Hooligans: Knowing the Score*. Oxford: Berg.

Armstrong G. and R. Giulianotti. 1999. *Football Cultures and Identities*. London: MacMillan.

Armstrong, G. and R. Harris. 1991. 'Football Hooligans: Theory and Evidence'. *Sociological Review*, 39(3): 427–458.

Armstrong, G. and J. Mitchell. 2008. *Global and Local Football: Politics and Europeanization on the Fringes of the EU*. Abingdon, Oxon: Routledge.

Arnold, M. 2006. *Culture and Anarchy*, edited by J. Garnett. Oxford: Oxford University Press (originally published 1869).

Back, L., T. Crabbe, and J. Solomos. 2001. *The Changing Face of Football: Racism, Identity and Multiculture in the English Game*. Oxford: Berg.

Bairner, A. 2001. *Sport, Nationalism, and Globalization*. Albany, NY: State University of New York Press.

Besnier, N., S. Brownell, and T.F. Carter. 2018 *The Anthropology of Sport: Bodies, Borders, Biopolitics*. Oakland, CA: University of California Press.

Bradley, J. 2004. *Celtic Minded: Essays on Religion, Politics, Society, Identity and Football*. Glendaruel: Argyll.

Brett, R. 2011. 'Moz: art: Adorno Meets Morrissey in the Cultural Divisions'. In *Morrissey: Fandom, Representations and Identities*, edited by E. Devereux, A. Dillane, and M. Power. Bristol: Intellect.

Brooks, O. 2019. *Football, Fandom and Consumption*. Abingdon, Oxon: Routledge.

Brown, A. 1998. *Fanatics: Power, Identity and Fandom in Football*. London: Routledge.

Crawford, G. 2006. 'The Cult of Champ Man: The Culture and Pleasures of Championship Manager/Football Manager Gamers'. *Information, Communication & Society*, 9(4): 496-514.

Delaney, T. 2007. 'Pop Culture: An Overview'. *Philosophy Now*, 64: https://philosophynow.org/issues/64/Pop_Culture_An_Overview

Dixon, K. 2016. 'Fandom'. In *Studying Football*, edited by E. Cashmore and K. Dixon, Abingdon, Oxon: Routledge.

Dunning, E., P. Murphy, and J. Williams. 1988. *The Roots of Football Hooliganism: An Historical and Sociological Study*. Abingdon, Oxon: Routledge.

Dunning, E., P. Murphy, I. Waddington, and A.E. Astrinakis. 2002. *Fighting Fans: Football Hooliganism as a World Phenomenon*. Dublin: University College Dublin Press.

Ekblom, B. 1994. *Football (Soccer)*. Oxford: Blackwell Scientific.

Esplin R. and G. Walker. 2007. *It's Rangers for Me? New Perspectives on a Scottish Institution.* Ayr: Fort.

Gehrmann, S. 1997. *Football and Regional Identity in Europe*. New Brunswick, NJ: Transaction Publishers.

Giddens, A. (ed.) 1997. *Sociology: Introductory Readings*, Cambridge: Polity Press.

Giulianotti, R., N. Bonney, and M. Hepworth. 1994. *Football, Violence and Social Identity*. London: Routledge.

Giulianotti, R. 1995. 'Participant Observation and Research into Football Hooliganism: Reflections on the Problems of Entree and Everyday Risks'. *Sociology of Sport Journal*, 12(1): 1–20.

Giulianotti, R. 2000. *Football: A Sociology of the Global Game*. Cambridge: Polity.

Giulianotti, R. and R. Robertson. 2009. *Globalisation and Football.* London: Sage.

Hall, S. 2009. 'The Rediscovery of Ideology: The Return of the Repressed in Media Studies'. In *Cultural Theory and Popular Culture: A Reader*, edited by J. Storey, 4th edn, Harlow: Pearson Education.

Herrera, E. 2018. 'Masculinity, Violence, and Deindividuation in Argentine Soccer Chants: The Sonic Potentials of Participatory Sounding-in-Synchrony'. *Ethnomusicology*, 62(3):470-499.

Hodges, A. 2020. *Fan Activism, Protest and Politics: Ultras in Post-Socialist Croatia.* Abingdon, Oxon: Routledge.

Hughson, J. 1998. 'Among the Thugs: The "New Ethnographies" of Football Supporting Subcultures'. *International Review of the Sociology of Sport*, 33(1): 43–57.

Irak, D. 2019. *Football Fandom, Protest and Democracy: Supporter Activism in Turkey*. Abingdon, Oxon: Routledge.

Ingham, R., S. Hall, J. Clarke, P. Marsh, and J. Donovan. 1978. *Football Hooliganism: The Wider Context*. London: Inter-Action Inprint.

Kossakowski, R., P. Nosal, and W. Woźniak (eds.) 2020. *Politics, Ideology and Football Fandom: The Transformation of Modern Poland*. Abingdon, Oxon: Routledge.

Krustrup, P. and D. Parnell (eds.) 2019. *Football as Medicine: Prescribing Football for Global Health Promotion*. Abingdon, Oxon: Routledge.

Macionis, J. 2018. *Sociology*. Harlow: Pearson.

Marsh, I. and Keating, M. 2006. *Sociology: Making Sense of Society*. Harlow: Pearson.

Newson, M., T. Bortolini, M. Buhrmester, S. R. da Silva, J.N.Q. da Aquino, and H. Whitehouse. 2018. 'Brazil's Football Warriors: Social Bonding and Inter-Group Violence', *Evolution and Human Behavior*, 39(6): 675–683.

Newson, M. 2019. 'Football, Fan Violence, and Identity Fusion'. *International Review for the Sociology of Sport*, 54(4): 431–444.

Owonikoko, S.B. 2020. 'Game of Hope; Game of Addiction: Rising Football Betting Among Nigerian Youths and Its Implications for Peace, Security and Stability'. *Soccer & Society*, 21(7): 821–833.

Pearson, G. 2012. *An Ethnography of English Football Fans*. Manchester: Manchester University Press.

Redhead, S. 1993. *The Passion and the Fashion: Football Fandom in New Europe*. Aldershot: Avebury.
Reershemius, G. 2019. 'Lamppost Networks: Stickers as a Genre in Urban Semiotic Landscapes'. *Social Semiotics*, 29(5): 622–644.
Sandvoss, C. 2003. A *Game of Two Halves: Football, Television and Globalisation*. London: Routledge.
Spaaij, R. and Testa, A. 2017. 'Football Hooliganism'. In *Routledge Handbook of Football Studies*, edited by J. Hughson, K. Moore, R. Spaaij, and J. Maguire. Abingdon, Oxon: Routledge.
Storey, J. (ed.) 2015. *Cultural Theory and Popular Culture: An Introduction*, 7th edn, Harlow: Pearson Education.
Sugden J. 2006. 'Teaching and Playing Sport for Conflict Resolution and Co-Existence in Israel'. *International Review for the Sociology of Sport*, 41(2):221–240.
Taylor, I. 1971. 'Football Mad – A Speculative Sociology of Soccer Hooliganism. In *The Sociology of Sport*, edited by E. Dunning. London: Cass.
Testa, A. and G. Armstrong 2010. *Football, Fascism and Fandom: The UltraS of Italian Football*. London: A&C Black.
Williams, R. 1985. *Keywords: A Vocabulary of Culture and Society*. New York: Oxford University Press.

Part I

Sound and violence in football culture

Chapter 1

Kicking metaphors of the body around in the mediation of self and other

Conceptual metaphor in the *multimodal* construction of football songs and chants

Simon McKerrell

Introduction

This chapter focuses in on the social semiotics of belonging where football and music collide; both human activities that are at once embodied, emotionally powerful and yet, until recently, historically marginal to academic research. The turning of our attention towards football (and concomitantly to the musical life of football) is now understood not as marginal or tangential to our lives, but indeed, as areas that are often crucial to our sense of Self, identity, belonging and, critically, to our understanding of our Others. This volume, and this chapter, sit within an ongoing discourse within Anglo-American scholarship that has licensed the critical, sociological and anthropological understanding of everyday lives that began (on British soil) with the outputs of the Birmingham School of Raymond Williams and Dick Hebdige amongst others, continued to grow based on the critical insights of authors such as Pierre Bourdieu and Max Weber, and has in this particular field developed a social constructivist view of the symbolic significance and discursive agency based upon the contributions of Harry Edwards, Jay Coakley and Richard Giulianotti. But beyond this emergence of the legitimacy of sport and vernacular culture more widely, research after the post-modernism of the last century has significantly prioritized the importance of our affective lives, and how we feel about ourselves and behave towards others.

What is striking about the emergence of both the sociology of sport and various '-ologies' of music is the gradual appearance and acceptance of the significance of the body. Since the turn of the century the previously quite singular scholarly discourses about the body, often focused on the extreme or licentious capacity for physical hedonism, have been shaken off, and the move to more serious engagement with embodiment has been growing across many disciplines scientific, artistic and humane. This recognises the important social and foundational somatic aspects of our behaviour on or about our bodies across many domains of life. Today, there is widespread acknowledgement across many disciplines that our somatic Selves are not only fundamental to understanding the relationship(s) between our bodies and our minds, but that our somatic understanding is also crucial to understanding how we feel about others and our sense of identity and belonging. This embodied turn (see Shilling 2012), in the social life of music has been grounded in key contributions from Richard Shusterman (1999, 2008, 2012), Mark Johnson (2007) and, at the more cognitive end, from contributions about the science of embodied cognition from Godøy and Leman (2009), Sloboda (2005) and Zbikowski (2009). Both football and music depend in a visceral way on our ability to feel through our bodies. What this means for everyday culture is that our bodies are not simply present at the match, or with our friends, but that we take part in football and singing as embodied action, where our sense of Self is grounded not only in our emotional attachment to the club or game, but where we literally 'feel' our sense of belonging through mirror neurons and a thousand small acts of embodied cognition as fans. Enhanced (as in all things), when we sing together, to experience a sense of somatic connectedness that literally *moves us*, we can examine through phenomenological experience, but also, as in this chapter, in the social semiotic analysis of our collective use of metaphor, language and music.

I believe that most forms of communal belonging, identity and social conflict are grounded in our bodies. One of the best ways of studying this is to examine the ways people talk and sing about football (or any other collective group activity or social phenomenon). This usually emerges in the multimodal discourse that we use every day, and that is a powerful analytical tool to consider the hidden social relations and somatic foundations of our relationships with other people in things like football songs. Mark Johnson articulates it more powerfully when he suggests that:

> The key to my entire argument is that meaning is not just what is consciously entertained in acts of feeling and thought; instead, meaning reaches deep down into our corporeal encounter with our environment … [and] most theories of meaning focus exclusively on the conceptual-propositional skeletal structures of meaning, while entirely overlooking the emotional flesh and blood of actual human meaning.
>
> (2007, 25, 53)

Conceptual metaphor and the body

A conceptual metaphor is a widely understood concept from cognitive linguistics where one domain of human activity is understood in terms of another. The importance of conceptual metaphor, as Lakoff and Johnson (1980) first showed, is that they are not just linguistic structures whereby one thing is understood as another. For example, in relation to football, examples of common metaphors might include, a 'penalty shootout' or 'they've smashed their own record'. Metaphors reveal much more about the way we think and how we structure our understanding of the world. Understanding how these metaphors manifest themselves in everyday communication is therefore one of the key ways in which we can understand how we structure our social interactions.

Lakoff and Johnson's key idea is that metaphor underlies almost all meaning through its ability to map from one domain onto another founded upon embodied sensorimotor knowledge in the form of conceptual metaphors and image schemata. A conceptual metaphor is a cognitive mapping between two different domains. Lakoff proposed most recently that primary conceptual metaphors relate to our early experience and involve basic bodily feelings. Thus, primary metaphors include up–down; warm–cold; where warmth is mapped onto 'up' and cold is mapped to 'down', giving us the ability to discuss temperatures rising and falling and to understand how others are feeling too. 'Conceptual metaphor' is essentially therefore the neural means by which these basic image-schemata are mapped between domains. Thus, AFFECTION-IS-WARMTH is one of the key conceptual metaphors that occur in many languages. Lakoff and Johnson (1999) also suggest that primary metaphors such as MORE-IS-UP are potentially universal across cultures although not always linguistically expressed. In fact the 'verticality metaphor' they convincingly show permeates much of our thinking: HAPPY IS UP, SAD IS DOWN (e.g. 'I'm feeling low, I'm in high spirits' etc.); HIGH STATUS IS UP, LOW STATUS IS DOWN (e.g. she's at the peak of her career, he's climbing the ladder'.

Elsewhere, in social semiotics, Van Leeuwen (1999) theorised the sense of spatial metaphor through the volume, timbre and aural perspective of the voice. Other scholars such as Dockwray and Moore (2010) established the 'diagonal mix' and the sound box for notions of spatiality in recorded music. Zbikowski has similarly theorised the sense of social intimacy through a semiotic reading of the interacting modes of text, rhythm and chords/melody to demonstrate how singers can produce an aural sense of intimacy or social distance (2009). Ian Cross (2011) emphasises the rhythmical synchronisation of the focused attention of group of people to enable participants to align their sense of time together to produce a sense of shared purpose (entrainment), and Johnson (2007) and Shusterman (2008) have also made significant contributions to a somatic and embodied approach to understanding perception and musical metaphor. I have introduced the concept of *tonal gravity* as a means to describe the underlying metaphor for semiotic space in the musical mode (McKerrell 2015).

This chapter makes use of Lakoff and Johnson's insights, which have been adapted in many fields, and combines them with the theory of conceptual metaphor developed by Kövecses (2010) alongside an interdisciplinary analytical framework broadly configured for a social semiotics of music developed by Van Leeuwen (1999, 2004), Johnson and Larson (2003) and others such as Machin (2010), Machin and Richardson (2012) and Zbikowski (2009). The power of this approach is that it emphasises metaphor as a means of explaining the structure of communication, and how metaphor can reveal the social life of communication, whether that be on or off the pitch.[1]

In a social semiotic approach to communication, we all use different 'modes' of communication, and a mode is usually understood as a socio-cultural channel of communication such as talk, written text, gesture, image (both still and moving) or musical sound, etc. Scholars of social semiotics regard all communication as socially situated, and this is a very powerful way of thinking about music. When one begins to consider football songs as acts of socially embedded communication, they reveal analytic potential that goes far beyond the more simplistic notions of song as a sonic object or as a static text. Furthermore, almost all communication is multimodal; our verbal communication is almost always accompanied by gesture and visual communication, songs are inherently multimodal as they involve both words and music, almost all social media is nowadays multimodal because of the ubiquity of image alongside text (and indeed, sound too). This has consequences for how we understand the world, and how we understand sporting communities as well as any other community of practice or sense of group identities founded in shared participation.

Football is rich with multimodal communication: football is most often consumed via the television, with both moving images and commentary providing a rich stream of communicative detail for fans, and indeed, now further enhanced by the interactivity of the 'red button' on our smart televisions. Our interactions online and face to face are almost exclusively multimodal in that we use text and talk, images and video, all saturated with the rich symbology of club colours, emblems and other socially agreed signs of belonging. Football players also regularly employ multimodal metaphors on the pitch: Think of the striker who kisses or holds up their club badge on their shirt after scoring a goal; the metaphor has no words, but the gesture of love and belonging to the club are effortlessly understood by fans of any age. Or the gesture appeals to referees that signify (often manufactured) indignation against a decision – again, no words here are necessary, but we share a social canon of human gesture that allow us to read the meaning of gestures.

Metaphor and football

In football, my analysis suggests there are several key conceptual metaphors that structure thinking about the game and our social relationship with other people that we identify with (the in-group or social Self) and the opposite side (the out-group, or collective Other). In most football songs, I suggest that the home club, or social group of the fans, is understood through the Centre-Periphery metaphor, where CENTRE-IS-SELF and this is expressed through various spatial and musical concepts in song. The other key organising metaphors in football in my analysis include FOOTBALL-IS-WAR, OTHER-AS-DISEASED and the universal verticality metaphor, HIGH-IS-GOOD, summarised here:

Source	*Target*
WAR	FOOTBALL (ALL BALL GAMES)
CENTRE-MARGIN	SELF-OTHER
DISEASE	THE OTHER AS DISEASED
VERTICALITY	HIGH IS GOOD

At first listen, much of the language of football employs metaphors when we talk about 'attack' or 'defence'. Strikers 'shoot', players can be 'caught in the crossfire' or 'pierce the defence'. Much of the action is described through the language of war which goes further than simple metaphorical use of terms such as 'shoot' and 'defence' to include more subtle metaphors such as 'close range pass' where the spatiality of the pitch is understood as the spatiality of the battlefield. Managers and players talk about 'tactics' too, which is set within a context of what I term *the primeval battle* between two directly opposing teams, that stands in directly for a metaphor for the Self and Other. The primeval battle is a clear battle, unobscured by the normal complexities of multiple actors, layered and mythologized identities, invented histories, misattributed intentions, unequal agency and general ethical mud of *real* human conflict. The primeval battle involves only two, cleanly defined identities: the collective Self, and the collective Other – perfectly modelled in the home and opposition football teams. This simplicity of purpose and identity is one of the key attractions to the social belonging of a football club. Indeed, Manchester City have a Latin motto, 'Superbia in proelia', meaning 'pride in battle'; a metaphor well-recognised in the game and amongst fans.

One of the great football songs in Britain was the Chaz and Dave hit, 'Ossie's Dream', which reached no. 5 in the UK charts in 1981.[2] The song directly compares Tottenham Hotspur with an army going into battle at Wembley and is framed around Tottenham's Argentinean player Osvaldo Ardiles ('Ossie'). Lyrically, the song demonstrates clarity of belonging; the 'We' of this song are the Tottenham Hotspur fans. The collective Other will be the opposing team who qualify for the final, as yet unknown, but guaranteed to be opposed in the primeval battle of Self and Other. In the song, the protagonist 'Ossie' is reimagined, as are the football team, as an 'army' that are 'marching off to war' to 'capture the cup'. The Tottenham Hotspur manager at the time, Keith Burkenshaw, is referenced as 'General Burkenshaw' who is leading the team, which is described both as an army, and at one point as 'Keithy's soldiers'. Lyrically, the song is an unambiguous recasting of the FOOTBALL-IS-WAR metaphor, supported both in the martial language of the lyrical content but also through the use of the tune.

The tune amplifies the signification of the lyrical content, drawing as it does upon the globally popular melody known by many different names such as 'the conga tune', 'Cuban Pete's song' and many others, but which Gustavo Pérez Firmat (2008) suggests can be thought of as one of the most popular 'Latunes': Latin melodies that have been popularized and given English lyrics. The tune was made popular and reinforces the militaristic metaphor, through its setting as 'I came, I saw, I conga'd' by Edmundo Ros in 1941 (itself yet another historically thick intertextual reference to the popular mythologization of the Roman emperor Caesar's 'Veni, Vidi, Vici'!). The characteristic and emphatic tune has appeared right across Anglophone and Lusophone cultural materials for decades, including appearances in *Strike up the Band* with Judy Garland, as an advertising melody to sell 'Cosifit' nappies, and even sung by Rachel in the ubiquitous 1990s

American sitcom *Friends*. It has a long and wide history like many catchy melodies in football chants and songs. The basic contour and rhythm of the opening bars of the song (the 'incipit' for musicologists) is used for football chants by teams including West Ham United, Rangers Football Club and many, many others. Therefore, both the lyrical content and the contextualisation and re-contextualisation of the melody used for this song support the analysis of the FOOTBALL-IS-WAR metaphor.

The song, 'the Billy Boys', is one of the most viscerally offensive football songs; it invokes a frame of war in the conceptual metaphor, and through the gestures associated with the performance of the song. The song is sung by Rangers Football Club supporters and deals with direct historical references to their Glaswegian rivalry with Celtic Football Club. The 'Billy Boys' were

> a violent, Protestant, and proto-fascist street gang, based in the East End of Glasgow, that violently opposed Irish-Catholic immigration. Named after the protestant King William – 'King Billy' – it was led by Billy Fullerton and was active during the 1920s and 1930s.
>
> (Millar 2015)

The song is not only used by Rangers fans, but also is regularly used on Orange marches in the West of Scotland and Northern Ireland and is thereby directly sectarian both in lyrical content and in the performative context. Indeed, Rangers Football Club and UEFA ordered that the song be banned in 2006, but it has continued to appear at matches and been implicated in various legal cases surrounding offensive and hate speech cases in Scotland since that time. The lyrics themselves make direct reference to the killing of Irish-Catholic Scots:

> Hello, Hello,
> We are the Billy Boys,
> Hello, Hello,
> You'll know us by our noise,
> We're up to our knees in Fenian blood,
> Surrender or you'll die,
> For we are the Bridgeton Billy Boys

In this football song, the words are clearly divisive at the surface level, invoking images of blood for 'Fenians' who are clearly identified through the local chain of assumptions as Catholic, Celtic Football Club supporters (see Millar [2015] for a more detailed historical understanding of the song, and Goodall et al. [2015] for more detailed ethnographic examples of this interpretation). Musically too, the rising tune at the start of the song indicates a form of assertiveness where the group identity is established. However, this sonic material is sometimes combined in the football stadium with gestures by Rangers fans pointing at their socks in the stands, often thought to represent the phrase 'up to our knees in Fenian blood' in the Billy Boys song. All this symbology and discourse aims to construct a total dominance over the Other in a war. These songs are often combined by Rangers fans with other non-textual signifiers of dominance and conflict with the Celtic fans, such as the use of adapted flags indicating dominance of the 'Irish-Catholic' Other of the Celtic supporter, or the colours of Orange and Blue, historically associated with Protestantism and its dominant place in the West of Scotland. Celtic fans also have their own repertoire of war-related discourses when Othering Rangers football fans. Celtic fans use the term 'huns' to label Rangers supporters, which collocates Rangers fans with the Nazis in British vernacular usage, clearly invoking the FOOTBALL-IS-WAR metaphor in Celtic fan discourse.[3] Football discourse, and more specifically, fan discourse, is saturated with FOOTBALL-IS-WAR metaphors that use text, image and sound.

Verticality metaphor

Another core conceptual metaphor at use in football is the 'verticality metaphor' which is one of a series of fundamental orientational metaphors that establishes a scale of meaning in our minds. Most often the verticality metaphor establishes a collocation between a dualistic domain of social, emotional or moral action as high or low. Johnson (2007, 21) suggests in his later work that these various fundamental forms of meaning derive from our earliest sensorimotor movements, beginning in the womb, and are generally experienced below consciousness: for example, containment; linearity; force/exertion. These movements are combined with structures and patterns that we learn in early life (which are, technically, sometimes called 'image schemas'), and typical examples of these would include: source-path-goal; up-down (verticality); into-out of; toward-away from; and straight-curved.

Musically, the verticality metaphor is primarily how Western cultures discuss things like pitch (high pitches being high-frequency sounds and low pitches being low-frequency sounds).[4] Equally, the verticality metaphor structures many social relations across many domains of life such as social status (e.g. social caste, categories of social events, military rank, etc.) and is reflected literally in the physical arrangement of social space, where 'higher'-ranking people in businesses and organisations were historically positioned 'higher' up in buildings, in rooms, space or on the land. The positive associations with greater height and the negative relations with being 'low' extend into almost limitless discursive spaces. For instance, consider metaphors around use of force where CONTROL IS UP or BEING CONTROLLED IS DOWN, e.g. 'I have control over her, I am on top of the situation, he's at the height of his power' (Lakoff and Johnson 1980: 'orientational metaphors'). The orientational metaphor of high = good and low = bad has extended into our understanding of musical sound also in that generally, low, repetitive (and often dissonant) sounds are key to the construction of a threatening or dangerous ambience in music. But the orientation of verticality is pervasive and extends to physical and social well-being, emotions, organization of the environment, etc.

It is therefore unsurprising to find the verticality metaphor used in football songs, to equate the collective SELF AS UP and the OTHER AS DOWN. It is also a widely used metaphor in football commentary, where it is often used to describe both the physical orientation of the field (despite it being flat and on only two planes) or to communicate the moral and perceived equity of the game: e.g. 'Ratcheting up the tension' (blended), 'Up there in the field', 'On the level', 'they've hit rock bottom', etc. Celtic Football Club sing a song, 'The Flag that Flies on High' which describes this use of verticality and association with the sense of Selfhood for supporters. The use of flags as potent symbols of football belonging is now common across many clubs. For instance, the verticality metaphor is used to position a sense of belonging and positivity, with Shelbourne FC fans in the League of Ireland who sing a version of the song, 'The Red Flag', a widely used song thick with intertextual political meanings, including its (now) traditional performance at Labour Party conferences and by various communist parties around the world for many years:[5]

So raise the scarlet standard high,
Within our dreams we'll live and die,
Through coward's flinch and traitor's sneer,
We'll keep the red flag flying here,
Oh flying high, up in the sky.
We'll keep the red flag flying high,
From Tolka Park and far and near,
We'll keep the red flag flying here …

Manchester United fans have tended to combine conceptual metaphors, so that in this supporters song 'Glory, Glory Man United', they invoke the verticality metaphor to position Manchester United as higher and therefore proud and positive, combined with the musical signification of the use of the old militaristic 'Battle Hymn of the Republic' which has a thickly semiotic and intertextual history of over 200 years and has a particularly complex history of recontextualization and intertextuality (Randall 2004). The song has been used in many songs of solidarity as well as to incite conflict, division and military meaning (Richardson 2017). The use of that tune here for the Manchester United song 'Glory, Glory Man United', is, I think, reinforced by the song's origins as a signifier of social justice which originally emerged to commemorate anti-slavery abolitionists. The song deals with strong elements of Self and Other in racial social life, common to many war anthems, and is perhaps why it is so popular as an ideal melody for tribal Selfhood in football fandom:

Glory glory Man united,
Glory glory Man united,
Glory glory Man united,
As the reds go marching on on on!

Just like the busby babes in days gone by,
We'll keep the red flags flying high,

You're gonna see us all from far and wide,
You're gonna hear the masses sing with pride.

United, Man United,
We're the boys in red and we're on our way to Wembley!

Metaphor 3: Self as healthy, Other as diseased

One of the key metaphors in sporting and social division and conflict, is to construct the Other as Diseased in contrast to the health and vitality of one's own team and collective Self. Common metaphors map illness, disease or disfigurement onto the Other and also relate to our bodies as the fundamental site of human meaning. Many football fans will know their own club's often-disgusting expressions of denigration for the opposing team, and many people regard these as simply 'ordinary banter' in football. The debate over prejudice, racism and the limits to freedom of expression in football is particularly present in Scotland today in relation to sectarianism (see, for instance, Millar 2016), but also throughout the global game now, where previous expressions of dominant ideological racism or prejudice are now being called out on a regular basis by minority groups, and even by players themselves.

Many fans will of course know their own versions of these metaphors, but some of the obvious ones that deal with the Other as Diseased include Newcastle United supporter's specific ridiculing of Sunderland AFC club's fans:

You are a Mackem, An ugly Mackem,
You're only happy, On giro day.
Your mum's out thieving Your dad's drug dealing,
So please don't take my hubcaps away...

Similarly, Celtic Football Club are sometimes referred to by Rangers fans as 'Septic' football club, and on the Rangers FC online forum followfollow.com, the code word for Celtic is 'the filth', which clearly indicates dirt, disease and Otherness.[6] Rangers embody these metaphors in quite vile chants about Celtic supporters, and some Rangers fans refer to Celtic Park as 'the piggery', connecting it in the discursive mind to filth and animal behaviour. The following example uses the vernacular slang term for Catholic in Northern Ireland and the West of Scotland of 'taig', which is used as a sectarian term, accuses Celtic fans of being smelly and directly implicates religious sectarianism through the use of this term and the term 'Fenian' which carries a chain of assumptions of denigrating Catholics:

If yer feelin lonely or if yer feelin sad
just go doon tae Ibrox park and ye wulny feel so bad
but if ye ur a smelly taig yul hear a massive cry
get tae fuck ya fenian cunt before ye fuckin die!

Another of the Rangers' supporters chants invokes the metaphor of Otherness through disease,

Nacho Novo[7] is the best
always better than the rest
Dundee United and Celtic
pish their pants every match
they are wee smelly rats.

Manchester United's 'Build a Bonfire Chant' also suggests a virulent purging of the Other via fire, which has traditionally been used to eradicate diseased bodies at times of extreme infection:[8]

Build a bonfire,
Build a bonfire,
Put the Scousers on the top,
Put the City in the middle,
And we'll burn the fucking lot.[9]

Interestingly, the use of the OTHER AS DISEASED metaphor, although widespread, can also be observed in football in its antonymical expression; to signify one's love for the perfect, whole and healthy Self and football team. In an unusual use of the metaphor, Celtic fans have inverted the metaphor to express an almost transcendental 'super-self' expressing their love, closeness and intimacy for the team. The lyrical content is unusual too and runs as follows (sung to the tune of Depeche Mode's 'Just Can't Get Enough'):

Du, du, du, du, du, du, du, du, du, du, du, du,

When I see you Celtic, I go out of my head,
I just can't get enough,
I just can't get enough,
All the things you do to me and all the things you said,
I just can't get enough.
I just can't get enough
We slip and slide and we fall in love and I just can't seem to get enough of.[10]

In this example, we see the metaphor reversed and the somatic metaphor is used to suggest that if the Other is diseased, then Celtic provides a perfect Self, where fandom is conceived of almost a sexualized experience via conceptual metaphor. The metaphor here is a container metaphor, very common in everyday discourse; here it constructs fandom as love which fills the container of ordinary life with joy and strong emotional attachment to the football club. Lakoff and Johnson show that container metaphors are primal metaphors for humans to organize the world because we have a clear sense of being bounded as physical beings by our bodies and skin, where the external world is always experienced as outside our bodies, giving us a natural sense of 'in' and 'out' of containers or our bodies. We use the container metaphor across many social domains, and not just for clear in-out contexts such as a room or a house (e.g. 'he *entered* the house'), but also for more abstract physical containers such as countries, e.g. 'she is *in* France'. Or in the case of a sporting race, the race itself can be organised as a container; 'are you *in* the race on Sunday?' (Lakoff and Johnson 1980: 'Container Metaphors'). The container metaphor is also used in relation to football, where people discuss the activities of players and managers in terms of being *in* or *out* of the game, e.g. '*outside* of the game he does great charity work', 'players are *in* or *out* the team selection', or 'they're *out* of trouble now'.

In this song's context, the metaphor suggests that the container of life cannot be filled because football fandom is an addiction which changes one's own sense of Self, and of the metaphor. In this way, the fans signify and use both SELF AS HEALTHY as well as the container metaphor, FANDOM AS ADDICTION, in the song text.

Conclusion

In conclusion, football, like any social activity, is deeply social and relies on our somatic awareness of our bodies and draws on long histories of talk and text to express our fandom. The musical elements of football songs, although not properly explored here, are often highly significant too, and the underspecified nature of musical communication enables very wide affordances but also significantly problematic legitimation strategies. The lyrics of football chants and songs most often set up the supporter's team as the collective Self, and the opposing team as Other. In the case of long-established regional rivalries such as Newcastle/Sunderland or Rangers/Celtic, the specific socio-cultural attributes of the Other are used in the construction of football songs and chants. In music, our bodies map onto the tonality of the song; Self as the most important chords (Self as tonic chord, for instance), Other as more tonally distant indicating social distance (see McKerrell 2015). And, like almost all social life, football is multimodal; football involves moving images, sound and symbols such as flags, songs and chants and is a very rich field of social interaction. As such, it is useful to understand the somatic basis for many of the underlying conceptual metaphors used in football that provide and give meaning to the construction of the supporter's own team, the Self, and the collective Other in the form of the opposition. This clearly defined sense of two opposing groups is what I term the primeval battle because it involves very clear division, and a temporally limited field of conflict (i.e. the 90 minutes on a Saturday) whereupon one side or the other can declare a clear victory or loss. This clarity of personal belonging is one of the key reasons why football continues to be so popular around the world.

The metaphors used by fans to express this primeval battle between Self and Other revolve around the central conceptual metaphors of FOOTBALL IS WAR, SELF IS UP, SELF IS GOOD, THE OTHER AS DISEASED, SELF AS HEALTHY, and NORMAL LIFE IS A CONTAINER, and all of these are flavoured with the unique contextualizing references to local teams, regions and players. The use of conceptual metaphor underscores the importance of our bodies in meaning making, and in discourse analysis more broadly, and can provide an underlying intertextual coherence through time, such as in the use of tunes and songs like 'The Battle Hymn of the Republic' and 'The Red Flag'. The power of all this is that it provides not only a discursive and social framework for football, but also a neurological basis for football because all of these metaphors rely upon the use of our own neural networks and mirror neurons, which perhaps explain in part why the experience of football fandom can be so overpowering for some. The significance of music and singing is that it amplifies the mirror neuron effect in our brains which transforms metaphor from language to embodied metaphor. This means we literally, collectively, *feel* the sense of belonging and of division through the neural connections made in singing together, and this results in a powerful sense of Self and Other.

Football is a particularly tribal activity, not only deeply social but, as research is now demonstrating, an arena where psychosocial phenomena and research are moving towards efforts to reduce violence and recidivism. Research on the discursive and multimodal conceptual metaphors used in football songs can in some senses be thought of as the 'soft gates' of interdisciplinarity in the academy. 'Soft gates' in the sense that it deals with social interaction through song, chant and offline and online discourse. If one thinks of the 'hard gates' of interdisciplinary research as biological or neurological networks, such as mirror neurons and the brain, then it is possible to imagine a future research trajectory that draws on interdisciplinary research where we 'double hinge' the soft gates – in order to allow disciplines as disparate as sport sociology, discourse analysis and (even) ethnomusicology to work alongside psychologists and cognitive anthropologists to combat football violence and conflict in the real world. Work in this domain has already begun with research by Martha Newson, for instance, who has shown how identity fusion amongst football hooligans can happen, and how understanding this sort of behaviour could potentially lead to ways to deal with hooliganism and violence with extreme fans (Newson et al. 2018; Newson 2019; Bortolini et al. 2018). It remains to be seen whether applied work on football songs and chants could lead to the sort of conceptual metaphor substitutions, that might provide, for instance, 'win-win' metaphors in football, reducing the sense of Otherness and hate that extreme football hooligans feel for the opposing team (in contradistinction to the ordinary, non-extreme healthy sporting rivalries of the majority of fans). This, amongst many other possible applications, provides a sense of how interdisciplinary research from within the sociology of sport and music might begin to tackle some of the intractable problems that emerge from the visceral love of the game.

Notes

1 For a more detailed explanation of this approach, see Way and McKerrell (2017).
2 Source: https://www.youtube.com/watch?v=gnYjI17lPso [Original recording: Top of the Pops, 21 May 1981; date accessed: 22 November 2017].
3 Historically, there are various explanations for the etymology of the description of Rangers fans by Celtic fans as 'huns'. One prevalent mythology suggests that it is derived from an incident in the 1960s, when Rangers travelled to play Wolverhampton Wanderers and their supporters ran riot through the town. In an article appearing in the English media shortly afterwards, they were described as 'coming across the border like marauding huns' (thanks to the editors for pointing this out).

4 In other cultures around the world, these metaphors are arranged differently, so some cultures use OLD-YOUNG or FAT-THIN to describe musical pitch demonstrating that verticality is but one way of organizing binary concepts such as pitch (see Zbikowski, 2002, 67–68).
5 For a more detailed historical and semiotic reading of this well-known song, see Millar (2020).
6 'If yer feelin lonely …': http://terracechants.me.uk/club/chants/Rangers/best/3/ [date accessed: 20 November 2017].
7 A famous player for Rangers, Ignacio Novo, a Spanish Catholic.
8 This chant is also used by fans of other clubs too, including Celtic supporters' adaptation to target Rangers fans and by Hearts also.
9 'Build a Bonfire: MUFC song, www.fanchants.com, https://www.fanchants.com/football-songs/manchester_united-chants/build-a-bonfire-12/ [date accessed: 14 January 2020].
10 https://www.youtube.com/watch?v=7wcYdyPusmU [date accessed: 20 November 2017].

Bibliography

Bortolini, T., M. Newson, J. Natividade, A. Vázquez, and A. Gómez. 2018. 'Identity Fusion Predicts Endorsement of Pro-Group Behaviours Targeting Nationality, Religion, or Football in Brazilian Samples'. *British Journal of Social Psychology*, 57(2): 346-366.

Cross, I. 2011. 'Music and Biocultural Evolution'. In *The Cultural Study of Music: A Critical Introduction* (2nd edition), edited by M. Clayton, T. Herbert, and R. Middleton. London: Routledge.

Dockwray, R., and A.F. Moore. 2010. 'Configuring the Sound-Box 1965–1972', *Popular Music*, 29(2): 181–197.

Firmat, G.P. 2008. 'Latunes: An Introduction', *Latin American Research Review*, 43(2): 180–203.

Godøy, R. I., and M. Leman. 2009. *Musical Gestures: Sound, Movement, and Meaning* New York, NY: Routledge.

Goodall, K., S. McKerrell, J. Markey, S.R. Millar, and M.J. Richardson. 2015. 'Sectarianism in Scotland: A 'West of Scotland' Problem, a Patchwork or a Cobweb?', *Scottish Affairs*, 24(3): 288–307.

Johnson, M. 2007. *The Meaning of the Body, Aesthetics of Human Understanding*. Chicago, IL; London: University of Chicago Press.

Johnson, M. L. and S. Larson. 2003. '"Something in the Way She Moves" - Metaphors of Musical Motion', *Metaphor and Symbol*, 18(2): 63–84.

Kövecses, Z. 2010. *Metaphor: A Practical Introduction*. New York, NY; Oxford: Oxford University Press.

Lakoff, G. and M. Johnson. 1980. *Metaphors We Live By*. Chicago, IL; London: University of Chicago Press.

Lakoff, G. and M. Johnson. 1999. *Philosophy in the Flesh: The Embodied Mind and Its Challenge to Western Thought*. New York, NY: Basic Books.

Machin, D. 2010. *Analysing Popular Music: Image, Sound and Text*. London: Sage.

Machin, D. and J.E. Richardson. 2012. 'Discourses of Unity and Purpose in the Sounds of Fascist Music: A Multimodal Approach', *Critical Discourse Studies*, 9(4): 329–345.

McKerrell, S. 2015. 'Social Distance and the Multimodal Construction of the Other in Sectarian Song', *Social Semiotics*, 25(5): 1–19.

Millar, S.R. 2015. 'Musically Consonant, Socially Dissonant: Orange Walks and Catholic Interpretation in West-Central Scotland', *Music and Politics*, 9(1). http://dx.doi.org/10.3998/mp.9460447.0009.102.

Millar, S.R. 2016 'Let the People Sing? Irish Rebel Songs, Sectarianism, and Scotland's Offensive Behaviour Act', *Popular Music*, 35(3): 297–319.

Millar, S.R. (2020). *Sounding Dissent: Rebel Songs, Resistance, and Irish Republicanism*. Ann Arbor, MI: University of Michigan Press.

Newson, M. 2019. 'Football, Fan Violence, and Identity Fusion'. *International Review for the Sociology of Sport*, 54(4): 431-444.

Newson, M., T. Bortolini, M. Buhrmester, S.R. da Silva, J. N. Q. da Aquino, and H. Whitehouse. 2018. 'Brazil's Football Warriors: Social Bonding and Inter-Group Violence', *Evolution and Human Behavior*, 39(6): 675–683.

Randall, A.J. 2004. 'A Censorship of Forgetting: Origins and Origin Myths of "Battle Hymn of the Republic"'. In *Music, Power, and Politics*, edited by A.J. Randall. New York, NY: Routledge.

Richardson, J.E. 2017. 'Recontextualisation and Fascist Music', in *Music as Multimodal Discourse: Semiotics, Power and Protest*. London: Bloomsbury Academic.

Shilling, C. 2012. *The Body and Social Theory* (3rd ed.). London: Sage.

Shusterman, R. 1999. 'Somaesthetics: A Disciplinary Proposal'. *Journal of Aesthetics and Art Criticism*, 57(3): 299–313.

Shusterman, R. 2008. *Body Consciousness: A Philosophy of Mindfulness and Somaesthetics*. Cambridge, New York, NY: Cambridge University Press.

Shusterman, R. 2012. *Thinking Through the Body, Essays in Somaesthetics*. Cambridge & New York: Cambridge University Press.

Sloboda, J. A. 2005. *Exploring the Musical Mind: Cognition, Emotion, Ability, Function*. Oxford University Press.

Van Leeuwen, T. 1999. *Speech, Music, Sound*. Basingstoke: MacMillan.

Van Leeuwen, T. 2004. *Introducing Social Semiotics: An Introductory Textbook*. Oxon: Routledge.

Way, L.C.S., and S. McKerrell. 2017. *Music as Multimodal Discourse: Semiotics, Power and Protest*. London: Bloomsbury Academic.

Zbikowski, L. 2002. *Conceptualizing Music: Cognitive Structure, Theory, and Analysis*. Oxford; New York, NY: Oxford University Press).

Zbikowski, L. 2009. 'Music, Language, and Multimodal Metaphor'. In *Multimodal Metaphor*, edited by C. Forceville and E. Urios-Aparisi. Berlin: De Gruyter Mouton.

Chapter 2

'You call this democracy?'

FC Saint Pauli supporters, football chants, and the police

Max Jack

Filling the normally quiet regional train with loud conversation and cigarette smoke, the ultras – hardcore fans of FC Saint Pauli – disrupt the normally quiet ride from Hamburg to the small town of Rathenow in East Germany. Placing stickers over the cameras built into the train carriage, there is purposeful care amongst the ultras to avoid being watched. Upon arrival, the train doors open and several hundred supporters with open bottles of beer walk out, ready for the team's German Cup game against lower-division side FSV Optik Rathenow. As the crowd exits through a tunnel that leads toward the street, riot police are waiting. One policeman begins filming the fans as the unit follows the crowd down the road.

Chants erupt sporadically as the crowd moves down the road toward the stadium. Riot police in vans park outside the ground while others stand around in groups with their helmets in their hands. Hanging out on the dirt road outside the stadium, many of the fans drink and chat while ignoring the line of police vans that are trying to get through. Out of frustration and impatience, an officer drives his van forward and bumps several fans resolutely standing in the way. Fans spring to their defence, open the unlocked van door, and grab the officer by the jacket. After pulling him out of the van halfway, they shove him back in and slam the door. Glass beer bottles fly through the air and hit the van, spraying beer into the open window.

After we enter the stadium, the ultras sing for the entirety of the match. The police, looking more relaxed, watch the game and chat with one another now that the fans are safely within the caged confines of the visitor section of the stadium. After a win for Saint Pauli, tensions escalate on the trip home. As the crowd sings and moves along the platform toward the idling train, one supporter veers toward the cops. With arms outraised, he shoves his face within an inch of a policeman's who remains in control and does not move – save for a look of disgust. On the second leg of the journey, riot police enter the train. Asking supporters to move out of the stairwell, the police are met with no acknowledgement as chatting amongst the fans continues. Words are exchanged, and suddenly, a policeman begins viciously punching a fan. Supporters fight back and the brawl begins to bottleneck up the stairs of the two-tiered train car. Riot police come from both ends to quell the melee. I am stuck in between the converging mass of bodies. A cop in full body armour screams at me to sit down and I stare at him in disbelief until he shoves me into a nearby seat. At the other end of the train a man is being held by the police. 'You call this democracy?!?' shouts a fan from across the aisle. As the train pulls into Hamburg Central Station, supporters surround the police standing on the platform. They try to remain nonchalant as supporters begin to chant, 'All of Hamburg hates the police!'

Forming a mutually constitutive relationship between ultras and the state, violence has become a key feature of hardcore fandom and social life at FC Saint Pauli. Defined in part by conflict with the police as a common experiential thread amongst ultras globally, *ultra* can be characterized as a transnational fan movement positioned against the commercialization and mediatization of professional sport (Gabler 2010). Particularly wary of rising ticket prices and the diminishment of standing terraces in many stadia across Germany, which threaten their lifestyle as hardcore fans, the ultras have carved out an enclave at FC Saint Pauli in which participatory crowd performance and consistent attendance are key to socialization and membership within the fan scene. Crowd action and illegal pyrotechnics, then, are in part motivated by rebellion against the financial prerogatives of the German Bundesliga, resultantly placing the hardcore fans in direct confrontation with a state apparatus designed to streamline public safety on match day (Jack 2019).

While most ultra groups across Europe avoid discourse around institutionalized politics, Ultra Saint Pauli (USP) are arguably the most well-known ultra group to integrate antifascist themes into the stadium space. Adopting and adapting the diffuse and varied logics of Antifa as a transnationally networked movement aimed at eliminating right-wing extremism from the public sphere, USP overtly positions themselves against homophobia, racism, sexism, and capitalism in the stadium space. While the social politics of the Saint Pauli fan base have proven fashionable in popular culture and the global media,[1] crowd action coordinated by the ultras also functions as a collective rhetorical device that publicly critiques the intertwined logics of commercialism and the state's management of public space, which together heavily influence the format of the modern professional football event. In contrast to scholars in ethnomusicology who have pointed out the role of music as a pathway toward mediation and conflict resolution (Brinner 2009; O'Connell 2010), crowd performance at FC Saint Pauli instead operates as a rhetorical device in which many forms of violence are conceived by its participants as an engrained dimension of social life (Cusick 2006; Araujo 2010; McDonald 2013; Daughtry 2015).

***

Capitalizing on the local fan base's subcultural affiliations, FC Saint Pauli has developed into a global brand that represents a confluence of antifascist and anarchist ideologies underscored by punk and hip-hop visual aesthetics. Offering a counternarrative to anxieties around hooliganism and right-wing extremism at football matches in the public sphere (Clarke 1973; Hall 1978), Saint Pauli has become associated with progressive social politics while simultaneously evoking a nostalgia for traditional fandoms in places like England where high ticket prices and all-seater stadiums have eliminated standing terraces and consistent attendance. Beginning in the 1980s, FC Saint Pauli began attracting new followers as a contingent of fans from the city's biggest club, Hamburg SV, looked for an alternative to the right-wing extremist rhetoric within the broader fan base. Residents of the Saint Pauli neighbourhood also began attending their club's matches in the 1980s, many of whom were living in squatted buildings as autonomous collectives (Davidson 2014). Adopting and trademarking the skull and crossbones that once waved outside the squats on Hafenstraße, FC Saint Pauli has embraced the historical narrative and current social politics of the neighbourhood while adopting fiscal strategies such as merchandising and sponsorships that facilitate its continued existence as a competitive team in the German second division.

While subculture and ethnicity have often been repackaged and sold to consumers for profit (Hebdige 1991; Wheaton 2004; Comaroff and Comaroff 2009), sports fandom is increasingly grounded in the consumptive and mediated aspects of participation, such as merchandising and televised viewership (Armstrong and Giulianotti 2001; Giulianotti 2002). Embracing and marketing the politics at the roots of their fan base, FC Saint Pauli boasts merchandise sales that rival the most successful clubs in Germany, such as Bayern Munich and Borussia Dortmund. Further, the club has acquired a transnational following because it projects a fan base with a political edge and a punk aesthetic whose performative ethos in the stadium represents an emotional purity and an 'honesty of experience' (Moore 2002, 213) that distinguishes them from their sporting competitors as 'alternative'.[2] As the most dedicated supporters, the ultras have immense value to the club because their expressive capacity authenticates the club and projects its left-wing political affiliation. Their cultural capital as fans who attend every match and their affective labour serve as resources from which FC Saint Pauli can sell a stadium experience with high atmosphere in addition to merchandise that has come to represent a broader cultural association with progressive left-wing politics. The club administration, then, accommodates dissonant ideologies of localized and globalized fandom by maintaining cheap ticket prices and standing terraces, which enable the ultras' lifestyle while simultaneously developing a transnational fan base that attends few if any matches at the Millerntor Stadium. In contrast to the club administration's pragmatic approach to fiscal survival and competitive success through global merchandising, the anarchist, anti-capitalist, and antifascist logics that inform the politics of the Saint Pauli neighbourhood influence the ultras' position against the commercial priorities of professional football and the state.

As such, USP, like many ultra groups, occupies a paradoxical position as both culture bearers and 'problem fans' in the eyes of football club administration, the state, and the German Football Association (Jack 2019). Claims to moral authority justify actions that propel ongoing antagonisms between ultras and these governing apparatuses. In this way, USP publicly protests the commercial priorities of the league through the use of pyrotechnics and provocative crowd choreographies, bringing them into conflict with the police who present themselves as the arbiters of public safety (ibid). In response, government-sanctioned use of physical force is a tacitly accepted means of re-exerting control over public space. Chants, however, challenge this power – exhibiting the equally ominous potentiality of the crowd. Contrary to the notion that peace characterizes the status quo of social and economic life (Araujo 2010, 219), I argue instead that violence forms *a mutually beneficial and consensually antagonistic relationship* between ultras and the police. Playing a key role in cultivating the ideologies and world views of the fan base, friction between the ultras and the apparatuses of the state that aim to discipline them reinforces the anarchist and antifascist political ideologies that undergird the epistemologies of hardcore fandom at FC Saint Pauli. Crowd performance creates atmospheres, which in conjunction with heavy police presence facilitates and perpetuates the repeated actualization of physical violence between police and fans. Resultantly transforming violence into a spectacle that publicly performs the terrifying resources of the state, police repression ironically reaffirms the authenticity of the FC Saint Pauli brand as a community on the edge of radical political activism and legitimizes the epistemologies of fandom that make ultra a movement defined by its opposition to commercialism and the state.

Culturally valuable and socially deviant

The day after travelling to see Saint Pauli play in the small city of Aalen, I headed over to a party that the ultras had organized in the neighbouring Schanzeviertel. I had just entered the Rote Flora – a theatre turned squatted building – which the police had been unsuccessfully trying to vacate for decades. In Germany, squats often serve as community and cultural centres, operating their downstairs as cheap bars, running kitchens that serve vegan food, and hosting various events that engage with issues such as nationalism, state monopoly of violence, and the privatization of public space. Opening its doors to many different community groups, the Rote Flora makes itself available rent-free for bands, sports groups, Vokús (cheap community dinners), and even a food co-op (roteflora.de). Symbolic of the left-wing autonomous and antifascist movements in Germany, the Rote Flora is one of the best-known squats in the country. To help raise money for the group's legal fees and fines issued by the government, USP had gotten permission to host their *Soliparty* (solidarity party) at the Rote Flora. Inside the building, the grandeur of the architecture has been redesigned with intricate graffiti covering the walls. At the party, DJs played techno while rappers performed in the smoke-filled, dimly lit basement. The residents at the Rote Flora are in constant tension with the government, manoeuvring to assert their lasting claim to the building as the changing government officials of the city oscillate between seeing the Flora as culturally valuable and socially deviant. Meanwhile, the political edge and the unique cultural flavour of the neighbourhood have ironically led to its gentrification.

In reputation, Saint Pauli is perceived as the antithesis to the surrounding neighbourhoods of Hamburg, whose beautiful white buildings, trees, and lakes reflect the overall wealth of the city and its residents. This comparative grit of Saint Pauli, however, has ironically made the neighbourhood the most fashionable and sought-after area to live in the city. Lined with sex shops and strip clubs, Saint Pauli's main street, called the Reeperbahn, has become one of the primary tourist attractions in Hamburg. Away from these heavily trafficked destinations, hip cafes and bars line every block. Comprised of old apartment buildings with beautiful facades, the walls, trash cans, and lamp posts on every street are almost entirely covered by graffiti, street art, and stickers. USP are especially prolific graffiti writers in this area, and the group's tags can be seen on almost every building on every street. Their stickers also express slogans and graphics associated with Antifa: fists smashing swastikas, *No One Is Illegal*, and *Refugees Welcome* logos pepper the lamp posts, articulating the neighbourhood as a left-wing space. Emerging out of this urban milieu, fashionable clothing stores have opened up matching the graffiti and punk aesthetics of the neighbourhood. Every day I walked by the store *Kauf dich Glücklich* (Shop Yourself Happy), whose main window was fully cracked by what appeared to be a well-aimed rock.

A heterogeneous and uneven process of social marginalization that repurposes historically and culturally valuable neighbourhoods and populations (Novak 2019, 6), urban development has transformed Saint Pauli into a site of tension over the neighbourhood's changing socio-economic demographics and the rising value of real estate, both of which threaten the survival of the surrounding punk scene, music venues, and squatted communities. Kai, a veteran member of USP, mentions to me that he doesn't come to Saint Pauli anymore unless he is going to a match or an event at the Rote Flora. Capitalizing on the visibility and notoriety of the punk and antifa scenes, new bars, tourists, and rising rent prices increasingly alienate residents and the hardcore fans of FC Saint Pauli from the imagined identity of the neighbourhood.

My own subject position as an ethnographer articulates the varied transnational interests in Saint Pauli and the resultant insularity of communities wary of outsider attraction to the neighbourhood. Drawn to the political dimension of football fandom and bolstered by the ample journalistic and academic resources on the club, I planned to conduct my field research year in Hamburg during my graduate studies. In expressing my interest to accompany the ultras and engage in participant observation, many members of the group had doubts that I could understand their subject positions at all, let alone that they could trust me to protect their identities and daily whereabouts from the government. Perceived as authenticators of Saint Pauli's antifascist and political mythos through the collective practice of participatory performance in the stadium, the ultras attempted to live the changes they wanted to see by running the group as a consensus-based collective that overtly critiqued capitalism and the state in ways that attracted both police intervention and outsiders like me who ultimately posed a risk to their lifestyle. This created a paradoxical scenario in which the group created a collective social life that aimed to mitigate the weakened social cohesion and isolating effects of neoliberal capitalism (Gershon and Alexy 2011), which required them to insulate themselves from outsiders with potentially harmful interests.

The Authenticity (and Profitability) of Radical Fandom

Similar to the tension around the shifting biopolitical makeup of the neighbourhood, ultras position themselves against the financially driven logics that structure professional football, which have dramatically changed the cultural landscape of modern fandom. As a means of achieving competitive success on the field through strategies that maximize football clubs' revenue, the modernization of professional sport has been accompanied by rising ticket prices, an ongoing transition from standing terraces to all-seater stadiums, and a greater emphasis on televised spectatorship designed for mass-mediated accessibility – a process that has created increasingly diffuse fan communities in which attendance is not a prerequisite for identification with the football club (Armstrong and Giulianotti 2001). Supplemented by occasional visits to see the team play 'live', consumption of pay-per-view, social media, merchandise, and magazines have become a standard means of expressing affinity for one's team.

In opposition to this cultural trend, ultras cultivate atmosphere in the stadium through 'participatory performance' (Turino 2008) as an alternative to the consumptive aspects of modern fandom (Jack 2019). Gaining public attention for their overt commentary on current events, USP use crowd action to merge the terrain of professional football with political discourse. Kai and the others in the group used the stadium space as a means of addressing issues such as the impending G20 summit in Hamburg in 2017, ongoing police violence in the neighbourhood, and even the Turkish invasion of Syria in 2019 (which earned the club a fine from the DFB). In addition to fines for inflammatory content of banners and chants, the ultras' graffiti and pyrotechnics received the most attention from police and media outlets like Bild, who report on and consistently sensationalize football-related violence.

Public perception of ultras as deviants in conjunction with state strategies to repress their use of pyrotechnics have further radicalized and alienated them in the process. Exercising their authority to arrest and fine ultras who light pyrotechnics and write graffiti around the city, Pauly[3] pointed out to me that the police would often arrest ultras at random if they didn't have a confirmed culprit. Surveillance is used by the police not only to catch illicit activity, but also as a means of constructing profiles on the members of Ultra Saint Pauli. This information is often put into a federal database called the *Gewalttätersportdatei* (Violent Criminal Offender Database) that law enforcement across the country can access. Fans, however, aren't explicitly informed if they are on it. From this perspective, the ultras' banner advertising their party at the Rote Flora came as little surprise – a police officer with the head of a pig was holding bloody hooks and wearing a butcher's apron. It read:

Die Polizei:
Dein Feind
und Schlächter!

(*The Police*
Your Enemy
And Butcher!)

While the state's attempts at repressing the ultras' crowd activities have reinforced the ultras' resolve in creating alternatives to social life aimed at circumventing consumption, the social politics of anti-racism and anti-homophobia have proven broadly popular amongst media outlets who often nostalgize the Saint Pauli experience. Carefully curated as an alternative football experience, the outside walls of the club's home ground, the Millerntor Stadium, are covered in commissioned street art while the inside has been painted by the fans. A prominent message extends along the standing terrace, which reads 'No Place for Fascists'. Two men in a passionate embrace are painted along the gangway that leads to the field above a slogan that reads, 'Love is Love'. Cigarette smoke hangs in the air before kick-off as the loudspeakers blare punk rock. The players walk onto the pitch to the opening guitar riff of AC/DC's 'Hell's Bells' until the ultras take over, who lead the chants from behind the goal for the entirety of the match.

In response to the changing urban space and cultures of modern fandom, the overlapping antifascist and ultra scenes in Hamburg emerge as forms of radical citizenship through the cultivation of social milieus that aim at reclaiming public space explicitly without aim for financial gain. At the same time, the ultras' affective labour in the stadium is an integral component of the sporting event at FC Saint Pauli – that which authenticates the stadium experience and the club's brand. From the ultras' position, however, crowd action serves as a means of political commentary and a symbol of resistance against modern football and the isolating effects of capitalism at large – a performative strategy responding to the decline of standing terraces, the waning of attendance-based fandom, and the increasing prevalence of capitalist strategies of accumulation in modern football.

Violence as a spectral threat

To understand the cultural response and performative protest of USP, the marginalizing logics of urban 'revitalization' and the 'modernization' of professional football must be conceived as a type of violence that is 'structurally central to social norms' (Araujo 2010, 218) in Saint Pauli. In response to the ultras' public and at times inflammatory critiques of neoliberalism, various state apparatuses have built up around the fan scene as a means of repressing the fans' expressive potential. The state's monopoly of physical violence serves as a performative means of communication and coercion (Schmidt and Schröder 2001), which displays the physical (and later the judicial) repercussions of confronting riot police in public space. Physical violence also performs the spectacle of state power through the police's claim to a morally justified application of 'force' (Taussig 1997; Larkins 2015). Force, however, is not a social interaction that wins the future ideological consent or even necessarily the cooperation of its recipients. It can also enculturate in its participants a cynicism around the efficacy of governance and its overall legitimacy of the nation-state (Appadurai 1996, 2006). As we talk outside the stadium, even Lars the club social worker[4] is wearing a No Borders T-shirt – a sentiment representative of the fan scene's position toward the state at large.

Negative institutional perceptions and (mis)representations of ultras as 'problem fans' also work to validate their radical positionality. Research stemming from the Leicester School of Sociology, for instance, has framed sport-related conflict primarily as *fan* violence (Dunning et al. 1992; Dunning 2002; Poulton 2005). In contrast to public anxieties around football-related violence, however, The Birmingham School examined the 'bourgeoisification' of professional football and identified hooliganism as a site of class struggle and resistance to these changes in the 1970s and 1980s (Clarke 1973; Hall 1978). In spite of this counternarrative offered within the field of cultural studies, decades of media reporting and films have engrained the connection between football fandom and violence in the public imaginary. Having chatted about my research with my landlord, she introduced me to a friend of hers named Daniel who agreed to take me to the next home match against Sandhausen. She mentioned that he had laughingly called himself a 'Saint Pauli hooligan'. She wasn't sure how to interpret the label – was he?

Clarifying these blurred perceptions, Lars explained that as hooliganism waned in the 1990s, the ultra style of crowd support developed in popularity, instilling new anxieties amongst authorities due to its performative reminiscence to fighting subcultures. Replacing the physical confrontations that marked fighting fans as deviant in the public sphere, the crowd now performs the group's ability to publicly criticize the DFB and the police, at times through the illegal use of marine flares. The performative aesthetics of crowd action don't require physical violence to be interpreted as violent and forceful in public space. There is, then, a fear of violent *potential*, which has resulted in pre-emptive attempts by the government to contain and control coordinated activities of the crowd by stationing riot and civil police at the grounds (Honigstein 2014). As a means of securing public order on game day, riot police focus their collective attention on surrounding the crowd in the streets until fans can be contained within the fenced terraces of the stadium.

In consideration of the legacies of violence at professional football, governance operates upon 'ecologies of fear' where 'threat becomes spectral' in and around the stadium space (Goodman 2010, 71). Goodman argues that ecologies of fear entail preventative measures that work to inadvertently 'actualize the future in the present' even though the future event need not necessarily occur. It is sound, Goodman argues, which creates an immersive atmosphere that impacts mood (ibid, xiv) and 'beckons the event' (ibid, 71). However, it is important to note that ecologies of fear do not create situations in which there is a clear dichotomy between peace and violence. Instead, it is essential to regard the relationship between synchronous performance and violence as inhabiting a 'seamless aesthetic loop' where both interact fluidly (McDonald 2009, 62). The relationship between chants and physical violence is an intimate one. Exemplified by the tensions before and after the match in Rathenow, ultras can create hostile atmospheres as a means of subjecting riot police to environments that allude to the crowd's own potentiality – that which displays what they could do if they wanted. While the ultras comprise a small minority of fans in the stadium, they are able to harness vast numbers of surrounding fans that are ideologically and performatively considered to be 'ultra-oriented'. Such displays of participatory power work to compound the police's fear by underscoring their helplessness. In this way, force can be applied sonically without the physical application of one's body onto another. Performance replaces physical violence as a means of emotive retribution toward the police that is within the law but often works to actualize 'the real thing' (Graeber 2009, 519).

What's so scary about ultras?

Pulling a crowd cover over all the fans in the South Stand, a number of the ultras pull balaclavas over their heads to avoid being identified by the police while taking marine flares out from their clothing. Once lit, pyrotechnics stain their surroundings a bright neon orange as the smell of burning gun powder fills the air. Flares have emotive power not only for the visual spectacle they create, but also because people's emotions feed back into the atmosphere in the stadium. The movements and emotions of the crowd in the South Curve *are enhanced in public moments of successful violation of the law*. When the flares have burned down, the crowd cover goes back up and members of USP take off their masks, sometimes even swapping out articles of clothing that could be used to identify them when they exit the stadium. 'Normal fans see it as a really aggressive thing, which I guess it is in a way', Sal reflected during our interview. 'But for ultras it's the best way to show the emotion you have for your football club'. The conflicting affective responses to flares create a dynamic tension in the stadium that both attracts and repels onlookers, making the South Stand the most popular area of the stadium while driving others away who fear the ultras' deviant activities.

More broadly, USP operationalizes the crowd as a means of making participants and onlookers *feel and react* in polarizing ways to the (im)morality of state violence. At Saint Pauli's home game against Sandhausen, USP had prepared a crowd choreography, which served as a fitting response to the altercation with the police on the train coming home from Rathenow. Upon the entrance of the players onto the field, large black banners were raised depicting a burning police van and a cop shooting unarmed citizens. Thousands of small German flags were distributed with the yellow stripe torn off, transforming a nationalist symbol into the anarchist red and black to be waved by the crowd in the South Stand. Along the wall of the terrace, a long banner was unfurled that read, 'We are the Red and Black Front', referencing the lyrics from a track by the anarchist band, Ton Stein

Scherben, who are well known to the Saint Pauli punk scene. Repetitions of 'Sankt Pauli, Sankt Pauli, Sankt Pauli!' transitioned into 'Alerta, Alerta, Antifascista!' as the players lined up to be introduced by the announcer. The alignment of antifascist sentiments within the hardcore fan scene at FC Saint Pauli provide the ultras the opportunity to cultivate a heightened atmosphere in the stadium based upon the fan base's political dispositions.

Able to be seen and heard in the stadium, the overarching theme of the ultras' crowd choreographies, flags, banners, and even personal appearance, focus on addressing the manifestations of government authority and modes of control that violate the fans' fundamental ideals of economic and social equality. Saint Pauli supporters, for instance, have responded to the Syrian refugee crisis with shirts, banners, and crowd choreographies ranging from those that simply state, 'No One is Illegal', to others which read, 'FCK SPD' (the acronym for Germany's centre-left-leaning political party). In this way, performing Saint Pauli occurs through the presentation of varied visual and sonic symbols, which have fused an association of left-wing political ideals with Saint Pauli Football Club itself. These performative responses to such frustrations do not go unnoticed and are often met with various institutional sanctions. In this instance, the Hamburg police banned the sale of beer in the stadium for the next match for the ultras' crowd choreography.

In contrast to the ultras' politically charged stadium activities, collective movement and chants on the street raise immediate tensions in ways that the very same chants in the stadium do not. My point is that the anxiety and fear ultras create pertains not only to the ideological content of their public performance but also because of *how* their collective discourse is conducted. Such intensive government strategies aimed at undermining the ultras' affective potential allude specifically to the state's fear of the crowd as a source of deviancy – that there is in fact something illiberal to it because it leads to the 'dissolution of the individual' (Gaonkar 2019) and functions instead as a collective (Stokes 2018, 105). Dilip Gaonkar argues that 'within the liberal imaginary, the individual is the bedrock of social ontology, moral responsibility, and economic calculation and the crowd jeopardizes all those invaluable assets' (ibid). In this context, the current political economy is caught within a contradiction that covets crowds as essential to certain aspects of the economy (i.e. crowd sourcing or the consumer crowd) (ibid), while simultaneously fearing a loss of control. Noting this trend, Stephen Connor argues that the crowd is increasingly called upon and harnessed as an informational resource rather than a form of kinetic power in contemporary public culture (2016, 21). Contrary to this position, however, I point toward the ongoing relevance of the crowd as a culturally productive resource, which has become a point of fascination in the public sphere and popular culture for the very characteristics that mark it as outdated and deviant.

The ultras' use of the crowd lends its performative content an ideological momentum through its capacity to make its participants *feel* while also serving a presentational function, which elicits anxiety in onlookers through perceived displays of aggression, masculine tropes, and the volatility of sonic and physical synchrony. Such performances, learned through repetition inside the stadium, accentuate the division between insidership and outsidership in the streets. Meant to be contained by the state, the collective direction and synchrony of ultras operate within spaces where they are permitted to exist yet are simultaneously feared. Chants, by disrupting the everyday soundscapes of urban life, contest and claim territory through the ritual performance of collective expression. It is in this sense that the crowd at FC Saint Pauli supersedes its own 'political' content, which through collective voicing rejects normative pathways of restrained discourse in the public sphere.

If the police are perceived by the ultras as the most visible antagonists of a larger government apparatus, then chants and pyrotechnics become the primary strategy in which to display collective power in ways that challenge the state's ability to effectively maintain order in urban space. Crowd performance amongst football supporters serves as an emotive rhetorical device, which creates a tinderbox in which one misstep can spark a wave of physical violence. In response, random arrests, surveillance, and use of physical force by the riot police in and around the city on match days serve as the vehicle for the state to publicly perform a recalibration of the normative logics of public life.

Conclusions

My goal throughout this chapter has been to show how violence is structurally central to the social life of the hardcore fans at FC Saint Pauli in ways that authenticate the antifascist mythos of the club as a global brand. Informed by the marginalizing social impacts of gentrification and the commercialization of their own football club (and the Bundesliga in general), the ultras' public (and at times illegal) protests open up urban space as a site in which the state performs the extent of its martial capacity as a means of restoring the normative logics of public space. The physical violence performed by riot police, however, serves as an enculturating process for ultras – it affirms the state as *Feindlich* (hostile). In response, ultras implement the emotive force of the crowd as a performative display of power, which emphasizes collective resilience and potentiality. Through this process violence becomes spectral – always in stages of actualizing itself.

While ultras and supporters in the stadium contest government policies that they believe restrict movement and reinforce economic inequality, it is the crowd activity in the streets which allows supporters to experience just how this status quo is maintained. Crowd performance thus plays an integral role in actualizing the now common narrative in which the police are oppressors and supporters are a force of subversive political ideology. Synchronized sonic and physical aspects of crowd performance on the streets are often threatening because they contest standardized modes of conduct and display alternative order. Tensions with law enforcement do not persuade the dispersal of the crowd but instead work to enhance group unity and validate their political positionalities. This leads to the potentially uncomfortable acknowledgement that encounters between ultras and police on match day not only reinforce the epistemological tensions between the state and fans, but further create moments of conflict in public space which are in fact *enjoyable* for the participants involved.

While Dick Hebdige observed the fusion and de-fusion of subculture through the commoditization and commercialization of style (1991), Ultra Saint Pauli's insularity has contrastingly created a tensely maintained social enclave at the Millerntor Stadium in spite of the team's global popularity. The performance of violence by the state and the ultras' performance in the stadium space serve as intertwined social relations that bolster the legitimacy of both sides to their respective sympathizers. Revealing the antagonisms inherent within liberal democracy at large (Mouffe 2009), participatory performance, the conflict that follows, and the residual legal repercussions for many ultras complete a cycle that develops and reaffirms perceptions of the government as that which represses those willing to seek alternatives to the isolating and alienating effects of millennial capitalism. Specifically, Ultra Saint Pauli's protests emerge in opposition to the neoliberal logics that reorganize social life as consumptive leisure in and outside of the context of football in their neighbourhood. Their perceived marginalization coupled with an ongoing friction with the state echoes the young man's cries on the train home from Rathenow – 'You call *this* democracy?'

Notes

1 Left-wing politics have become a key dimension of fandom at clubs such as Celtic FC (Scotland), Hapoel Tel-Aviv (Israel), AC Omonia (Cyprus), Standard Liege (Belgium), and the Portland Timbers (USA), to name only a few.

2 Alan Moore's work on authenticity in rock and country music scenes are remarkably similar to the underlying perceptions of what soccer chants are supposed to express, which in their 'purest' form should be true to the participant's experience and represent his or her sincere feelings for the club.

3 I have changed the names of all my interlocutors to protect their identities.

4 All teams in the top three divisions of German football are aided by social workers who provide safe meeting spaces for the fans to spend time during the week and before games. For FC Saint Pauli, 'The Fanladen' is located at the stadium underneath the main standing terrace.

Bibliography

Appadurai, A. 1996. *Modernity at Large: Cultural Dimensions of Globalization. Public Worlds, v. 1*. Minneapolis, Minn: University of Minnesota Press.

Appadurai, A. 2006. *Fear of Small Numbers: An Essay on the Geography of Anger. Public Planet Books*. Durham, NC: Duke University Press.

Araujo, S. 2010. 'Sound Praxis: Music, Politics, and Violence in Brazil'. In *Music and Conflict*, edited by J. Morgan O'Connell and S.E. Castelo-Branco. Urbana, IL: University of Illinois Press.

Armstrong, G. and R. Giulianotti. 2001. 'Afterword'. In *Fear and Loathing in World Football.* Oxford: Berg.

Brinner, B.E. 2009. *Playing Across a Divide: Israeli-Palestinian Musical Encounters. Oxford*; New York: Oxford University Press.

Clarke, J. 1973. *Football Hooliganism and the Skinheads.* Birmingham: Centre for Contemporary Cultural Studies, University of Birmingham.

Comaroff, J. and J. Comaroff. 2009. *Ethnicity, Inc.* Chicago, IL: The University of Chicago Press.

Cusick, S. 2006. 'Music as Torture/Music as Weapon'. *Transcultural Music Review* 10.

Daughtry, M. 2015. *Listening to War: Sound, Music, Trauma, and Survival in Wartime Iraq.* New York: Oxford University Press.

Davidson, N. 2014. *Pirates, Punks & Politics: FC St. Pauli: Falling in Love with a Radical Football Club.* York: Sports Books.

DFB. 2019. Deutscher Fußball-Bund e.V. *'Sperre der Südtribüne und Geldstrafe für den BVB gefordert'.* Accessed 2 December: http://www.dfb.de/news/detail/sperre-der-suedtribuene-und-geldstrafe-fuer-den-bvb-gefordert-161807/.

Dunning, E. (ed.). 2002. *Fighting Fans: Football Hooliganism as a World Phenomenon.* Dublin: University College Dublin Press.

Dunning, E.G., P.J. Murphy, and J.M. Williams. 1992. *The Roots of Football Hooliganism: An Historical and Sociological Study.* London: Routledge.

Eisenberg, A. 2013. 'Islam, Sound, and Space: Acoustemology and Muslim Citizenship on the Kenyan Coast'. In G. Born (ed.), *Music, Sound, and Space: Transformations of Public and Private Experience.* Cambridge: Cambridge University Press.

Gabler, J. 2010 Die Ultras: Fussballfans Und Fussballkulturen in Deutschland. *Neue Kleine Bibliothek 156.* Köln: PapyRossa.

Gaonkar, D. 2019 'After the Fictions: Notes Towards a Phenomenology of the Multitude'. *E-Flux* 58. Accessed November 29, 2019. https://www.e-flux.com/journal/58/61187/after-the-fictions-notes-towards-a-phenomenology-of-the-multitude/.

Gershon, I., and A. Alexy. 2011. 'Introduction'. *Anthropological Quarterly* 84(4): 799–808.

Giulianotti, R. 2002. "Supporters, Followers, Fans, and Flaneurs: A Taxonomy of Spectator Identities in Football." *Journal of Sport and Social Issues* 26(1): 25–46.

Goodman, S. 2010. *Sonic Warfare: Sound, Affect, and the Ecology of Fear.* Cambridge, MA: MIT Press.

Graeber, D. 2009. *Direct Action: An Ethnography.* Edinburgh: AK Press.

Griggs, G. 2012. "'Carlsberg Don't Make Football Teams... But If They Did': The Utopian Reporting of FC St Pauli in the British Media." *Soccer & Society* 13(1): 73–82.

Hall, S. 1978. 'The Treatment of "Football Hooliganism" in the Press'. In *Football Hooliganism: The Wider Context.* London: Inter-Action Inprint.

Hebdige, D. 1991. *Subculture: The Meaning of Style. New Accents. London*; New York: Routledge.

Honigstein, R. 2014 'Ultras Play with Fire as Bundesliga Engulfed by Flares and Violence'. *The Guardian*, 26 November 2012. Accessed December 15 2014. http://www.theguardian.com/football/blog/2012/nov/26/bundesliga-flares-violence-safety-measures

Jack, M. 2019. 'Deviant Subjectivities: The Ultra Movement and the Governance of Public Affects'. PhD Dissertation, University of California Santa Barbara.

Larkins, E. 2015. *The Spectacular Favela: Violence in Modern Brazil.* Oakland, CA: The University of California Press.

McDonald, D. 2009. 'Poetics and the Performance of Violence in Israel/Palestine'. *Ethnomusicology* 53(1): 58–85.

McDonald, D.A. 2013. *My Voice Is My Weapon: Music, Nationalism, and the Poetics of Palestinian Resistance*. Durham: Duke University Press.

Mouffe, C. 2009. *The Democratic Paradox. Repr. Radical Thinkers*. London: Verso.

Novak, D. 2019. 'The Arts of Gentrification: Creativity, Cultural Policy, and Public Space in Kamagasaki'. *City & Society* 31(1): 94–118.

O'Connell, J. 2010. *'Introduction: An Ethnomusicological Approach to Music and Conflict'*. *Music and Conflict*. Urbana, IL: University of Illinois Press.

Poulton, E. 2005. 'English Media Representation of Football-Related Disorder: Brutal, Short-Hand and Simplifying?' *Sport in Society* 8(1): 27–47.

Schmidt, B.E., I. Schröder. (eds.) 2001. *Anthropology of Violence and Conflict. London*; New York: Routledge.

Stokes, M. 2018 'The Musical Citizen'. *Etnomüzikoloji Dergisi* 1(2).

Taussig, M. T. 1997. *The Magic of the State*. New York: Routledge.

Trautwein, A. 2017. 'Rote Flora: Seit 28 Jahren ist die Flora infiltriert'. *Die Zeit*. 22 June, sec. Hamburg. https://www.zeit.de/hamburg/2017-06/rote-flora-verdeckte-ermittler-prozess-interview.

Turino, T. 2008. *Music as Social Life: The Politics of Participation*. Chicago, IL: University of Chicago Press.

Weidman, A.J. 2007. *Singing the Classical, Voicing the Modern: The Postcolonial Politics of Music in South India*. Calcutta: Seagull Books.

Wheaton, B. 2004. 'Introduction: Mapping the Lifestyle Sport-Scape'. In B. Wheaton (ed.), *Understanding Lifestyle Sports: Consumption, Identity and Difference*. London: Routledge.

Whitehead, N.L. (ed.). 2004. *Violence. School of American Research Advanced Seminar Series*. Santa Fe: School of American Research.

Chapter 3

Sound, violence and gender performances in Brazilian football

Pedro Silva Marra

Sou, sou Galoucura, eu sou
Vou dar porrada eu vou
E ninguém vai me segurar, nem a PM [1]

In an old song frequently chanted in Brazilian football arenas, *torcidas organizadas* present themselves as true war machines. Organized fan clubs, *torcidas organizadas* are the Brazilian equivalent to European Ultras. They differ from Ultras, however, in their institutionality: they register their members; manage headquarters; are governed by statutes; finance their activities through sales of products, such as uniforms and other souvenirs; and are structured around a relatively rigid hierarchy (Toledo, 1996). Violence is a recurrent theme in the lyrics of a great part of the sonic repertoire sung by *torcidas organizadas* and other fans in the stands in the country. These songs and chants threaten or insult opponents, sports organizers, and state institutions, and are sometimes even aimed at other *torcidas organizadas* for the same team. They also tell stories of clashes against rival groups and the police. Episodes of violence involving the clubs are constantly reported by the media, and academic research has explored their relationship to such different topics as fan culture and its dynamics of rivalry (Toledo, 1996; Alabarces et al. 2000), a search for excitement (Dunning, 2011), gender and class relations (Spaaij, 2008, Gastaldo, 2010, Alabarces, 2014), identity fusion (Theodoropoulou, 2007; Newson et al., 2018), and the revolt against mismanagement both in football itself and in society as a whole (Palhares and Schwartz, 2015).

This chapter explores what I call a sonic technique[2] (Marra, 2016) that football fans utilize in some of their violent practices in Brazil. Examining sound practices in sport, it questions some common themes in the literature on sports and violence. In addition to acting as 'weapons' in conflicts that take place inside the stadiums, sound is an important mediator of social, cultural and affective issues.

Football, violence and sound

A common interpretation of violence in research on sports states that conflicts and clashes are exclusively negative and therefore should be solved in service of peacemaking. Studies which concede that aggressive acts are part of fan culture usually understand violence as juvenile delinquency (as in street fighting by *torcidas organizadas*), anomie or social breakdown (in their acts of vandalism).

Thus, even when they do not propose policies that are punitive or seek social control and regulation as solutions to the problem of violence in arenas, they adopt condescending claims about the issue. As such, violence is constantly understood as outside society, as something to be eradicated or unacknowledged so that differences between groups and social collectives do not destroy the possibility of common life.

While I do not disagree that conflict can cause harmful consequences, this chapter aims to take a different theoretical path. It prefers to situate violence as one of the engines of society (Clastres, 1979, 2004), as something that constitutes human activity, even outside of crisis contexts (Araújo, 2006). It seeks to unveil the ubiquity of violence in a political project that articulates social relations in contemporary societies, including at their most local level, especially those marked by precarious situations, what Achille Mbembe (2018) describes as necropolitics. That is, where social and economic networks deteriorate or are unevenly distributed, as is the case in Latin America, violence is especially salient in the articulation of social relations. High-performance sport is a privileged site of social practice for understanding these dynamics: global capital and neoliberal marketing logics flow through it (Wisnik, 2008), and competition and conflict is also inherent to its own logic. After all, although in football there is not always a winner and a loser – a draw is a possibility – there is always a champion. As Hans Ulrich Gumbrecht (2007) reminds us, the actions of an athlete on the pitch always take place against the opponent's effort, both agents trying to resist the tactical, strategic and sensory tricks of the rival.

Gumbrecht (2007, p. 109) argues that, for some audiences, sporting violence produces fascination – the gaze is attracted by, and becomes entangled with, the specificities of the event. Rugby and American football, for example, involve clashes between opponents' physical bodies, at which fans cheer intensely. On these occasions, according to Gumbrecht, one gains an aesthetic experience in the sports context, even though the event that catalyzes what he characterizes as an 'epiphany' is steeped in violence. In this sense, he defines violence as 'all acts and all forms of behaviour that occupy or block spaces through bodies, against the resistance of other bodies' (Gumbrecht, 2010, p. 6). With this definition, Gumbrecht intends to highlight the mobilizing power of physical aggressiveness, without confirming its frequent association with criminal behaviour; at the same time, contra Foucault, he avoids treating it as an unwelcome or spiritual phenomenon.

In this definition of violence, sound is central, as it occupies space (Daughtry, 2014) and, therefore, can be instrumentalized as a device (DeNora, 2004) that mediates the issues that animate, explain, justify or instigate aggression. The role of protest songs in contexts of demonstrations, armed conflict, and resistance against authoritarian regimes is well documented (Zan, 2013; Correa, 2017) and their public performances are considered political actions in themselves, as they mediate 'spatial, political and cultural relationships with the uprising' (McDonald, 2013, p. 197). Over the past two decades, research on the relationship between sound and violence has emerged as a major focus within the field of sound studies, after scholars identified the use of sound and music as a fundamental element of the 'shock and awe' campaign undertaken during the Iraq War. Studies range from the various types of music to be used incidentally as a 'weapon', as a means of performing torture without touch (Cusick, 2006), to the affective power of sound to make explicit how sonic expressions of the capitalist world – the ubiquity of portable music devices, for instance – constitute a politics of frequency (Goodman, 2010).

These studies argue that sound's capacity to disturb an individual's spatial orientation, sense of balance and motor coordination allows agents to use it as means for aggressive actions, an agency that articulates sonic vibrations, listening and technologies (Daughtry, 2015) in the production of hyper-sensory events in which the semantic features of the audible are overwhelmed by its material presence. In such contexts, sound colonizes territories, whether they be places or bodies. The violent use of sound in everyday life has been documented by various researchers: Marra and Madeira (2020) examined sound as a mediator of religious, class, racial and political conflicts; Trotta (2019) argued that compulsory music listening – music one is obliged to listen to either because it is ubiquitous or because a neighbour plays it so loud that it invades the place one is in – affects well-being; and Johnson and Cloonan (2009), coined taxonomies of the ways in which music is accessed in violent actions. I agree with Stock (2018, pp. 99–100) that these studies show that 'if once we focused on the relationships between violence and music, we now attend equally to the sound of violence and to the violence of sound'.

The spectacle of soccer – especially in acoustic terms – is largely hyper-sensory. While a single person's voice does not have the ability to make a noticeable impact on one's skin, a crowd roaring the same motto, or low bass and loud sounds, can. In Brazil, the sound of arenas is intense and often chaotic, since several *torcidas organizadas* for the same team, each one with their own percussion bands performing different songs, occupy different sections of the stands. The neighbourhoods within which these arenas are located frequently complain of the ruckus that assaults their streets. It is, therefore, by sound – and not only by the semantic content of the messages and words chanted – that fans perform not only symbolic but also physical acts of violence.

Drawing on research conducted during Galo matches, I argue that most of the audible experience of cheering consists of fans constantly deciding whether and through which song, chant or moto they need to sound. It might also shift to a more traumatic experience when clashes erupt in the stands. Moreover, fans tell a story of the game as they try to understand which song opponent supporters are singing in order to sonically 'counterattack', aiming to silence rivals. People who live near football arenas – sometimes some kilometres away from the pitch – also share this narrative, as they can guess what is happening in the game through sound: the crowd uproar means the home team scored; silence means it lost the match. Football listening experience is learnt through time, as fans attend matches in the arenas and learn when and through which repertory they can make their presence audible from each section of the audience to players on the pitch. It also tends to force supporters to tirelessly emit sounds aiming at boosting players' performances and disturbing the opponents' game. Fans also use sound to colonize the stands and confirm the arena as their territory.

This research also shows that sound is employed in violent practices in at least three processes: (1) performances of gender, (2) territorial disputes over the arena space and (3) identity fusion. Here, I focus only on the first – via an analysis of swearing and male performances in practices of sonic torture – as the two other topics will be discussed in future articles. Thus, in the following section, I put recordings obtained in my investigation in dialogue with a body of research on gender relations, the education of future athletes, rivalry, jocularity and violence in football fan practices.

The aggressive sounds of heteronormative insults in male fan performances strain, reinvent or re-enact gender biases in football arenas through sonic modulations of swearing. Immersed in a misogynistic culture, fans access the repertoire they have in hand to protest, taunt or hate upon their rival. Therefore, fans always walk a thin line between legitimate aggression against abuse and the violent reproduction of normal, non-deviant masculinity. By playing between these two poles, they look for excitement, as, for fans, name-calling is often one of the principal forms of entertainment. Through these offences they also work out or sublimate their aggression, to the extent that joke-like symbolic violence can prevent physical violence from taking place. Therefore, I conclude the chapter with notes on an ethical sounding in which I try to evaluate whether violence becomes insurrectional and creates autonomous zones (Newman, 2011) in football. I argue that in such cases, legitimate violence is practiced – in which there is a correspondence between the forms and amplitudes of violent acts and the oppressions and asymmetries they fight against (Hardt and Negri, 2009) – in order to overcome conflict.

Sonic torture and gender performances

In the final match of a tournament, your football team plays against its arch-rival at the football arena. The stands are so packed that the intensity, size and weight of the collective voice forces every fan to sing. The opposing defender fouls your team's player on the boundary line. The stands roar for the penalty, but the referee only assigns a free kick. Outraged, the crowd roars, 'Hey referee, take it in the ass!' You are also angry about the referee's decision and – just as you had previously entrained to the club anthem – feel compelled to echo the offense despite its homophobic content. Eventually, you give in to the weight and intensity of the shout that takes over the stands. A few moments after the incident, you realize you just took part in a manifestation of prejudice that you would otherwise fight against. To overcome the guilt for what you just have done, you remember that football fans usually naturalize actions like these as male jocularity. You also recollect memories from your childhood, when you and your friends used to jokingly insult one another with heteronormative curse words and insults that disapproved of practices linked to homosexuality by common sense. That was not homophobia, or hate crime at that time.

The narrative just presented highlights sound as a mediator of violence in the fan's gender performances. There is a certain ambiguity here in this aggressive act. On the one hand, we find the symbolic violence of reproducing heteronormativity in a swearing phrase that attributes negative meanings to erotic practices linked, in everyday understanding, to male homosexuality. On the other hand, there is the indignation of the fans against a sports injustice that takes place in the match. In another article (Marra, 2018), I demonstrated how the sound of cursing is directly linked to the offensiveness of these terms. In the context of football, an offense such as 'take it in the ass' only reaches its maximum state of intensity when collectively sung throughout the stadium simultaneously, in a guttural vocal register. Cursing with this sonority is usually deployed in three ways:

a) As in the case presented earlier, it may refer to referees, football management institutions, the administrators of the team one is supporting, or to city, state or national politicians. During these occasions, it usually expresses an indignation of the fans, who protest against unfair or incorrect decisions that undermine the club they support in that game, championship or season;
b) It may take the form of insults that resonate with society's broader social demands, serving as complaints against corruption, police violence, and other issues that hinder the daily life of fans, beyond sport.
c) Curses may be collectively launched throughout the stadium with a guttural voice in reference to opposing fans, athletes or team managers, loudly expressing the rivalry that constitutes high-performance sport.

In order to describe such cases of violence through the use of collective and loud swearing, I borrow the term sonic torture, as coined by Susanne Cusick (2006) – that is, the use of strategically deployed extreme sounds aimed at undermining a detainee's morale. What makes this use of sound 'torture' is neither the sonic material nor its specific features, nor the perpetrators, the targets it is turned against or even the wartime or interrogation situations in which it is practised. Rather, it is the fact that it is strategically and continuously used in certain situations in which one agent intends to break another, building up a protocol for a violent use of sound intended for specific purposes. The United Nations Human Rights Commission, in its Convention against Torture and Other Cruel, Inhuman or Degrading Treatment or Punishment, held in December 1984, defines torture under broad terms in which violence, either physical or symbolic, is instrumentalized, be it in order to force someone to give in or do something they do not want to concede, or to cause loss of courage or self-confidence, resulting in fear or timidity. Thus, it can be used not only to retrieve information and objects, or to convince a person to perform a certain action they previously did not want to do, but also to strip someone of their agency.[3]

While UN regulations and academic research focus on strategic and continuous violence committed by the state against civilians or military officers, I expand Anna Papaeti's (2013, p. 84) claim that 'revisiting and broadening the definition of torture is an urgent necessity'. This stretching of the term, in a sense, is exactly what authors do when they engage with the term sonic torture, as they document that the use of music during torture is not commonly seen as part of violence itself by its perpetrators, although it is often present in the victims' accounts. As I will argue here, systematic, aggressive and loud homophobic swearing is employed collectively by football fans in the arena in order to punish referees, or to lower players' or a team's performance on the pitch. This is done in specific moments when the target's attention is already down, as when the victim has just committed a mistake, or when the opponent has a good opportunity to score.

Episodes of sonic torture at Galo games are quite common when the team faces Cruzeiro, its arch-rival. These sounds are often triggered at the beginning of the match and are very commonly addressed to their goalkeeper, Fábio, an athlete who has been playing on the team for over a decade and therefore identifies strongly with it. Goalkeepers are often targets of sonic torture, both because they play at the ends of the field, which brings them closer to the crowd and increases the possibility of hearing the insults, and because their performance is critical to the outcome of the contest. After all, these players' mistakes are likely to result in goals against the team they defend. Fans can also swear in unison with a guttural voice at an athlete from their own team who repeatedly commits mistakes, causing an adverse result for their club. It is, then, an act of sonic torture that cuts two ways: it can draw the player's attention, so that he performs better in following games, or it can make the coach substitute him with another. Some players never manage to play again in certain clubs because of the insistence of swearing coming from their own club fans.[4] As a result, they have to play somewhere else, which can increase the use of this sonic torture against them on later occasions, as a kind of punishment for the treason of playing for another team.

Thus, swearing in football holds another feature in common with the use of music and sound in violence: academic research has shown that a typical side-effect of sonic torture is trauma, which brings back painful memories triggered by sound. Jean-François Augoyard and Henry Torgue (2005, p. 88) recall a story told by Pierre Sansot of 'a rugby touch judge who would hear the "booings" and "cheers" of the public only the day after and who collected in a way a "treasure of hearing" – exemplary remanence'. As Arley Sander Damo (2005) demonstrates in his ethnography of the education of future professional football players, building psychological barriers to the audience's cursing is key for athletes' performance and becomes an important part of their training. Damo documents cases of young and promising players who don't live up to the expectations around them, as they can't cope with the pressure from fans swearing in the stands and are dismissed by the clubs in which they are training. A performance in a game, or even a professional career, can be damaged by this sonic torture, which makes 'players fear the audience' (Damo, 2005, p. 387).

Often the same insult can be used by isolated supporters, addressed to a friend or acquaintance of the same team or a rival, with an ironic voice, with intensity levels close to that of everyday speech. In this case, the curse word refers to jocularity (Gastaldo, 2006) that denotes intimacy between two individuals who enter into an exchange relationship: the one who swears jokes with the one who is cursed, while accepting that they will switch positions at a future time. Jocularity is governed by unspoken but well-defined rules that establish who can make fun of whom: winners make fun of losers. There are also limits to the intensity of the offence. Crossing the boundary of what is acceptable to fans, by issuing an exaggerated offence, can cause physical clashes. The sonorities of jocularity, therefore, articulate the rivalry between opposing fans on a milder level of violence. Through jokes, fans re-enact and rearticulate the traditions and rivalries of their teams.

Torcidas organizadas also often use guttural collective cursing in their songs and mottos. Most of these sonorities narrate clashes with fans of rival teams, in extended lyrics and syncopated rhythm, which makes it difficult for other fans to memorize. Other songs are parodies of the adversary's sound repertoire. At times, these fan groups insert rival offences in pieces of the common sonic repertoire of the team that did not have these terms previously. However, these sounds are often restricted to the region in which they start, finding no echo in the rest of the stands. This is a performance in which the timbre of the voice denotes a high heteronormative masculinity. Through the aggressiveness of the guttural voice, exaggerated at times when the curses are sung, *torcidas organizadas* aim at delimiting the identity of their team's fans within quite narrow, homogeneous limits that oppose those attributed to the opponent. This is done in a male vocal performance in which violence overlaps with sexual ethics and courage.

Sound, legitimate violence and insurrection

Throughout the examples discussed in this chapter, one may have noticed a contradiction between forms of violence and seduction through the use of sound. Frequently, one body hinders the action of another through forms of blocking; sometimes such barriers exert a force, convincing individuals on the somatic level to echo or move in directions they might not otherwise have taken. Such ambiguity raises questions about the legitimacy of violent acts. When is it justified for the actions of one body to disturb the agency of another? To what extent do sonorities that colonize space materialize disputes based on asymmetrical power relations?

Magowan and Donnan (2019, p. 3) point out that resistance as 'modes of subverting, obfuscating or silencing the powerful other' is 'a destabilizing, amorphous, provocative and ambiguous concept, that may or may not produce beneficial results'. They also offer 'resilience' as a term commonly used by scholars in the study of dynamics of power and control in contexts of hegemony or subordination, as a means of accruing resources for well-being. These two terms refer to the survival of the weak in a context of oppression, in which unequally included groups find ways to negotiate their forms of life against stronger forces that intend to crush them, or to continue existing despite the adverse conditions in which they are forcefully immersed. But, in their ambiguity, those concepts also convey a sense of maintenance of the social order, as they usually address local issues and micropolitical processes, not necessarily engaging in the production of new macro structures and systems of production and distribution of resources, or of subjectivities or meaning.

To these two terms I would like to include in this discussion concepts like revolution and insurrection in order to address the use of violence in dynamics of social transformation that operate on both micro and macro levels and aim at fracturing the social structure in such a way that it would cease to exist, or at least lose its hegemony. This would permit the appearance and emergence of new and more inclusive systems of production. In other words, focusing on processes in which violence is employed, I seek to point towards ways of overcoming social, economic or symbolic issues in football.

Discussing the possibility of combating inequalities and social transformation in contemporary times, Saul Newman argues that the avant-garde/Jacobin model of revolution, understood as a rupture with, and taking control of, the state, is no longer sustainable. The author argues that this traditional revolutionary model 'imagine[s] an event that encompasses everything' (Newman, 2011, p. 350), and thus fails to account for the complex networks that articulate and structure various spheres of society. Thus, he proposes considering revolution in terms of a multiplicity of spaces of autonomy and insurrection, understood as those that would foster 'alternative forms of life, new relations and intensities' (Newman, 2011, p. 353). In the process of creating and defending these spaces, confrontations with the state may occur. However, autonomy and insurrection work better as micropolitics that supplement policies at the macro level than ways of supplanting macropolitics. This political model of autonomy would also require a democracy that is built against the state and no longer linked to it. In exploring the criteria that define revolutionary violence, Hardt and Negri (2009) raise the following questions: what weapons and strategies are most effective in achieving victory? Which weapons are most beneficial for multitude building? In this context, it is assumed that legitimate violence is the one in which the oppressed turns against the oppressor. However, not all legitimate violence would be revolutionary and therefore necessary.

The case of Coligay, a gay fan group active from the turn of the 1970s to the 1980s, offers us one possibility to think over both the creation of spaces of autonomy and insurrection and revolutionary violence. This group was led by homosexual fans who would attend the matches of Gremio – a major club from the large southern city of Porto Alegre. They would dress in female clothes, dance choreographies interpreted by other fans as North American cheerleading, and sing their own homo-affective chants (Anjos, 2018). They had their own drumming band – composed of hired heterosexual musicians from samba schools from the city – which played what was considered by other fans as 'good music' throughout the 90 minutes of the game. Coligay was also recognized by their cheerful and shrill noise and screams and by their refusal to boo, contrasting with the typical Gremio fans' grumpy performance at the time. Their gay fan performances were rejected by other fans at first, but they later achieved some recognition, as soon as they proved their bravery in clashes against other clubs' *torcidas organizadas*: Coligay fans took karate classes and would get into fist fights only to defend themselves against aggression. Thus, they found some economic support from Gremio itself, getting funding for trips to matches in other cities, a room at Gremio's Olimpico Stadium to keep their flags, and eventually a place in the permanent exhibition at the club's museum. Coligay inspired homosexual fans of other clubs throughout Brazil to create their own gay fan groups during the period, such as Flagay (Flamengo) and Galo Gay, though there is no documentation of those gay fan groups' attendance at their clubs' matches. The fan group had its own gender politics ambiguities, however, as the presence of cross-dressing and transgender fans remains in dispute.[5]

Conclusion

Some of the cases of violence raised in this chapter, such as the homophobia employed against rivals, seem clearly illegitimate. Others, such as the outrage of the fans at an unfair sport decisions, are legitimate. A third kind of violence, though, presents a grey area in which the terms used in violent action are understandable, although the meaning of the agency does not seem justifiable. This is the case of the friends who cheer for opponent clubs playfully swearing at each other in the dynamics of jocularity. More than *ginga*,[6] survival strategy or disrupting the norms that constitute societies, these violent sonic practices highlight the violent social structures to which we are subjected and the poison/remedy character of football, as José Miguel Wisnik points out: 'exposed equally to all the manoeuvres of capitalist advertising, it is nevertheless the place where one finds something that is lacking in "capitalist daily life" ... a recognizable symbolic code capable of expressing and crossing cultural differences' (Wisnik, 2008, p. 429).

It is in this sense that the recent emergence of queer supporter groups in Brazil (Mendonça, 2014) could point toward some political ways of using cursing and heteronormative swearing words, manipulated in their sound so as to expand on Coligay's practices and make football 'a critical instrument rather than a target' (Gumbrecht, 2007, p. 30). Galo Queer,[7] Gaivotas Fiéis[8] and Bambi Tricolor,[9] for instance, are names of LGBTQ+ fan groups that appropriate offensive terms in order to delineate an inversion of values that brings about the power to question constituted norms, to redistribute the sensible. Yet, for fear of physical aggression from other fans (Bandeira and Seffner, 2013), such groups do not attend the arenas in a visible or audible manner. If such groups were heard in the stands, perhaps fans' indignation and ferocity could shift to more legitimate causes.

Notes

1 This is an old song sung by a large number of *torcidas organizadas* from different teams in Brazil. Each of these groups insert their own name in the verses. Thus, *Galoucura* is an interchangeable term in these lyrics and can be freely substituted according to the singing group that chants it. A free translation of the lyrics goes: I am Galoucura, yes I am/I'm gonna kick some ass, I am/And no one will stop me, not even the police.
2 In my PhD research, I define sonic techniques as protocols for the use of a repertoire of sounds in order to achieve certain accomplishments.
3 Those regulations are available at OHCHR (1984). For the Commission's definition, read article 1.
4 The list of football players banned from a club by fans' swearing in Brazil includes successful athletes such as Rivelino, Roberto Carlos and Alexandre Pato (O Estado de São Paulo, 2015).

5 At that time, in Brazil, transgender people and cross-dressers were commonly perceived as being homosexual.
6 Popular Brazilian slang denoting the tricks necessary to survive in precarious situations. It also refers to the movements of a skilfully dancing body.
7 Information on the LGBT fan group Galo Queer at Facebook (2015) and Oliveira (2014).
8 Information on the Gay *torcida organizada* Gaivotas Fiéis at Facebook (2013) and Extra (2013).
9 Information on the Facebook page created by São Paulo supporters to discuss machismo and homophobia in the club's arena at Laurentis (2013).

References

Alabarces, P. 2014. *Héroes, machos y patriotas: el fútbol entre la violência y los médios*. Buenos Aires: Aguilar.

Alabarces, P., R. Coelho, J. Garriga Zucal, B. Guindi, A. Lobos, M.V. Moreira, J. Sanguinetti, and Á. Szrabsteni. 2000. 'Aguante y repression: Futbol, violencia y politica en la Argentina'. In *Peligro de gol. Estudios sobre deporte y sociedad en América Latina*, edited by P. Alabarces. Buenos Aires: CLACSO.

Anjos, L. A. 2018. De 'São bichas, mas são nossas' à 'diversidade da alegria': Uma história da torcida Coligay. Unpublished thesis (PhD), Universidade Federal do Rio Grande do Sul.

Araújo, S. 2006. 'A violência como conveito na pesquisa musical; reflexões sobre uma experiência dialógica na Maré, Rio de Janeiro'. *TRANS – Revista Transcultural de música* [online], 10. Accessed July 9 2020: http://www.sibetrans.com/trans/articulo/148/a-violencia-como-conceito-na-pesquisa-musical-reflexoes-sobre-uma-experiencia-dialogica-na-mare-rio-de-janeiro.

Augoyard, J. F. and H. Torgue. (2005). *Sonic Experience: A Guide to Everyday Sounds*. London: McGill-Queen's University Press.

Bandeira, G. A. and F. Seffner. 2013. 'Futebol, gênero, masculinidades e homofobia: Um jogo dentro do jogo'. *Espaço Plural*, 29, 246–270.

Clastres, P. 1979. *A Sociedade contra o Estado. Investigações de Antropologia Política*. Porto: Afrontamento.

Clastres, P. 2004. *Arqueologia da violência. Pesquisas de Antropologia Política*. São Paulo: Cosac e Naif.

Correa, P. G. 2017. 'Performance e Resistência no Festival Phono 73'. *Anais do XXIX Simpósio de História Nacional – Contra os Preconceitos: História e Democracia* [online], 1–10. Accessed July 9 2020: https://www.snh2017.anpuh.org/resources/anais/54/1502795338_ARQUIVO_PerformanceeResistencianoFestivalPhono73textocompletojulho2017.pdf.

Cusick, S. 2006. 'Music as Torture/Music as Weapon'. *TRANS – Revista Transcultural de Música* [online], 10, Accessed: July 9 2020 http://www.sibetrans.com/trans/articulo/152/music-as-torture-music-as-weapon.

Damo, A. S. 2005. *Do dom à profissão: Uma etnografia do futebol de espetáculo a partir da formação de jogadores no Brasil e na França*, Unpublished thesis (PhD), Universidade Federal do Rio Grande do Sul.

Daughtry, M. 2014. 'Thanatosonics: Ontologies of Acoustic Violence'. *Social Text*, 32 (2 119), 25–51.

Daughtry, M. 2015. *Listening to War: Sound, Music, Trauma and Survival in Wartime Iraq*. New York: Oxford University Press.

DeNora, T. 2004. *Music in Everyday Life*. Cambridge: Cambridge University Press.

Dunning, E. 2011. '"Figurando" o esporte moderno: Algumas reflexões sobre esporte, violência e civilização com referência especial ao futebol'. *Revista de Ciências Sociais, Fortaleza*, 42 (1), 11–26.

Extra. 2013. 'É lançada a primeira torcida gay do Corinthians'. *Extra* [online], available: https://extra.globo.com/esporte/e-lancada-primeira-torcida-gay-do-corinthians-gaivotas-fieis-10459169.html [Accessed April 30 2020].

Facebook. 2013. 'Gaivotas Fiéis'. *Facebook* [online]. https://www.facebook.com/GaivotasFieisOficial/ [Accessed April 30 2020].

Facebook. 2015. 'Galo Queer'. *Facebook* [online]. Accessed April 30 2020: https://www.facebook.com/Galo-Queer-941232029242434/.

Gastaldo, E. 2006. 'Futebol e performances de gênero: Notas etnográficas sobre as relações jocosas futebolísticas'. *Anais do 30o Encontro Anual da ANPOCS* [online], 30, Accessed July 9 2020: https://www.ludopedio.com.br/v2/content/uploads/071216_Gastaldo%20-%20Futebol%20e%20performances%20de%20genero_%20notas%20etnograficas%20sobre%20as%20relacoes%20jocosas%20futebol.pdf.

Gastaldo, E. 2010. 'As relações jocosas futebolísticas. Futebol, sociabilidade e conflito no Brasil'. *Mana*, 16 (2), 311–325.

Goodman, S. 2010. *Sonic Warfare: Sound, Affect and the Ecology of Fear*. Cambridge, MA: MIT Press.

Gumbrecht, H. U. 2007. *Elogio da beleza atlética*. São Paulo: Companhia das Letras.

Gumbrecht, H. U. 2010. 'Is There Anything Wrong with Violence? About the Beauty of Rugby and American Football'. *Philia&Filia*, 1(2): 67–73.

Hardt, M. and A. Negri. (2009). *Commonwealth*. Cambridge, MA: The Belknap Press of Harvard University Press.

Johnson, B. and M. Cloonan. 2009. *Dark Side of the Tune*. Surrey: Ashgate.

Laurentis, F. (2013). '"Bambi Tricolor" Ganha Adeptos Na Internet, Mas Medo De Repressão Breca Ação Em Estádios' *UOL* [online]. Accessed April 30 2020 https://www.uol.com.br/esporte/futebol/ultimas-noticias/2013/06/06/bambi-tricolor-ganha-adeptos-na-internet-mas-medo-de-agressao-breca-acao-em-estadios.htm.

Magowan, F. and H. Donnan. 2019. 'Introduction: Sounding and Performing Resistance and Resilience'. *Music and Arts in Action*, 7(1): 1–10.

Marra, P. S. 2016. Vou Ficar de Arquibancada pra sentir mais emoção: Técnicas Sônicas nas dinâmicas de produção de partidas de futebol do Clube Atlético Mineiro, Unpublished thesis (PhD), Universidade Federal Fluminense.

Marra, P. S. 2018. '"Ei, juiz, vai tomar no cu": Políticas torcedoras e do futebol e sonoridades de xingamentos em performances masculinas'. *FuLiA/UFMG*, 2, 55–79.

Marra, P. S. and Madeira, T.V. 2020. 'Sonic Politics: Sonority, Territoriality and Violence in Urban Cultural Practices in Brazil'. *Journal of Sonic Studies* [online], 19, Accessed July 9 2020: https://www.researchcatalogue.net/view/824264/824265.

Mbembe, A. 2018. *Necropolítica*. São Paulo: n-1 edições.

McDonald, D. A. 2013. *My Voice is My Weapon: Music, Nationalism, and the Poetics of Palestinian Resistance*. Durham, NC, London: Duke University Press.

Mendonça, R. 2014. 'Ambiente "hostil e oppressor" afasta torcidas gays dos estádios'. *BBC Brasil* [online]. Accessed July 29 2015: https://www.bbc.com/portuguese/noticias/2014/09/140919_homofobia_futebol_rm_rb.

Newman, S. 2011. 'Postanarchism and Space: Revolutionary Fantasies and Autonomous Zones'. *Planning Theory*. 10 (4): 344–365.

Newson, M., T. Bortolini, M. Buhrmester, S.R. da Silva, J. N. Q. da Aquino, and H. Whitehouse. 2018. 'Brazil's Football Warriors: Social Bonding and Inter-Group Violence'. *Evolution and Human Behavior*, 39(6): 675–683.

O Estado de São Paulo. 2015. 'Na linha de Maicon, relembre 10 jogadores "enxotados" pela torcida'. *O Estado de São Paulo* [online]. Accessed June 24 2020: https://esportes.estadao.com.br/noticias/futebol,na-linha-de-maicon-relembre-dez-jogadores-enxotados-pela-torcida,1645767.

OHCHR. 1984. 'Convention Against Torture and Other Cruel, Inhuman or Degrading Treating or Punishment'. *Office of the High Comissioner of United Nations Human Rights* [online]. Accessed April 30 2020: https://www.ohchr.org/en/professionalinterest/pages/cat.aspx.

Oliveira, L. 2014. 'Torcida gay do Atlético se esconde em jogos e sofre até ameaça de morte'. *UOL* [online]. Accessed April 30 2020: https://www.uol.com.br/esporte/futebol/campeonatos/copa-do-brasil/ultimas-noticias/2014/11/26/torcida-gay-do-atletico-se-esconde-em-jogos-e-sofre-ate-ameca-de-morte.htm.

Palhares, M. and G. Schwartz. (2015) *Não é só a torcida organizada: O que os torcedores organizados têm a dizer sobre a violência no futebol?* São Paulo: Editora UNESP.

Papaeti, A. 2013. 'Music, Torture, Testimony: Reopening the Case of the Greek Junta (1967–1974)'. *The World of Music*, 2(1): 67–89.

Spaaij, R. 2008. 'Men Like Us, Boys Like Them: Violence, Masculinity and Collective Identity in Football Hooliganism'. *Journal of Sports and Social Issues*, 32(4): 369–392.

Stock, J.P. 2018. 'Violence'. *Music and Arts in Action*, 6(2): 91–104.

Theodoropoulou, V. 2007. 'The Anti-Fan Within the Fan'. In *Fandom: Identities and Communities in a Mediated World*, edited by J. Gray. New York, NY: New York University Press.

Toledo, L. H. 1996. *Torcidas Organizadas de futebol*. Campinas: Autores Associados/Anpocs.

Trotta, F. 2019. 'Música, afeto e Bem Estar Uma Conversa com Alicia e Peter'. *El Oído Pensante*, 7(1): 7–23.

Wisnik, J. M. 2008. *Veneno Remédio – O Futebol no Brasil*. São Paulo: Companhia das Letra.

Zan, J. R. 2013. 'Secos e Molhados: Metáfora, Ambivalência e Performance'. *ArtCultura*, 15(27): 7–27.

Chapter 4

Capital culture, political performance

Listening to football in Ottawa 2014–2015

Jordan Zalis

Prelude to the afternoon: Riot games

The Stony Monday Riot took place in Bytown, Province of Canada (British North America), in 1849 (18 years before Confederation, while pre-Canadians were still re-configuring the colonies). Now a historic walk through the heart of Ottawa, Ontario (the nation's capital and seat of political power), Bytown was first an emerging and aspirational logging community settling into the south bank of the Ottawa River ('near the canal area', one supporter put it, pointing north to the city's UNESCO World Heritage Site). Pitting Loyalists against Reformers (Reformists), the Stony Monday Riot marked an expression of difference between colonial parties – two antonymic groups at odds over the newly signed Rebellion Losses Bill (introduced to compensate provincial Canadians whose property was lost or destroyed during the Rebellions of 1837 and 1838). Working to leverage the occasion, the Reformers gathered inside a public house, hoping to celebrate the Governor-General (Lord Elgin) for, among other things, 'Giving Royal Assent' to the indemnifying legislation. Catching wind of the committee (meaningfully being differently), the Loyalists rallied – rustling for Reformers outside the same ByWard Market pub ...

Kick-off.

Oral history recounts that fists turned into firearms and then into cannon fire over the course of two long days in September. During the riot, one bystander, David Borthwick, was killed when he 'took a rock to the head'. Stony, lumbering, powdered, and violent, Bytown built a reputation for being rough and tumble, a different place before there was an Ottawa incorporated 'using the river's name'.

Names; languages; politics; place

'Ottawa' was claimed (named) contextually (politically), by the Dominion of Canada with respect to the earlier 17th-century fur trade. There and then (from an Anglo/Franco-political, settler-Canadian, colonial-economic perspective), the Anishinaabe Odawa first nation (sometimes 'Ottawa') worked as important middlemen to the French Canadian voyageurs who were transporting goods and critical supplies through the area (from Lake of the Woods to Montreal). Per English-language Algonquin history, there and then, the Odawa were a nation of trading people.

To the Odawa (and to other groups held within their Algonquian language family), the river was (and still is) 'Kichi Sibi', meaning, 'the Great River' or 'big river'. Towards a time immemorial, Kichi Sibi carried Omàmiwininìwak (the Algonquin people in the Algonquian language) as they traded, hunted, and processed complex exchanges.

Indeed, what is now Ottawa (the city) was once big river running through old-growth forest – climax by colour-change and evergreen. During the 19th century, early-Canadian industrialists 're-organized' the 'resource', affording enormous 'wealth' to key players in the timber trade ('resource', in scare quotes, because 'losing the forest for the trees' is keen to extract 'wealth' from a thing of beauty). Now, in the 21st century, the Ottawan (Ottawa's contemporary residents, cosmopolitan people who live in the city) might be found enjoying traditional craft offerings from the family-owned Kichesippi Beer Co.

Violence, quarrels, performing, sonorities

What happened to David Borthwick was an example of real violence – sticks and stones, to use the popular saying. What I focus on with the rest of this chapter is not the same thing. And because, in Ottawa, the supporters' 'quarrel' is more strictly and categorically performing (McCrae and Ferres 1918, p. 2), we must remember that citing death, destruction, and the weight of more than four complicated centuries can really mean blowing things out of proportion (this is written unwittingly – *of course* we should inquire of history; we are always already awake in its performance). In this chapter, I work in sonorities ('sonoridades'; phenomenology in ethnomusicology), making artillery out of supporting.

The Stony Monday Riot: Sound, supporters, listening

Pre-game: Meeting

Through 2014–2015, I conducted participant observation and ethnographic fieldwork with the Stony Monday Riot (SMR), a group of football supporters for the Ottawa Fury Football Club (OFFC), in Ottawa, Ontario, Canada.[1] The SMR were music makers – singing, gesturing, drumming, and chanting – bantering in public, and living out loud around OFFC matches. On matchday, the SMR set to 'riot' in and around the freshly renovated TD Place Stadium (named for the Toronto-Dominion Bank in Canada). For two summers I 'rioted' with the SMR, making field recordings and taking notes so that later, I could write in thick description (Geertz 1972).

Gathering

As the SMR assembled, our rendezvous point was 'the Rock', a monument dedicated to Princess Patricia's Canadian Light Infantry. Staking claims within a pedestrian T-junction in front of the old exhibition hall inside Lansdowne Park (held for leisure and entertainment since the middle of the 19th century), meeting at the Rock was advantageous for a few reasons. First, at the end of a broad pedestrian laneway, the Rock was easy to pick out (literally and figuratively, the Rock 'stood out'). Second, by space and sound (spatio-sonically), we knew very well that while occupying the Rock, our calls would reach 'everybody' contained within the resto-bar/patio and shopping area. Third, symbolically (subsuming a performative force called 'history'), gathering around the rough-cut piece of Laurentian pink granite attuned our presence to a group of brave Canadians who, a century earlier, prepared for 'the war to end all wars' overseas (now World War I): 'A proud Regiment was born here in August 1914'. One hundred years later, the supporter, Will, poured rum into his soft drink, 'FURY!'.[2]

Sounding; supporting

Musically, the SMR were spontaneous, engaging and practising 'improvisation'. The SMR were an 'on the spot' collective (although they did reuse and recycle some of their best work, turning improvs into repertoire). Spanning a broad range of source material, the SMR re-purposed rhythms, lyrics, and melodies from a diverse set of musical genres: Canadian new wave, Hollywood movie soundtracks, indie folk rock, hardcore American hip-hop (gangster rap), rock and roll, the blues, military music, rhythms and songs from other stadia – really, whatever they could wrap their voices and drums around (over three games in 2014, for example, I recounted 39 musical pieces appearing over 141 unique instances). Out loud, the SMR held a kickabout. A few foundational forms lent space to be filled with banter.

And when the SMR made music, they called it 'support'. The SMR were supporters. This is important. The SMR were not ultras (Jack 2018), nor hooligans; the SMR were football supporters. We include this because the SMR contained a smaller subgroup of three younger, rowdier men – newcomers into the section – who liked to refer to themselves as the 'Ottawa Hooligans' (although their 'hooligan' seemed more like 'stirring the pot' rather than violent 'hooliganism').

Phenomenology; ethnomusicology; soundscape; anthrophony

Singing, dancing, clapping, and drumming recognizes an incredible number of bodies – some of them real, some of them more imaginary. 'Too many to count' is a number that can be used here appropriately. We frame these bodies any number of ways, but in every case, we are bound to leave out some bodies; we can grapple with only so many things. This is how we deal with football, politics, and popular culture – we deal with them by grappling with bodies. For the sake of argument, we will call this collection of bodies 'everything' (e.g., people, presences, modes, forces).

Making meaningful music matter during Ottawa Fury football games

Think about every sound in every stadium – every sound on every terrace – each and every sound in each and every football setting. This is the study object – 'football's soundscape' – all sounds to do with footballing ('soundscape', from Schafer 1994, paraphrased as an idea and practice that signifies all sound is music and all sound-makers are musicians; 'sound and football' from Back 2003). Ecologically, Krause (2012, p. 157) insists we are studying 'anthrophony'. Indeed, these are the sounds that people made (and some of them, of course, were music).

Expressive culture; meaning; stance; grappling

Musical meaning (expressive cultural meaning; 'Meaning') comes about as the result of a complex engagement between human subjects and cultural objects (although at times, the subject/object relationship can become 'obscured' – 'slippery' – even, 'fuzzy'). We constitute our experience engaging these objects with a clear sense of pragmatic grappling. The valual quality assigned to this grappling is our *stance* (Berger 2009).[3] Everybody in every role of the production, distribution, and reception cycle of expressive culture has a stance relationship with the object of expressive culture being produced, distributed, and received.

For example, in constituting a piece of music in experience (a match day chant, reacting to a football match), Paula might sense that her club needs a lift, thereby taking a moment to find the right expression with which she can imbue and communicate endless support for her footballers (for the Ottawa Fury, an obstinate, repetitive, 'OFFC!' comes to mind, for example); this is Paula's composer's stance. In constituting the same piece in experience, while mediating the idea, Paula might turn the letters out loud, inflecting her call with rhythm, gesture, melody, and drums, signalling when and how the other supporters might join in her song. For example, while calling 'OF!', Paula might extend her arm out to her right side, looking and pointing her drumsticks away from her instrument before smashing inward, drawing two big bangs out of her standing bass drum (the big bangs are struck between the first part of the chant, the 'OF!', and again after the complimentary response, 'FC!'). Here, Paula holds a performer's stance (and simultaneously, something like a conductor's stance). In constituting the same piece in experience, a different supporter – in a listener's stance, say, Terry, for example – might perceive the participatory nature of the new music (the two big bangs and straightforward acronymic call), catch Paula's gestures, make manifest a sense of solidarity, and then proceed to join in with Paula, singing, drumming, and pointing along (here, Terry quickly switches to her performer's stance). And again, in constituting the same piece in experience, another listener in another listener's stance – perhaps a footballer on the opponent's team, taking a deep breath, about to take a free kick; say, Mendes, for example – might perceive both Paula's encouragement and Terry's solidarity and in turn adopt a (hypothetically) antithetical stance to where within, Mendes might imagine thinking something akin to, 'a goal here would really shut them up'.

And so it goes. There are many other forms of stance (and forms of stance relationship) held by different people positioned differently in the stadium (as there are many other calls with which we might perform this exercise, 'THIS IS OUR HOUSE!', for example). But keeping with 'OFFC!', we might imagine another alternative 'listener's stance' with respect to the different footballers on the different football clubs (and the more regular fans, the owners and operators of the teams, the coaches, the other musical acts hired to perform during match day, the beer vendors, and the list goes on). For example, members of the Ottawa Fury FC might indeed sense 'support', 'dig a little deeper', and find the strength to keep running (or maybe this helps the Fury's goalkeeper focus, blocking out all the other distractions).

Here, not only does every actor involved in the production, distribution, and reception cycle of expressive culture ('OFFC!' in performance) have a stance relationship with the expressive cultural object, but every actor also has a stance relationship with all the other actors attending to the same performance piece (and even further, every actor also has a stance relationship with the higher orders of situated large-scale context).

Stance relationships inflect the constitution in experience of expressive culture, affecting the interpretations of its meaning.[4]

Intentionality

Theoretically (Berger 2009), both stance and the grappling rely on the idea that consciousness is intentional – consciousness is always consciousness *of* something. And as social practice, both stance and the grappling are actively achieved by a person – by we, the people who engage the world – reaching out – grappling with real and imaginary bodies. Every actor (defined broadly) engaging with expressive culture (also defined broadly) finds any number of bodies to grapple with affectively.

Everybody held meaning. This was the basis for support; support held a meaningful ontology. In support we found others with whom and how we engaged the world, grappling with real and imaginary bodies (e.g., symbols, materials, objects, environments).

Platforming

SMR members held a similar stance and grappled with a similar collection of bodies. Together, the SMR could hold something up – this was the idea that the SMR members were 'platforming' (we held up a 'platform'; our forces were 'platformative'; our field was in and as of 'platformativity'). For the SMR, support was the basis for the platform, and somehow, the support aided and abetted 'our' Ottawa Fury FC. The Fury could stand on the SMR; 'crush' the SMR, metaphorically speaking (to be clear, here, the supporters would be 'underneath' the platform, being crushed, holding the Fury FC 'up'). 'FURY SAMBA!', we were singing, dancing, and drumming.

Musical discovery

Support was a discovery; support was a possibility; support was a becoming. We found support somewhere between our bodies; somewhere between expression and collection; between movement and rhythm; between sticks, skin, tension, and friction. Counter-traditional (meaning, 'in and as of tradition') support felt like a liberating resistance ('Do you feel better now?', 'I do', we relieve, after emoting). But tradition in the New World is trans-Atlanticism, *Non Ultra Plus*, and everything that goes along with them (colonial parties, forced migration, labour slavery, and the subjugation of the non-white body, for example).

Tradition; technology; custom; grandiloquence

Tradition is technology – the means to an end and a human activity (Heidegger 1977). By this rite, tradition must consume something that is already there already (a big river, perhaps). Tradition reads with a hint of mystery – sublime collectivity – being with others (as one) in unity. Framed as technology, tradition in Ottawa honoured loyalty and pedigree: order, ideas, leverage, and authority. Indeed, tradition climbed a chain of mastery; over each other and over the environment, objectively.

Tradition sought to represent the 'longstandingness' of something – whether or not the longstandingness was real or imaginary (i.e. continuity). To Hobsbawm (2012, pp. 2–3), tradition was the robe and wig the judge was wearing. Tradition was how we dressed up what was customary.

In Ottawa, tradition found energy and festivity (Eichberg 2009). In Ottawa, tradition found football, hand-painted instruments, and 50 to 75 people singing. Beneath the capital, these passions burned resourcefully (the mascot Sparky was a flame, for example). It was us, the supporters, who filled the reserve (revealing the matrix, 'reverse utility', and 'utility in reverse').

Canadiana; Canadians; Canadiens; Canadiennes; Canadi-x ...

Tradition applied the past to the present strategically (like retention, protention, and immediacy). In Ottawa, we had all sorts of people, but the capital's institutions were skewed towards pre-Canadians through to the early 17th century: British politicians, Irish labourers, French Canadiens, and Algonquian-speaking traders (men, almost exclusively). Facing this romantic discord (the idea that most Canadians trace their roots to non-Canadian wellsprings), Canada maintains itself one country – one political entity that in 2017 celebrated 150 years being 'True North Strong and Free'.

This is not easy; we are not family.

Indeed, it is in this space that football functions sociologically; football in Ottawa helps shape a sense of belonging. Gab informed me that nobody in the group was actually from Ottawa, like 'Ottawa natives [in air quotes]'. The whole football culture in Ottawa, while writing, was tied to this legacy (i.e. displacement and association). The whole supporters' culture was about staking claims to space – 'place-making' directly (getting people used to the situation) – 'taking place'. Indeed, in Ottawa (especially in the newly renovated TD Place Stadium), belonging sometimes felt like 'taking it'. In Ottawa we acknowledged that we were building on the traditional, unceded territories of the Algonquin nation, and inasmuch, we held responsibility to the Algonquin people and a responsibility to adhere to Algonquin cultural protocols; but how can football be so?

And these words would be substantiated ('[this] sounds like bragging, doesn't it?', Sylvain asked slyly). Understood as performance art – 'unconcealing' reality – football throws forth this set of circumstances, obviously; the 'emotion without reserve' – the 'spectacle of excess' – football in Ottawa ought to be read alongside Barthes's (1972, p. 13) studies in wrestling. Football is apparent, but in football we sense a moral ambiguity.

Doing music; sitting down; cosmopolitan bonding; musicking

But as it were, from 2014 to 2015 the SMR supported the Fury. For in and around TD Place Stadium, the supporters enacted what Christopher Small (1998) calls *musicking* (an operative term turning music into a verb). The supporters were well within the musical community. Intuitively, the SMR were making music together, apart from all the other fans who were sitting, taking in the football more 'regularly'. The SMR were markedly different in the Canadian sports stadium ecology.

For example, in Ottawa, popular, mainstream, professional sports fans were encouraged to 'take it in' while sitting, drinking, and eating. In Ottawa it would be unusual to submit to extended periods of intense music making – the 'unendurable', arduous task – sustained, strenuous, 'participatory moving and sounding-in-synchrony' (the endurance is *aguante*, in Herrera 2018, p. 471). In Ottawa, it was the winter, ice-storm emergencies that demonstrated our 'bearing the unbearable' – fighting, suffering – throwing forth a similar sense of endurance (our athletes demonstrated aguante, sure, but here I am thinking instead about supporters and fans – everyday people). In Ottawa, fans stood up and got loud in anticipation (even sometimes incensed to pre-reflexivity), but they did not usually sing, dance, clap, and drum for the duration of the contest. Aguante was not the norm in Ottawa. Faced contrapuntally (by sitting, drinking, and eating), aguante presented an alternative model of match day performance (although contests of sitting, drinking, and eating would offer aguante up for their participants). In TD Place Stadium, it felt like we flirted with the aguante. Our group worked for it – we did – but sometimes we stopped the music and flag-waving. As leisure, perhaps, aguante is too exhaustive.

Instead of aguante, being-in-the-section (being-with) felt more like what Jocelyn Guilbault (2017, p. 101) describes as *cosmopolitan musical bonding*, a form of musical being-together presenting 'across places, times, and people'. At once a verb and an affect, cosmopolitan musical bonding establishes and nurtures relationships that highlight 'affinities with particular individuals or groups and with certain soundings, for the aesthetics they convey, the ethical values they enact, the political positioning they stand for, or the ideas they communicate' (ibid.). Cosmopolitan musical bonding contained a form of endurance, certainly, but in TD Place Stadium it was more about platforming, laughter, humour, and banter than demonstrating an endurance like aguante (the psycho-social force of this coming-together was written before as 'platformativity').

Making music together; tuning in; bantering; supporting

For two people to engage in social interaction (for two people to hold the same thing 'up'), they must coordinate the temporal dimension of experience. This *mutual tuning-in* (Schütz 1951) was described before as a bantering kickabout; here, a time together begins.

As a theoretical device, mutual tuning-in relies on an understanding of time made in and as of (at least) two different modes: (1) *inner-time* (the subjective flow of the temporal; the sense that time is flying by and dragging on, and so forth) and (2) *outer-time* (mechanical time that can be atomized and measured). In outer-time, for example, a length of time might have been measured to be about 30 seconds (using a stopwatch, a timer app, 30 'Mississippis', whatever). In inner-time, however, the length of the piece would have been impossible to measure. If, for example, the inner-time took place inside a penalty shoot-out during the World Cup Final, well, the experience might have 'felt like forever' rather than 30 seconds. And in another, alternative sense of inner-time, the supporters would have to work 'step-in-step' as their music making unfolds (being different than their audience; being with each other; bantering back and forth). And in outer-time (in another loop), the supporters would consider the same tempo, or that the match kicked off at 8:00 p.m. (football tends to clocks and calendars; so does music sometimes, too). This multiple sense of time affords all parties who participated in the event to experience a synchronized, vivid, present (ibid., p. 96). Multidimensional simultaneity results in acts of communication and mutual sharing. Mutual tuning-in turns the 'I' and 'Thou' into 'We' (ibid., p. 79). As supporters, we grow old together, meaningfully.

Half-time.

Football is music; soundscape; intentionality

Kick-off to start the second half.

With a well-tempered soundscape (tuned to the acoustic environment, 'everything'), movement begets musicality; football is music and music is football, eventually. Given this rite – that expressive cultural forms can be conceptualized as moving, meaningful, intentional bodies – we demonstrate the power of mind for one thing to stand in for another. Intentionality reveals substitution's technology (we are an excitable mess of meaningful bodies). Different people possess different substitutive capacities (both in real life and in the imaginary).

Physically; mentally; spiritually

The SMR broke out into spring, organized through summer, and celebrated into fall. We gathered around football matches – singing, dancing, clapping, and drumming. The extent of this was cathartic; to Gab, the outlet effectively popped the top off the 'Ottawa Box' (a local sense of diplomatic constriction).

Football in Ottawa was a massive gathering (average attendance hovered around 5,000 people). And all parties contributed to the performance. The crowd reacted to what was going on, sounding 'OOOOH!' and 'AAAAH!' as they followed the ball. The supporters were different; the supporters were attending support, helping hold the Ottawa Fury FC 'up'. Inasmuch, the SMR offered a strenuous physical, mental, and spiritual exercise ('team spirit' is what we are thinking, although the connections between football, organized religion, and 'Spirit' are well documented; e.g. Galeano 2013, p. 9).

For example, enraptured and impassioned, Daria once shattered the full-sized orchestral bass drum mallet the SMR used to draw sound from their biggest drum (this drum, named Borthwick, was hand-painted in red and black pinstripe, honouring the Stony Monday Riot's innocent fallen one). Daria kept smacking away – bashing the drum – not attending to the mallet. Here, Daria achieved 'freedom-from'. Passion was her input – out popped her platform. And logic held that the 'birth' supported our Fury (little kits for little babies push us to imagine dressing them up).

And in other ways too, somehow, the SMR's singing and drumming helped energize the footballers. Somehow, the SMR's sounding (pressure waves in atmosphere) helped synthesize adenosine triphosphate (yes, ATP, what muscles use for fuel, chemically).

Writing on sound, music, and magic in the football stadium, Marra and Trotta (2019, p. 76) conjure Lévi-Strauss, remarking the importance of 'beliefs' in this ideal equation; but what happens when we consider 'sound, music, and medicine'? It is understood that support has incredible benefits for physical, mental, and socio-communal well-being (the psycho-social force of collective singing, dancing, and drumming is undeniable), but how might the STEM fields (science, technology, engineering, maths) work the SMR's expressions into fuel to use for energy? These are questions for the passion industry (consider, 'sustainability').

Origin stories; capital region; musical communities

In June 2011, the National Capital Region (straddling the provincial border between English Ontario and French Quebec), 'Ottawa-Gatineau' was awarded an expansion team in the North American Soccer League. It was good football, but to be a supporter you had to be passionate for sport *against* a backdrop of mainstream national sport sensibility. Football was not, for example, Canadian football (think helmets and shoulder pads),[5] nor basketball, nor hockey in the popular cultural imaginary (although more Canadians were registered to play association football than any other organized team sport). As Gab explained it, a small group of people went to those early association football matches in and around the capital region, organizing something that resembled North American football culture, in part, because not many people were doing that sort of thing. The group decided to call themselves the Bytown Boys Supporters Club. As time went by there were 'some disagreements about how to organize, how to represent [ourselves] in the stadium and like amongst four of us … we decided instead of trying to fight over what the group [meant] we would step away and try something different'. Late in 2013, Gab and the others broke off from the BBSC, forming a newer, smaller unit, calling themselves the Stony Monday Riot (named for the riot that took place in Bytown in 1849).

Analytically, for Kaufman Shelemay (2011), there are three types of musical community formations: groups of dissent, descent, and affinity. Indeed, the supporters' groups in Ottawa worked in accordance with this model, affording ethnography the ability to recognize different bounded supporters' groups being the result of, if not all of them simultaneously, at least some combination of these three group-making forces.

Being-together; being differently

The SMR and the BBSC were actively different and made it a point to disagree on things like performance practice, social politics, and musical repertoire. However, stadium policy held that both supporters' groups were bound to the same Section W, so the SMR and BBSC took the time and effort to organize themselves at distance separately (Zalis 2020). As was the case, both groups projected their synthetic[6] aesthetic imaginaries, engaging the opportunities that emerged from their physical and political positions and their collective expressive capacity (albeit differently, e.g., the BBSC's capo would use a megaphone, whereas the SMR refused electronic sound-making).

Concerning practical difference, the most apparent distinction came about with the question concerning the *capo* (conductor); the SMR did not want a capo, have a capo, nor [almost] ever follow a capo (the SMR took turns leading, under inspiration; their style was flowing, they kept the 'ball' moving around). Point-counterpoint, the BBSC's capo was featured on the front cover of the Fury FC's 2015 Season Program (typically, the BBSC's capo stood at field level, facing the BBSC on a small platform in front of Section W). On top of this, Gab also explained socio-politically that being a 'boy' was diminutive of a man ('all the shit you [get] away with … for a laugh or a fun, right?'), and Lisa, Carla, and Emily were 'Riot Girls', anyway (Gab said, 'we didn't want to be just boys'). To the SMR, support in Ottawa was faced with a 'polyspectrality'; football's cultures were supposed to be open to anybody. With an optimism stemming from the

CAD300,000,000 stadium renovation project, inclusivity and pluralism would be held alongside the 2015 FIFA Women's World Cup (coming as it were the following summer).

Sound; music; supporting

Sound and music were fundamental to the lived experience of professional football. Typically, its soundscape was put on by supporters' groups, igniting the atmosphere so rightfully associated with the beautiful game. While professional football was gaining popularity in Canada, Ottawa's live local sports fans were not yet accustomed to this type of sounding environment (especially had the sports fans taken in their sport 'traditionally', meaning, 'of popular consumption by the mainstream rather than an ethos of co-creation and grassroots music making'). In Ottawa, the sound of sport was marketized and composed of popular music mediated through loudspeakers – even at amateur and youth levels – at odds with the sonic traditions that enveloped association football transnationally (Canadian and American football would both be examples of 'football' lived differently). Instead, the SMR and BBSC convinced the owners and operators to allow for the supporters' groups to compose football's live and improvised soundtrack, acoustically (making popular music that was, for the most part, *not* electronically mediated). In this sense, TD Place Stadium became a shared space for resisting the sonic diktat of North America's professional sportscape. This resistance was in contest, however, bringing with it layers of paradox and contradiction; support in Ottawa was a power play – played and playing in 'public intimacy' (we were loud in the stadium, but there was an inward, affective experience that came about simultaneously).[7]

Musical difference: Meaning and obedience

Supporters; pep bands; consumer experience

For the SMR, match day was an outpouring of passion, and this passion belonged to them. The Ottawa Sports and Entertainment Group (OSEG), however, heard music, saw the drums, and (hypothetically) thought, 'Let's bring in a marching band' *cum* 'How might we "MAXIMIZE" consumer experience?'. And while the SMR recognized this model, they felt that *they* ought to steward the acoustic environment. This resulted in conflict.

For example, the OSEG brought in the Carleton Conspiracy Pep Band one afternoon, to play before, during, and after the game. The Conspiracy spent the day roaming the place – posting up in different sections playing popular music arranged for brass, woodwinds, and drums (imagine an arrangement of Knowles, Harrison, Carter, and Record's 2003 'Crazy in Love', for example). At one point, the Conspiracy positioned themselves behind Section W, behind the SMR on the concourse level of the stadium. Striking up, the Conspiracy played Chicago's '25 or 6 to 4' (Lamm 1970).

In this instance, the SMR and the BBSC faced the offender, turning away from the field and towards the pep band, chanting, 'THIS IS OUR HOUSE!'. Staking claims and taking place, the supporters used the powers of sound to defend their sovereign territory. 'THIS IS OUR HOUSE!' – Section W, southwest side, TD Place Stadium.

Sonic sanctioning

Over a conversation in Facebook Messenger in early 2020, Gab referred to what the SMR were doing as 'sonic sanctioning' – making the implication (and confirming Rice's 2003 observation) that different members of the different musical groups (different people) experienced the same sounds – the same musics – differently. How this worked was a study in politicization (the SMR were conscious of their platform and positioning).

Taking bets; laughing; shouting

For example (and besides the pep band vignette in the previous section), sonic sanctioning became evident when SMR members were taking bets on how soon into the first half the BBSC would begin singing '[All We Are Saying Is] Give Us a Goal' (to Lennon and McCartney's 1969 'Give Peace a Chance'). The supporter, Devon, bantered as a bookie: 'Who wants to play an over/under game with me, eleven-and-a-half minutes?'. And the BBSC could hear Devon foretelling that the BBSC's performance would arrive too early (as, in a crude metaphor, 'boys' are wont to do). Sometimes too, the SMR would rap their drums, hoping to drown out the BBSC, or at least 'let them hear it'. In TD Place Stadium, this was parliamentary music.

Simon's silence

Silent sanctioning (i.e., 'the silent treatment'), another form of sonic sanctioning appeared when the SMR did *not* join in song, for example, while the BBSC were singing 'Walking in a Fury Wonderland' (to Bernard and Smith's 1934 classic, 'Winter Wonderland'). For the SMR, singing a winter (popular, Christmas) song in the summertime was not the point of the match day exercise. Instead, the SMR would stand and stare at the BBSC rather than singing along (confirming that indeed, sometimes the two groups co-created a meaningful intergroup sounding environment).

Rachel: Restraint; constraint; constriction

Ideally, the SMR wanted to include 'you' in their platform; the SMR were an inclusive group. In this sense, the SMR stood on openness and equity without any semblance of violence or hooliganism (nor stout central authority, nor bullying). To these efforts, the SMR confronted aggressions they perceived symbolically.

For example, one proud and vocal member of the SMR, Rachel, expressed her disdain for ableist chanting. She did not like hearing 'HELEN KELLER!' or 'I'M BLIND, I'M DEAF, I WANNA BE A REF!' directed at the officials (Helen Keller ought to be celebrated in music, not used to deride the referee). Gab agreed that we should not tease others using the example of deaf-blind people (and here Gab and Rachel explained connotation, interpretation, and incompassion to me). We stopped chanting the violent piece (although we learned 'THREE BLIND MICE!' was still okay because the referees were blind animals, not deaf-blind human beings).[8]

Rachel also suggested we snip off the 'WE DON'T HAVE EBOLA!' one match day; she was unimpressed that we were shouting as if FC Edmonton's footballers had Ebola like 'everybody else' from the western capital during the city's outbreak of the virus in late 2014 (Ebola in 2014 was of a smaller scale, but consider 'WE DON'T HAVE CORONA!' when supporters return to the stadia eventually). Rachel sanctioned what she valued as expressive culture being mediated in poor taste, even though she was a fellow SMR member.

Sometimes we caught ourselves or others being insensitive (forcing unjust attacks on a person) – making amendments – 'calling people out' – applying the vernacular: 'Guys? … Come on? … Seriously? … Guys?' But here, there were no definitive terms. These were personal politics (Bonaparte 1859, pp. 85–86). We policed ourselves because none of what we were doing could be classified as real violence or hate-speech (at least we never got into trouble for any of it, anyway). Sometimes we might bring up a chant while shaking our heads, 'remembering last match'.

Betweenness; Bakhtinians

We lived between two worlds, dialogically (Bakhtin 2013); we lived between conscious reflection and pre-reflexivity. For example, after shouting 'HOT PINK!' in support and encouragement of our keeper, Romuald Peiser (wearing an entirely hot pink goalkeeper's kit), one of our members, Gary, felt compelled to clarify his position explaining that 'HOT PINK!' was in no way meant to make light of breast cancer (nor breast cancer awareness), the 'HOT PINK!' kit's intentional cause. Gary understood that the chant might have been misinterpreted. He wanted to be supportive, not offensive towards anybody. This was around the same time Justin Bieber (2015) was questioning a similar policy: 'Is it Too Late Now to Say Sorry?'

The tossers and the tallboys; real and symbolic violence

Fascinatingly, however, there was an opportunity to observe the limits of propriety. For example, against Minnesota United (the Loons), mid-August 2015, the football became vicious, teetering on violence although never breaking out into any explicitly. The beautiful game became a contact sport; tackles were made with a sense of urgency. On the field went good, hard football, free of indignance, cheap shots, or intent to cause injury.

Being new to supporterdom and located in Section W (the pitch laid out only a few metres away), it was the first time I realized just how physically association football could be played. Because in Ottawa, professional football at the highest levels (UEFA Champions League, EPL, La Liga, etc.) came only by TV (TV is a technique here rather than a specific technology – being-in-audience by distance and feed), the 'spectator' went without a sense of real physicality; by TV, silent and slow-motion tackles could seem to be embellished with injury. Fans would imitate the televised players, joking around, 'Quick, get the magic water' or 'Give my ankle a spray' before 'Jumpin' Jack Flash' (Jagger and Richards 1968) back into the football game. This is not the case with the force of football only a few metres away. Football can be a loud, fast, violent game ('STITCH 'EM UP!', we commanded, pretending to be at a hockey game).

The evening against the Loons went tense and tied up late, 1–1, in the 93rd minute. A win or draw extended our undefeated streak to 13 games over the summer. As we, the supporters, were actively engaged – chanting and drumming our most popular piece, 'OFFC!', two of our Fury came together on our opponent's midfielder, fouling the Loon as he was turning towards a teammate. Directly in line with the goal post over our keeper's left shoulder, the United were awarded a free kick from about 30 metres straight away. The substitute, Daniel Mendes, took a deep breath …

'KABOOM!' … the ball shot over the wall and into the bottom left corner of our net.

For a brief moment, we must have stopped singing.

The goal scorer ripped towards our Section W (away from his teammates), taking his jersey off, leaping, and charging. Mendes cupped his hand behind his ear. 'I CAN'T HEAR YOU!' he communicated in gesture.

The striker started flexing in front of our section. We booed, facing his sneer – pointing, bashing our drums, firing away at the offender. The other Loons made for Mendes – wings stretched out – flying towards their champion (and towards our Section W).

Here, we were furious – frustrated that our boos (that our sounding-to-dos) were too weak to actually enforce any proportionately violent counteractivity. Our boos could not 'do' anything. Indeed we escalated lexically: 'MOTHER FUCKER!' and 'FUCK YOU, MOTHERFUCKER!'. Expressive supporters were punching fists forward, 'collapsing the football universe': 'FUCK YOUR MOTHER, YOU FUCKING LOON!'.[9]

Mendes wallowed in our calling, until 20 or 30 supporters – members from both supporters' groups – started throwing beer cans at the star performer.

We, the supporters (and the OSEG, frankly) were fortunate the Loons maintained their discipline and did not enter into Section W throwing punches. To say Mendes provoked us – as audience members, performers, and co-producers of the match day – was not good enough. We took it too far, both in real life and in the imaginary. But how did Mendes's gesture communicate cause for us to strike back in such a disorderly manner? More importantly, is real violence (transducing thought into word into flying aluminum) ever the appropriate and proportional response to violence performed symbolically?

In some cases, absolutely.

But here, we must remember that Mendes only took his shirt off. He was only 'flying hard', flexing, and cupping his hand behind his ear. Mendes was not signalling hatred, pointing names, being racist, a xenophobe, or even a bigot. Mendes was signalling that he had power over us; that his body won the match day (and in football, this was 'truth', so to speak; although we should note that Mendes did receive a yellow card for his dance routine). Yes, Mendes's actions were violent, sure, but more in the sense of not *really* ('truth; win; strong; man' are not necessarily violent things). It was us, the supporters, who were throwing stones, metaphorically.

On our end, nobody knew who tossed the first tallboy, and none of the supporters reported each other for throwing anything (and all told, the event was over pretty quickly). One supporter even wanted Mendes to apologize for starting the whole thing.[10]

Conclusion

Here, we queried match day and listened to supporters to learn about football, politics, and public performance (citing popular culture, poetry, folklore, and storytelling). We wrote about musical people, match day, and noted three key players in the stadium's acoustic environment: the Stony Monday Riot and the Bytown Boys Supporters Club (both of whom were groups of football supporters), and the Ottawa Sports and Entertainment Group (who owned and operated the Ottawa Fury Football Club of the North American Soccer League).

To engage the soundscape politically (while considering its contents with respect to real and imaginary bodies), we processed experiential data vis-à-vis intentionality (the power of mind for one thing to stand for another, the idea that cultural objects are bodies, and 'the idea that ideas are things'). Here, we learned about supporters' groups, identification issues, and how our simplest expressions ought to be inquired of and considered critically – imagine, 'THIS IS OUR HOUSE!' in face of Ottawa's truth and (re)conciliatory setting. Understanding these acts technologically (citing collectivity; belonging; leverage; authority), we learned about TD Place Stadium, and its representation (reproduction) of subject/object relations (i.e., 'tradition' was 'climbing over each other and over the environment', respectively).

Against the force of this striking incompatibility, we took a place to be together meaningfully. Achieving this musically, we examined our practice experientially. We learned about affective/subjective inner-time and the mechanical/objective outer-time – as we learned how step-by-step we were in a 'time-together' as we, the supporters, 'grew old'. Accepting this sentiment (i.e., embracing it, mutually tuning-in), we quested through proxemics – reaching out for feedback – building a vivid present while putting the past within it, strategically (as composers, performers, and audience members simultaneously). The result of this togetherness (our manifest platform) held 'up' the Fury FC (among other, institutional beings).

And in spite of all these contradictions (complications; complexifications), what emerged from the Ottawan match day was a visceral sense of oneness ('being-together') that somehow maintained a place for meaningfully being differently. These acts of personal nature became apparent when we considered Gab's 'sonic sanctioning'; we studied how indeed the SMR and BBSC *could* distance themselves, and how sound and silence did 'bridge the gap' im/materially. Indeed, we learned how the SMR worked their differences out into different relationships with the BBSC, the OSEG, the pep band, Minnesota United FC, and between different members of the SMR, themselves, tastefully.

Towards a meaningful theory of support (and a preliminary sense of platforming), we grounded our work in the politics of expressive culture, citing stance (often the pivot of meaning, from Berger 2009) and a transient, New World, cosmopolitan musical bonding (stressing, 'the political positioning they stand for' in Guilbault 2017, p. 101). The SMR could support their Fury because in some sense, we, the SMR, were being crushed by a similar sense of something. With this as the case, on match day we popped the top off – making music together until we felt better, collectively.

Full time.

Notes

1 I must thank and acknowledge Dr. Carolyn Ramzy and Dr. William Echard for their support and supervision during the fieldwork portion of this study.

2 Although the institutional names in this chapter have been maintained, all individual supporters have been given pseudonyms.

3 Extending a definitive note, Berger (2009, p. 137) writes: 'The word *valual* is the adjectival form of value. In everyday life, we experience things not only as having factual properties (size, shape, weight, etc.), but also as having qualities that involve their value for us. For example, we may experience an object on a store shelf as desirable or repellent, useful or useless, exciting or soothing, comfortably familiar or disturbingly strange'. Here, I wish to extend a similar sort of qualitative assessment to the objects of culture held within football's soundscape.

4 Here I must express warmth and gratitude to Dr. Harris M. Berger, whose patience, guidance, and clear contributions to phenomenological ethnomusicology inform most if not all my ongoing work in sport and musical performance.

5 In the same TD Place Stadium, the OSEG owned and operated the Ottawa REDBLACKS Canadian football team. To give a scale to popular cultural presence, the REDBLACKS averaged 23,225 people in attendance over their 2015 season.

6 'Synthetic', here, meaning 'a synthesis of parts', not a value judgement concerned with any artifice or inauthenticity.

7 Here I must give thanks and due respect to Dr. Jonathan Dueck, a mentor and fellow ethnomusicologist who, in personal communication and writing, shared this understanding of 'public intimacy' with me (clarifying that he himself adapted his understanding of 'public intimacy' from Dr. Byron Dueck's work on musical intimacies and Indigenous imaginaries; e.g., Dueck 2013).

8 Note: dehumanization.

9 Here, I cannot help but think about the stadium, the steam-valve (i.e., 'gas flare' or 'flare stack'), and the contextual nature of consequence. Imagine shouting 'FUCK YOUR MOTHER, YOU FUCKING LOON!' across the street, inside the local institutional Kettleman's Bagel? Somebody would intervene thinking it was lunacy. And even more risky behaviour should the performer be an Indigenous/Black/Person of Colour in Canada for whom police intervention into mental health crises turn lethal more frequently.

10 Thinking back, we never should have booed in the first place. We should have turned to our music; we should have ignored the Loons and supported our Fury. We should have been singing 'FURY, WE'RE ALWAYS WITH YOU!' (to the tune of Joel Plaskett's 2006 hit, 'Nowhere With You').

References

Back, L. 2003. 'Sounds in the Crowd'. In *The Auditory Culture Reader*, edited by M. Bull and L. Back. Oxford: Berg.

Bakhtin, M. 1984. *Rabelais and His World, translated by H Iswolsky*, Bloomington, IN: Indiana University Press.

Bakhtin, M. 2013. *Speech Genres and Other Late Essays, translated by V.W.* McGee Austin, TX: University of Texas Press.

Barthes, R. 1972. 'The World of Wrestling'. *In Mythologies, translated by Annette Lavers*, New York, NY: The Noonday Press.

Berger, H.M. 2009. *Stance: Ideas about Emotion, Style, and Meaning for the Study of Expressive Culture, Middletown*, CT: Wesleyan University Press.

Bernard, F., and R.B. Smith. 1934. *'Winter Wonderland', Track 1 of Winter Wonderland/ Water Under The Bridge*, Decca Records.

Bieber, J. 2015. *'Sorry', Track 4 of Purpose*, Def Jam.

Bonaparte, N.L. 1859. *Napoleonic Ideas, translated by J.A. Dorr*. New York, NY: D. Appleton & Company.

Dueck, B. 2013. *Musical Intimacies and Indigenous Imaginaries: Aboriginal Music and Dance in Public Performance*. Oxford: Oxford University Press.

Eichberg, H. 2009. 'The Energy of Festivity: Atmosphere, Intonation, and Self-Orchestration in Danish Popular Sports'. In *Sporting Sounds: Relationships Between Sport and Music*, edited by A. Bateman and J. Bale. New York, NY: Routledge.

Galeano, E. 2013. *Soccer in Sun and Shadow, translated by Mark Fried*, New York, NY: Nation Books.

Geertz, C. 1972. 'Deep Play: Notes on the Balinese Cockfight', *Dædalus* 101 (1), 1–37.

Guilbault, J. 2017. 'The Politics of Musical Bonding: New Prospects for Cosmopolitan Music Studies'. In *Perspectives on a 21st Century Comparative Musicology: Ethnomusicology or Transcultural Musicology*, edited by F. Giannattasio, and G. Giuriati. Udine: NOTA.

Heidegger, M. 1977. 'The Question Concerning Technology'. In *The Question Concerning Technology and Other Essays, translated by William Lovitt*, New York, NY: Garland.

Herrera, E. 2018. 'Masculinity, Violence, and Deindividuation in Argentine Soccer Chants: The Sonic Potentials of Participatory Sounding-In-Synchrony'. *Ethnomusicology*, 62(3): 471–500.

Hobsbawm, E. 2012. 'Introduction: Inventing Traditions'. In *The Invention of Tradition*, edited by E. Hobsbawm and T. Ranger, 20th ed., New York, NY: Cambridge University Press.

Jack, M. 2018. 'On the Terrace: Ritual Performance of Identity and Conflict by the Shamrock Rovers Football Club Ultras in Dublin'. *Ethnomusicology Review*, 18.

Jagger, M., and K. Richards. 1968. 'Jumpin' Jack Flash', Track 1 of Jumpin' Jack Flash, Decca Records.

Kaufman Shelemay, K. 2011. 'Musical Communities: Rethinking the Collective in Music'. *Journal of the American Musicological Society*, 64(2): 349–390.

Knowles, B., R. Harrison, S. Carter, and E. Record. (2003) *'Crazy in Love', Track 1 of Dangerously in Love*, Columbia Records.

Krause, B. 2012. *The Great Animal Orchestra*, New York, NY: Back Bay Books.

Lamm, R. 1970. '25 or 6 to 4', Track 8 of Chicago, Columbia Records.

Lennon, J., and McCartney, P. 1969. *'Give Peace a Chance', Track 1 of Give Peace a Chance/ Remember Love*, Apple Records.

Marra, P.S. and Trotta, F. 2019. 'Sound, Music, and Magic in Football Stadiums'. *Popular Music*, 38(1): 73–89.

McCrae, J. and J. Ferres. 1918. *In Flanders Fields*, Montreal: Stanley Court.

Plaskett, J. 2006. *'Nowhere With You', Track 7 of Truthfully*, Truthfully, Universal Music Canada.

Rice, T. 2003. 'Time, Place, and Metaphor in Musical Experience and Ethnography'. *Ethnomusicology*, 47:(2), 151–179.

Schafer, R. M. 1994. *The Soundscape: Our Sonic Environment and the Tuning the World*, 2nd ed., Rochester, VT: Destiny Books.

Schütz, A. 1951. 'Making Music Together-A Study in Social Relationship'. *Social Research*,18(1): 76–97.

Small, C. 1998. *Musicking: The Meanings of Performing and Listening*, Middletown, CT: Wesleyan University Press.

Zalis, J. 2020. 'Mais alto!' 'Faça algum barulho!' 'De pé!': Pensado através de um estatuto sônico, esporte professional e 'ficar sentado', in Castanheira, J., et al. (eds.) *Poderes do Som: Políticas, Escutas e Identidades*, translated by José Cláudio S. Castanheira, Florianópolis: Insular, 73–92.

Part II

Football and screen

Chapter 5

Kicking, not screaming

An examination of football (soccer) and female footballers in Australian screen-based narratives

Freya Wright-Brough and Lee McGowan

Though women have been playing football (soccer) in Australia for over a century (McGowan 2019; Downes et al. 2015; Williams 2007), their games have been available on screen only in the last decade. It was not until 2019 that all of the Matildas' (the Australian national women's team) matches were broadcast or at least live-streamed for the first time. Likewise, the national professional league competition, the Westfield W-League, has only recently entered into a deal with free-to-air national broadcaster, the Australian Broadcasting Corporation (ABC), to televise one club-level match per week with additional 'Finals' matches on delayed broadcast. This expands on access provided by pay TV broadcaster Foxtel (and their dedicated sports streaming service Kayo), whose coverage includes regular live and delayed W-League matches across the competition. Though women's football has not featured on Australian screens for long, it can attract a significant audience. The recent international friendly fixtures between Australia and Chile, a key component in Australia's 2023 Women's World Cup bid, attracted a substantial screen audience of 243,000 on Australian free-to-air coverage (Manning 2019).

Until recently, outside of live broadcasts of and accompanying commentary on professional male club and national matches, there are only a handful of instances where football has featured in Australian screen content. With very few exceptions, the football contained in these productions was played by male players and teams. Prior to 2016, stories about female footballers enjoyed very little presence on Australian screens. The lack of match broadcasting as well as Australian screen productions telling stories about female footballers has been a continuing central concern amid a range of issues and obstacles placed in the way of female footballers. This is because lack of support and coverage has limited awareness, participation and socialisation of the game at local, state and national levels (see Cauldwell 2011).[1] Increasing the visibility of women's football, by including more extensive television coverage of matches and supplementary reportage, expands awareness and increases participation rates (May 2020; Reece et al. 2017). The introduction of screen productions with female footballers as protagonists will arguably further inform and influence this process.

As of early 2020, three 'homemade' Australian productions about female footballers in three discrete formats are available to viewers on the streaming platforms DisneyNOW, CBBC iPlayer and the ABC's iView. *Back of the Net* (2018) is a feature-length Australian film with a Disney star in the lead role and a cameo from a highly successful Australian footballer; *Kick* (2017–2020) is an ABC documentary series focused on a group of young women playing for state and national teams; and *Mustangs FC* (2017–2020) is an ABC drama series, aimed at children from 8 to 12 years old (Keast 2017, p. 14), which follows the first all-female football team at the fictional Mustangs Football Club.[2]

These three screen productions represent the Australian screen industry's first representations of female footballers as protagonists at the centre of the story. In this chapter, we examine these significant screen text portrayals of female footballers in relation to broader representations of female footballers in the Australian media and the ways these productions resist previously totalising portrayals of female footballers. Levinasian (1969) notions of totality and infinity inform this exploration, and it is argued that these productions foster more 'ethical encounters' with female footballers.

We begin by contextualising the Australian media's treatment of women's football to date and introducing Levinasian notions of totality (the reduction of another) and infinity (the alterity of another who cannot be fully comprehended). A more detailed analysis of the three productions follows, examining how they may represent a departure from dominant totalising representations of female footballers. Finally, we conclude by discussing whether increased opportunities for female filmmakers has enabled stories about female footballers to emerge, identifying key methods the productions use to work towards more ethical relations with female footballers.

Representation of women's football in the Australian media

In Australia and elsewhere, women's football has become increasingly popular in terms of interest and participation. FIFA estimates suggest over 1.12 billion people consumed at least part of a match during the FIFA Women's World Cup in France in 2019 (Publicis Sport and Entertainment 2019). The tournament has since been positioned in the media as a watershed moment, 'a turning point' (Wrack 2019), for women's football. As football is the world's most popular sport in terms of audience and participation, it is not surprising that FIFA's signature global tournament for women has come to represent the rising tide for women's sport.

However, recent attention to women's football is noted by McLachlan (2019) as being part of a harmful pattern of representation of women's sport in the media. McLachlan (2019) analysed contemporary articles about women's sport between 2015 and 2017 and found a recurring theme of excitement over a boom in women's sport in Australia, including many examples focusing on growth in women's football. After examining articles from previous eras with similar representations of women's sport, McLachlan (2019, p. 20) concludes that this constant representation of 'boom' is 'potentially part of the very structure that prevents long-term change being achieved'. McLachlan (2019, p. 16) critiques the Australian media's common notion of a boom occurring because of unprecedented 'successes of Australian athletes on the world stage', and recognises that female athletes have often achieved similar successes on the world stage in years prior to the reports. By examining this pattern of representing women's sporting success as unprecedented, McLachlan (2019, p. 21) establishes a need for engagement in historical critique to generate more nuanced understandings of women's sport in Australia.

A lack of historical awareness of women's football in the Australian media is not surprising given that the history of Australian women's football is not well chronicled (Crawford and McGowan 2019). This has potentially contributed to repetition of 'boom' narratives in women's football reporting. In this chapter, we seek to acknowledge the increase in interest and participation in women's football that may have enabled female footballers to become protagonists on screen without erasing the successful history of the women's game in Australia or contributing to a simplistic narrative of continuous improvement in attitudes towards, or representations of, female footballers.

To put the popularity of women's football in context, on 17 March 2019, Atlético Madrid played Barcelona before an audience of 60,739 in the Metropolitano stadium Madrid. Globally, this is the largest crowd to ever attend a domestic club match between two female football teams. However, well-attended women's matches in Europe are by no means a recent phenomenon. In 1920 a women's match in England sold out, with 53,000 people watching and 14,000 locked out (Crawford and McGowan 2019, p. 14). The following year, women were banned from playing football, causing interest and participation in the women's game to substantially decline. In Australia, the recent Matildas match played at BankWest Stadium, Sydney, in November 2019 attracted 20,029, the largest ever attendance at an Australian women's football match. However, it must be noted that large crowds at Australian women's football are not new either. A match at the Brisbane Cricket Ground, The Gabba, on 24 September 1921 drew a crowd of 10,000 before the Melbourne-based British Association Interstate Conference elected to follow its European FA counterparts and not recognise women's football and ban women from playing on association grounds (McGowan 2019, p. 196). Women's football around the world and in Australia has a history of mass interest and participation together with obstacles and decline.

Currently, however, it appears that Australia and other nations are experiencing a rising interest in the women's game. According to estimates, 1.85 million Australians regularly participate in football; over 400,000 of these participants are women and girls (Sport Australia 2019). The Matildas' emergence into the mainstream coincided with the success of now world-renowned player Sam Kerr and the team's defeat of the US National Women's Soccer Team in the United States in the inaugural tournament of nations in 2017. Returning from their success in the US, their first home fixtures drew what were then unprecedented crowds – 16,800 at Penrith in September 2017. The domestic elite professional competition, the Westfield W-League, is now drawing crowds that are becoming comparable to their male counterpart A-League attendances – though this may in part be due to a decline in attendances at the men's league matches (Tuckerman 2019).

Despite the current demonstrated interest in participating in and watching Australian women's football, men's sport continues to dominate the Australian sports media landscape, meaning representations of women's football in the media continues to be diminished. Indeed, Caple et al. (2011, pp. 138–139) found that sports reporting is skewed to male sport and that horseracing received 'more airtime on Australian television news than women's sport'. They also found that 'news coverage of male athletes was subject to more sustained levels of reporting year-round' and that when women's sport was reported on, it received 30 seconds less time than reports on male sports (Caple et al. 2011, p. 139). In her more recent analysis of 'long-term trends of the framing of positive commentaries about women's sport', Fiona McLachlan (2019, p. 8) notes this skew continues despite reportage to the contrary.

Historically, female footballers have been represented in the Australian media patronisingly, as a novelty and/or as a sexual object. In 1903, a small group of women persuaded the secretary of the Clyde Engineering Sports Club, Sydney, to assist them in forming arguably Australia's first women's team (*The Cumberland Argus and Fruitgrowers Advocate* 1903, p. 5). When the CE Sports Club's secretary raised concerns about the dangers of the sport and what women would wear, the pioneering footballers assured him they would not engage with rough play and agreed to wear modern ladies' bicycle outfits (*The Cumberland Argus and Fruitgrowers Advocate* 1903, p. 5). In the 1940s, one commentator saw fit to attach comical sound effects to tackles during a women's match in Sydney suggesting that the match should not be taken seriously (British Pathé n.d.). The commentator (British Pathé n.d.) also confined the players to the role of sexual objects, stating that the largely male crowd were less concerned about the result than they were about the players' apparel. Representations of female football players as sexual objects persisted. For example, Hay and Murray (2014, pp. 627–628) highlight an article published in 1973 which asks if the women wear garters to hold up their socks. The accompanying photograph captured the 'Ladies of St George Budapest', one of the strongest teams in Sydney and consequently in the country, applying make-up and brushing their hair while dressed in their football strips (Hay and Murray 2014, pp. 627–628). During the run-up to the 2000 Sydney Olympics, the Matildas agreed to publish a nude calendar to raise monies essential to fund their campaign. Still one of Australia's fastest-ever-selling calendars, it received scathing editorial commentary suggesting the players had sought the attention of male fans and little more (Crawford and McGowan 2019, p. 95).

The sexualised images of female sports representatives are now being replaced with images of women as serious athletes and the coverage of women's football in what would be regarded as mainstream media is becoming more respectful.

However, representations of female footballers remain problematic in many ways, as Toffoletti and Palmer (2019, p. 5) note:

> the combination of grit and glamour that characterises contemporary imagery of empowered sporting femininity belies the challenges everyday women face in materialising a 'can-do' athletic subjectivity as well as the tensions women encounter in attempting to meet current social ideals of feminine athleticism that frequently reward a combination of strength, whiteness and (hetero)sexiness.

Football in Australian film and television

Despite the 100- to 150-year existence of men's (Syson 2018; Downes et al. 2015; Adair 2009) and women's football in Australia (McGowan 2019; Hay and Murray 2014; Williams 2007; Stell 1991), there has been very little screen content devoted to the women's game until recently. Free-to-air broadcaster the Special Broadcasting Service (SBS) initially had the monopoly on men's and women's football, as no other channel saw football as a key component of their sports programming. The partially government-funded broadcaster is also closely associated with the country's most diverse approach to programming and a substantial migrant viewership. More commercialised channels, Seven and Nine, have at times sought to capture the football audience following the incredible ratings success of the SBS coverage of the 2002 FIFA Men's World Cup in Japan and South Korea, but Channel Nine was heavily criticised for its broadcast of the 2006 Men's World Cup matches. The move was largely seen as an incursion into territory the commercial channels did not fully comprehend, which was reflected in their poor coverage and commentary during matches.

From 2009 to 2013, the ABC broadcast a weekly match from the W-League, but across a 12-week season, including finals, and dependent on outside broadcast capacity, this amounted to fewer than 50 matches. While coverage was intended to be regular, it was often impacted by 'higher priority' broadcasts. In one case, the 2014 Semi-Final play-off between Brisbane Roar and Sydney, a match that had gone into extra time and was to be decided in a penalty shootout, was cut off as the first penalty was taken. In this instance, it was not a matter of 'higher priority' but rather a simple error in programming – the next show on the schedule started. Viewers at home would not know the result until later, unless they were able to contact someone in the small crowd (Crawford and McGowan 2019).

In contrast, the men's national competition, the Hyundai A-League established in 2004, has had every match broadcast by Foxtel via their sports channels. While heavily supporting the League's development, Foxtel also exploited work done by SBS, which had until that point actively and successfully grown their football television audience through a long-established authentic and passionate advocacy for the game. SBS's sports coverage would, for example, feature more regular updates on the Matildas and included *Never Say Die*, the short documentary film of the team's fortunes at the 2007 FIFA Women's World Cup in China. Outside of the televised matches featuring the national team and the fixtures from the W-League broadcast by the ABC, it would be 2017 before we would see Australian female footballers on our screens on a more regular basis.

In terms of fictionalised screen content, the best-known football films have emerged from Europe and focus on male players. There is a rich tradition of male footballers in film (see Glynn 2018 for example) and in television, including recent examples *O11NCE* (pronounced 'Once') the Spanish language series produced by Disney (2017–2019) and four seasons of *Jamie Johnson* (2016–) produced by the British Broadcasting Corporation. However, there are several notable fictional screen representations of female footballers. *Gregory's Girl* (1980) was possibly one of the first films to feature a female footballer, a player so good she transformed a poor boys' high school team. The cross-cultural 'dramedy', *Bend It Like Beckham* (2002) – followed by its novelisation (Dhami 2004) and a successful West End musical (2015) – is regarded as groundbreaking because it focuses on women's football and has been the subject of much academic discussion exploring gender, identity and cultural representation (see Abdel-Shehid and Kalman-Lamb 2015; Ratna 2011; Walseth 2006). The film successfully drew on the cultural cache of former England player David Beckham, whose fame moved beyond playing football, to challenge traditional femininities and masculinities and illustrate a more openly inclusive world of women's football. In 2007, the US-made film *Gracie* achieved a degree of critical but not commercial success. Episodic series have been rarer still. In 2003, an Israeli football series, *Adumot* (2003–2004), featured a girls' team, and much more recently *The Kicks* (2018–), based on a book series co-authored by US soccer star Alex Morgan, also featured a young female team.

Australia has been very slow to broadcast football-related screen content, particularly series or films related to female footballers. It would seem then that this recent turn toward televising female football in Australia is about more than the emergence of female footballers into the mainstream. Before we examine the three works at the centre of this chapter, they will be contextualised with a brief consideration of football's presence in fictionalised, reality and documentary Australian screen content.

Filmed entirely in Adelaide, *Struck by Lightning* (1990) featured popular Australian actor Garry McDonald as a former schoolteacher employed by the male supervisor of a community support service for people living with intellectual disabilities to form a football team – the Heartbreakers. The film centres on the relationship between the two men – one old, one young – and the community they help build. The film's themes of acceptance of difference, the strength found in vulnerability and shared learning echo some of football's own struggles in Australian culture.

Few football films have made their mark more firmly on the Australian psyche than the acclaimed and commercially successful Australian film *Heartbreak Kid* (1993). The film plays to existing stereotypes of football in Australia as a game for predominantly European immigrants. It portrays the torrid affair between a teacher, played by Claudia Karvan, and her student, an angry young footballer, played by Alex Dimitriades. Karvan's teacher establishes a football team to help manage schoolyard tensions, but inadvertently finds herself the subject of the player's emotional attachment. Amid scenes highlighting their blossoming affection for each other, Karvan's character joins in a practice match – which could be the first time a female Australian character plays football on film. Alongside their fraught and taboo relationship, the film explores issues of nationalism and identity in multicultural Australia. The illustration of cross-cultural potential of football as a force for unity and a mechanism to challenge those barriers and boundaries created by patriarchal Anglo norms, norms that continue to dominate Australian society, offers rich terrain for further research.

The film's success led to the seven-season series, *Heartbreak High* (1994–1999). The first season picked up from where the film left off and included members of the original cast, focusing on the challenges faced by multicultural teenagers in an Anglo-centric fictitious suburb of Sydney. Football featured briefly in a small number of episodes in the first season, particularly episode nine where the primary narrative centred on the school's football team. In later episodes, as noted by Lesleyanne Hawthorne (1995), the 'ethnic' cast were almost all replaced with Anglo-Australians, basketball quickly came to the fore as the sport of choice, and the series moved to explore a different range of issues.

Running across the timing of *The Heartbreak Kid* and its spin-off, *Acropolis Now* (1988–1992), a comedy sketch show, openly poked fun at Australia's significant Greek culture while slyly casting glances at other Australian-based ethnicities and Anglo-Australians. Episode five in the show's third season features a now-famous sketch with a guest appearance by Russell Crowe, who plays football star Danny O'Brian, an Anglo-Australian footballer playing for the predominantly Greek, South Melbourne club. O'Brian (Crowe) goes on a date with a woman to an Italian restaurant. The ensuing comedy is derived from parodies and sweeping cultural generalisations and tensions.

The reality television series *Nerds FC* (2005–2007), which aired on SBS, used football as the basis for social experiment on 14 self-confessed 'Nerds', at a point when the cultural label held derogatory connotations. The men who had never taken part in active sport were trained as a group to play football. In one episode, the nerds' team play the Young Matildas and lose 11-nil and in Episode Seven, the Nerds get a rematch, this time losing only 5-nil. The Young Matildas are presented as an experienced and successful team. However, they are also positioned as an early test for the final match of the series against a men's A-League team.

Also aligned with the A-League, the three seasons of *Football Superstar* (2008–2010) featured a development process, though its intention was to focus on talent identification. Structured as a last-player-standing competitive show, the best player from each season was offered the opportunity to trial with an A-League club. Of the three young men who each won a season, only one would play in the A-League. The only female involved in the show's presentation and participation, was co-presenter and former Matilda Amy Duggan.

While the series aired and the A-League was gaining some traction in the mainstream media, an Australian feature film about football was being produced in South Australia. *Offside* (2009) is a little known, poorly distributed and low-budget romantic comedy about two brothers approaching the end of their careers and needing a win to save their club and their relationships. In brother Charlie's case, the relationships to be saved were with a stream of 'girlfriends'.

The 2017 National Indigenous Television (NITV) documentary *Australian Soccer's Dreaming* focused on the John Moriarty Football program and the National Indigenous Football Championship's capacity to provide pathways for young Indigenous footballers. Moriarty, Australia's first Indigenous national team player and civil rights activist, initiated his eponymous academy for young people, irrespective of gender, to develop football talent. The documentary features Shadeene Evans, a scholarship recipient, who regularly plays for the Young Matildas and in the Westfield W-League. The documentary was produced by NITV (part of the SBS network) and aired on the SBS On Demand platform. Alongside live airing of W-League matches, Australian government-funded screen practitioners have arguably been at the forefront of producing representations of female footballers seen in Australian screen content.

Resisting the totalisation of female footballers

Given the constrictive representations of female footballers in the Australian media, Levinas's notions of totality and infinity provide a useful way of thinking about resisting these narrow and limiting representations. Levinas (1969, p. 196) proposes that '[t]o know amounts to grasping being out of nothing or reducing it to nothing, removing from it its alterity', suggesting that attempts to know the Other absolutely are an act of totalisation and linking comprehension with possession (Raviv 2019, p. 67). In opposition to totality, Levinas presents the notion of infinity as a more ethical engagement with the Other. He describes this ethical engagement by stating 'to approach the Other in conversation is to welcome his [*sic*] expression, in which at each instant he [*sic*] overflows the idea a thought would carry away from it. It is therefore to receive from the Other beyond the capacity of the I, which means exactly: to have the idea of Infinity' (Levinas 1969, p. 51). Raviv (2019, p. 67) explains that for Levinas, 'ethical relations require the subject to give up her inherent tendency to force her own concepts onto what is different from her'. The notion of infinity provides a way of thinking about resisting oversimplified and narrow understandings of an Other, in this case, female footballers.

Although Levinas's notions of totality and infinity apply to face-to-face encounters and he opposes the application of his notions to art, many scholars argue that Levinas's work is applicable to the arts (Robbins 1995; Nowak 2010; Burke 2011; Burvill 2013; Balfour 2013). Nowak (2010, p. 274) argues that '[e] thics may at times involve representation which takes us away from the Other, while at the same time that same representation may refer us to that which is beyond representation'. There are particularly strong links between filmmaking and Levinas's work (Renov 2004; Cooper 2006; Saxton 2007; Nash 2011; Baek 2016; Colusso 2017; Raviv 2019). In line with Nowak's (2010, p. 274) logic that representations can in some instances refer their audience to what Levinas would call infinity, Saxton (2007) and Cooper (2006) both provide evidence that constructing narratives where the portrayal of a documentary subject frustrates the audience's desire to fully know them is one way of resisting totalising representations. In this chapter, we argue that the chosen screen texts, *Kick*, *Back of the Net* and *Mustangs FC*, also resist totalising representations of female footballers using similar techniques to refer their audience to what Levinas calls infinity.

Kick

Kick mostly follows the conventions of the expository documentary mode, constructing an informative tone by utilising 'voice of authority' narration, evidentiary editing and planned interviews which further guide the visuals of the narrative (Nichols 2017, p. 123). Miette Georgio's narration and the inclusion of video diaries from the other documentary subjects allow the series to incorporate elements of the performative mode as well. The show's origins reflect the same entrepreneurial drive that has informed the development of women's football in Australia. *Kick* began with 11-year-old junior footballer Georgio establishing a Vimeo channel as a showcase for footage of her team's matches. The channel features appearances from Matildas and Socceroos players and mock interviews with players and teammates. Georgio's father Dean supported Miette's passion for football filmmaking, and together they produced the 14-minute documentary *Time to Shine*. Since then, the concept has developed into the ABC TV multiseries documentary produced and filmed by Dean Georgio and Paul Zarogiannis.

Miette remains part of the filmmaking team, contributing as a content consultant, narrator and documentary subject within the narrative. The first series featured Miette playing for her local team. The second series followed Miette, aged 12, after being selected for the elite training program based at Victorian National Training Centre (NTC). The scope of the third season series is markedly larger, as it documents Miette and five other rising stars of football in Victoria. It was filmed over a two-year period in Victoria as well as overseas and interstate. The fourth season commissioned by the ABC (with Foxtel coming onboard) will document the junior Matildas on tour. Both channels also entered into an agreement to live-broadcast W-League matches from the 2019–2020 season.

Miette's involvement in the series may be representative of the current memoir boom described by Anderst (2017, p. 256) where documentarians tell their own stories or use 'bits and pieces of their lives in the service of projects focused on a wider group, place, or issue', in this case the wider group of female football players featured in *Kick*. Dowmunt (2013, p. 263) suggests that the current growth of personal documentaries 'may have been stimulated by the increasing availability of accessible digital recording technologies'. Accessibility of recording technologies and also distribution methods could be seen as a factor in the success of *Kick*. However, we note that access to technology does not equate to a democratic system of filmmaking and storytelling.

Miette's voice not only organises the film, it shifts the tone from authoritative to personal (Nichols 2017, p. 124) and provides a sense of authenticity. Nichols (2017, p. 153) suggests that such performative films 'share a rebalancing and corrective tendency with autoethnography', allowing for members of communities who are often spoken about to speak for themselves and represent their community in their own way. Given that female footballers in Australia have historically been sexualised or represented as a joke, *Kick* represents a marked difference in the way female players are represented. From the moment an episode begins, the documentary subjects are presented as serious athletes. For example, series three opens with a montage of the documentary subjects lacing up their boots, strapping their shin pads and staring down the lens with focused expressions. Spectators are also represented as legitimate fans who admire their skill as players. For example, a scene in series three depicts Kyra Cooney-Cross signing autographs for younger fans. Miette's continued presence as a narrator, filmmaker and member of the female football community represents the production team's commitment to welcoming the expression of the Other which Levinas (1969, p. 51) positions as a crucial part of an ethical relation. By continuing to welcome Miette's expression in the production, the series begins to resist the dominant representations of women's football in Australia.

Back of the Net

Back of the Net is a feature film released in Australian cinemas as well as on the Disney Channel in the United States. The film's protagonist, Cory, is a young science enthusiast who dreams of being on a research ship for a semester. But after catching the wrong bus and missing the research ship, she must complete a semester at football school instead. A number of other conflicts emerge as she must compete with the young woman who becomes her nemesis, top female player Edie who is captain of the 'E' – for excellence – team. After initially hating soccer, Cory makes friends with her misfit roommates and discovers a love of football through her scientific knowledge. When Cory is given an opportunity to return to her old life, her new friends convince her to stay, and the group wins the tournament. The frequent references to the game as soccer, and the inclusion of an American protagonist, along with Caitlin Foord, a successful female player in both the US League and the W-League, are made with the intent of the film being accessible to US audiences.

In a similar fashion to *Kick*, *Back of the Net* portrays female football players as serious athletes. Though Cory's team is not taken seriously in the first and second act because they are the 'worst of the best', many other female teams are presented as legitimate teams. Cory's bully and nemesis, Edie, is portrayed as the school's star player, with Cory's friends relaying rumours that Edie learnt to dribble the day she learnt to walk and that Pelé and Ronaldo are her uncles. Female football also appears to be taken seriously by male players, with the male leads turning up to watch the girls' grand final match (although it must be noted that one of those male players is romantically interested in Cory). By portraying female footballers as serious athletes, rather than comical because of their gender, *Back of the Net* begins to resist dominant representations of female football players in Australia as amateur players who should not be taken seriously.

Back of the Net also begins to resist dominant Hollywood representations of young female athletes as misfits. In her analysis of Hollywood children's sporting films featuring female athletes, Lieberman (2014, p. 57) suggests that while male children are often portrayed as participating in sport to fit in, females in sport are often positioned as misfits. She goes on to argue that 'the athletic prowess of a girl should not be the quality that makes her a "misfit"' (2014, p. 76). *Back of the Net* positions the protagonists as misfits because of their lack of sporting prowess, and they finally win acceptance with others in the school by improving their abilities as athletes. By inverting the trope of a children's sporting film, *Back of the Net* is able to overturn the message that athletic prowess makes girls misfits.

Though each individual character is portrayed as having a fixed and stable identity (e.g. the fashionista, the organiser, the scientist and the rich student), as a group, female footballers are represented as diverse in talent and background. Similar to the way Cooper (2006) and Saxton (2007) describe a documentary's ability to represent documentary subjects as unknowable, *Back of the Net* frustrates the audience's desire to fully know the female footballer as a fixed identity defined by amateur technique and sexualised beauty. This technique can also be seen in *Mustangs FC*.

Mustangs FC

Mustangs FC began production in 2017 and launched the same year on International Day of the Girl. The series has since aired its third season in early 2020. Amanda Higgs and Rachel Davis created and produced the show for Australian production company Matchbox Pictures and ABC's channel ABC Me with support from Screen Australia and Film Victoria. It has also screened in the United States on Universal Kids. The series is produced by a cast and crew that is 60 per cent female across the writing, directing, casting, cinematography, production design, costume and editing.

Set in suburban Australia, the series focuses on Mustangs FC, an all-girls football team. It has been described by one of its producers as 'celebrating female friendship in all its complexity' (Davis, in Keast 2017 *Inside Film interview*). Football is the catalyst which initiates those friendships and the vehicle through which they are sustained. While each player has a turn as protagonist across the episodic format, the show's overarching narratives tend to revolve around Marnie (Emmanuelle Mattana) who lives with her mother, Jen (Pia Miranda).

In series one, the protagonists struggle to be taken seriously as an all-girls team. Initially, the club will not provide the team with strips or keys to the changing room. Later, when the team makes the grand final, the club does not recognise this achievement. The girls team is often relegated to poorly kept pitches in competitions, and the boys team is also unsupportive, often making fun of the girls' abilities and refusing to lend their jerseys to the players for fear of 'boob dents'. The players must also convince their coach that girls can play soccer. Lieberman (2014, p. 58) notes that gender as an obstacle, rather than ability, is a common trope in Hollywood sports films which feature female athletes. This is true of *Mustangs FC* as the girls are often held back by gendered stereotypes rather than their skill as players. However, other obstacles such as fitness, relationships, mental health, body image and other facets of life also play significant roles in the narrative, allowing for the series to present gender as one of the many diverse and complex issues facing female football players.

Lieberman (2014, p. 76) also suggests that Hollywood sports films featuring female athletes lack female mentors, coaches and mother figures and that 'men have to initiate women into sport'. Lieberman's observation can be seen in *Mustangs FC* (and other female footballing stories such as *Bend It Like Beckham*) where a male coach features as the mentor character. In the first series of *Mustangs FC*, Marnie and her best friend Liv discover that their local shop owner once played in a World Cup many years ago and so the friends set about trying to convince him to coach them. Representing the only experienced mentor as a man positions the history of the game as male and consequently situates female football as relatively new. Though all three screen texts analysed here represent successful contemporary female footballers as figures of inspiration, none of the texts engage with the long history of women's football in Australia.

Despite this lack of engagement with the legacy of Australian women's football, *Mustangs FC*, *Back of the Net* and *Kick* begin to resist the dominant Hollywood representation of mentors as men by portraying female coaches in various capacities. While the key mentor in *Mustangs FC* is male, the team's rival is coached by a woman, and in series two Marnie is coached by a woman at a skills camp and is chosen to train with the state team by a female scout. In *Back of the Net*, the head coach is a woman, though she is presented as disorganised and plays no real role in the team's success other than to allow the players to execute their own plan. In *Kick*, female coaches and mentors are featured frequently and are positioned in the narrative as knowledgeable gatekeepers of the sport, often commenting on the progress of players and potential pathways the players might take. For example, Melbourne Victory assistant coach Kat Smith comments on the decisions made by Kyra Cooney-Cross in her footballing pathway, and Rae Dower, coach of the Junior Matildas, is portrayed as the figurehead of the team that all the documentary subjects dream of being a part of. She is also shown watching potential Junior Matildas players and deciding who will progress. Portraying women as mentors and gatekeepers of the sport represents a significant shift in the way screen texts present the power dynamics in female sport.

In a similar way to *Back of the Net*, *Mustangs FC* also represents female footballers as diverse in talent and background, frustrating the audience's desire to fully know the female footballer as a fixed identity defined by amateur technique and sexualised beauty. However, unlike *Back of the Net*, *Mustangs FC* also acknowledges the totalising representations of female footballers and draws the audience's attention to the complexity of representation. For example, throughout both series, players Liv and Ruby must contend with the perception that they are defined as players and as people by their ability to live up to conventional beauty standards of thinness and whiteness. In these moments both Liv and Ruby often discuss wanting to be perceived by others as complex rather than defined only by their size or skin colour. For example, in series two when Liv is called fat, she remarks 'I'm not bothered by being called fat, I have fat, I have toes too, I'm not just toes like I'm not just fat', and the voice-over compliments her dialogue, stating 'we're all lots of things'. These narrative choices directly confront the audience with the complexity of representation, encouraging them to interpret the female football playing characters in less totalising ways. The characters in *Mustangs FC* actively demand that the audience acknowledges their complexity and infinite nature.

Conclusion

Prior to *Kick*, *Back of the Net* and *Mustangs FC*, stories about female footballers enjoyed very little presence on Australian screens. Considering the circumstances which may have enabled these stories of female footballers to come to fruition allows us to identify some of the factors which may support the continued telling of female footballing stories. The previous lack of representation may be due to both the sports journalism and screen industries being largely dominated by male practitioners. In Australia, 'journalists reporting on sport are predominantly male' and 'sport journalism is a key area where male dominance is not only highly visible but arguably explicitly determines the nature and scope of coverage' (Caple et al. 2011, pp. 138–139). Just as a male-dominated sporting journalism industry influences the nature of women's sporting coverage, the male-dominated film industry in Australia has also influenced what stories are deemed worthy of telling. In 2015, Screen Australia released their gender matters report outlining the state of female participation in the Australian film industry, revealing very low numbers of women in key creative roles (Screen Australia 2015). The same year, French (2015, p. 142) found that in both Australian film and television there is a 'correlation between women in key creative roles and the number of women on the crew as well as in front of the camera'. She reports that female directors make films with female protagonists 74 per cent of the time, in contrast to male directors who feature a female character or subject only 24 per cent of the time (French 2015, p. 142).

As a result of their findings, Screen Australia released a suite of initiatives designed to support female filmmakers and set a self-imposed target of half of the projects that receive their production funding having women occupying at least 50 per cent of key creative roles by 2018–2019 (Screen Australia 2015). In August 2019, Screen Australia released a statement revealing that they had surpassed their goal by 6 per cent (Screen Australia 2019). All three of the screen texts analysed here report some form of support from Screen Australia, and both *Mustangs FC* and *Back of the Net* appear to satisfy women in 50 per cent of key creative roles. If we take the increase in production of screen sports narratives focused on female athletes, including the recent Rachel Griffith film, *Ride Like a Girl* (2019), it appears the convergence of increased support for female filmmakers with escalating interest in elite women's sport is enabling female Australian film and television makers to tell stories about female athletes that resist totalisation.

In mapping the innovative methods these three screen texts use to respond to the totalisation of female footballers, this chapter builds an initial foundation for future research focused on the representation of football on Australian screens. Women who play football have faced and continue to face many obstacles including limited and/or totalising representations of female footballers in the Australian media and screen industries. The three productions analysed in this chapter respond to the issue of totalisation by working toward more ethical relations with female footballers on screen. Given that there is a very limited number of Australian documentaries or fictional screen narratives featuring female football players, the three texts analysed here can only be compared to previous representations of female footballers in the broader Australian media and representations of female athletes in broader sporting screen narratives. However, it can be seen that *Mustangs FC*, *Back of the Net* and *Kick* all resist dominant representations of female athletes and female footballers in some way.

The three productions achieve this by representing girls and women as serious athletes, spectators as genuine fans of sporting prowess, female athletes as belonging through sports and female coaches as being able to open sporting pathways for younger generations. Furthermore, each of the productions are resisting totality and working towards more ethical relations with female footballers on screen by: welcoming the expression of female footballers in the productions (as seen in *Kick*); depicting female footballers as diverse rather than a fixed identity (as seen in *Back of the Net* and *Mustangs FC*); and by referring their audience to the complexity of representation (as seen in *Mustangs FC*). These methods for responding to totalisation are not completely unique to the productions analysed. Similar methods for responding to totalisation have been used in broader screen production practice. However, the screen texts analysed here represent a significant innovation in Australian screen productions depicting female footballers and in the representation of women's football in the Australian media landscape more broadly.

Notes

1 Promotion and foregrounding of female role models that break down stereotypes have proven to increase participation (Reece et al. 2017). As Jayne Cauldwell (2011) notes, where these activities have not occurred, it has proportionately limited awareness, participation and socialisation of female players.
2 *Kick* has very recently been commissioned for a fourth season by Foxtel, while *Mustangs FC* has recently aired its third.

References

Abdel-Shehid, G. and Kalman-Lamb, N. (2015) 'Multiculturalism, Gender and Bend It Like Beckham', *Social Inclusion*, 3(3), 142–152.

Adair, D. (2009) 'Australian Sport History: From the Founding Years to Today', *Sport in History*, 29(3), 405–436.

Anderst, L. (2017) 'The Self as Evidence and Collaborative Identity in Contemporary Autobiographical Documentary', *a/b: Auto/Biography Studies* 32(2), 255–257.

Baek, J. (2016) 'Turning Toward the Other: The Face of Humans, the Face of Things and the Face of Language in the Documentaries of Sylvian George', *Studies in French Cinema*, 16(1), 61–77.

Balfour, M. (2013) 'Refugee Performance: Encounters with Alterity', in Balfour, M. (ed.) *Refugee Performance Practical Encounters*, Bristol: Intellect, 213–228.

British Pathé (n.d.) 'Feminine Football 1944' [video], available: https://www.britishpathe.com/video/feminine-football/query/football+australia [accessed November 8 2019].

Burke, K. (2011) 'Audience of the Other: The Literary Arts and Ethics in Levinas', *Philosophy Today*, 55(1), 50–63.

Burvill, T. (2013) '"Politics Begins as Ethics": Levinasian Ethics and Australian Performance Concerning Refugees', in Balfour, M. (ed.) *Refugee Performance Practical Encounters*, Bristol: Intellect, 199–212.

Caple, H., Greenwood, K. and Lumby, C. (2011) 'What League?: The Representation of Female Athletes in Australian Television Sports Coverage', *Media International Australia: Incorporating Culture & Policy*, 140(Aug), 137–146.

Cauldwell, J. (2011) 'Gender, Feminism and Football Studies', *Soccer and Society*, 12(3), 330–344.

Colusso, E. (2017) 'The Space Between the Filmmaker and the Subject – the Ethical Encounter', *Studies in Documentary Film*, 11(2), 141–156.

Cooper, S. (2006) *Selfless Cinema? Ethics and French Documentary*, London: Legenda.

Crawford, F. and McGowan, L. (2019) *Never Say Die: The Hundred Year Overnight Success of the Australian Women's Football*, Sydney: New South.

Dhami, N. (2004) *Bend It Like Beckham*, New York: Welcome Rain.

Dowmunt, T. (2013) 'Autobiographical Documentary – the "Seer and the Seen"', *Studies in Documentary Film*, 7(3), 263–277.

Downes, G., Syson, I. and Hay, R. (2015) '"Not Merely an Isolated Game": Woman's Association Football in Australia', *The International Journal of the History of Sport*, 32(18), 2150–2170.

French, L. (2015) 'Does Gender Matter?', *Lumina: Australian Journal of Screen Arts and Business*, 14(May), 139–153.

Glynn, S. (2018) *The British Football Film*, London: Palgrave Macmillan.

Hawthorne, L. (1995) 'Soap Opera in a Multicultural Australia: Home and Away v. Heartbreak High', *Bureau of Immigration, Multicultural and Population Research Bulletin*, no. 15, 32–35.

Hay, R. and Murray, B. (2014) *The History of Football in Australia*, Sydney: Hardie Grant.

Keast, J. (2017) 'Girl Power', *Inside Film: If*, 177(Jun/Jul), 14.

Levinas, E. (1969) *Totality and Infinity: An Essay on Exteriority*. Translated by Lingis, A. Dordrecht: Martinus Nijhoff Publishers.

Lieberman, V. (2014) *Sports Heroines on Film: A Critical Study of Cinematic Women Athletes, Coaches and Owners*, North Carolina: McFarland & Company, Incorporated Publishers.

Manning, J. (2019) 'TV Ratings November 12: 10 Takes 7:30pm Demos with Amazing Race', available: https://www.mediaweek.com.au/tv-ratings-november-12-amazing-race/ [accessed November 25 2019].

May, C. (2020) 'Women in Sport', in *Clearing House for Sport*, available: https://www.clearinghouseforsport.gov.au/knowledge_base/organised_sport/sport_and_government_policy_objectives/womens_sport [accessed March 30 2020].

McGowan, L. (2019) 'Women's Association Football (Soccer) in Brisbane, Queensland 1921–1933: New Perspectives on Early Competition', *Sport in History*, 39(2), 187–206.

Nash, K. (2011) 'Documentary-for-the-Other: Relationships, Ethics and (Observational) Documentary', *Journal of Mass Media Ethics*, 26(3), 224–239.

Nichols, B. (2017) *Introduction to Documentary*. 3rd ed., Bloomington, IN: Indiana University Press.

Nowak, J. (2010) 'Out from Behind the Shadows: Levinas and Visual Art', *Philosophy Today*, 54(3), 265–278.

Publicis Sport and Entertainment (2019) 'FIFA Women's World Cup France 2019: Global Broadcast and Audience Report', available: https://img.fifa.com/image/upload/rvgxekduqpeo1ptbgcng.pdf [accessed November 26 2019].

Ratna, A. (2011) '"Who Wants to Make Aloo Gobi When You Can Bend It Like Beckham?" British Asian Females and Their Racialised Experiences of Gender and Identity in Women's Football', *Soccer & Society*, 12(3), 382–401.

Raviv, O. (2019) *Ethics of Cinematic Experience*, New York: Routledge.

Reece, L.J., Foley, B.C., McInerney, C., Bellew, B. and Bauman, A.E. (2017) *Women and Girls in Sport, Active Recreation and Physical Activity – a Participation Review*. Sydney: University of Sydney.

Renov, M. (2004) *The Subject of Documentary*. Minneapolis: University of Minnesota Press.

Robbins, J. (1995) 'Aesthetic Totality and Ethical Infinity: Levinas on Art', *L'Esprit Créateur*, 35(3), 66–79.

Saxton, L. (2007) 'Fragile Faces: Levinas and Lanzmann', *Film Philosophy*, 11(2), 1–14.

Screen Australia (2015) *Gender Matters*. Sydney: Screen Australia.

Sport Australia (2019) *Ausplay: Football/Soccer State of Play Report*. Canberra: Australian Government.

Stell, M. (1991) *Half the Race: A History of Australian Women in Sport, thesis (PhD)*, Australian National University.

Syson, I. (2018) 'Waiting for Association Football: Incipient Soccer in Australia, 1850–1880', *Soccer & Society*, 19(1), 154–167.

The Cumberland Argus and Fruitgrowers Advocate. (1903) '"A Ladies" Football Team', *The Cumberland Argus and Fruitgrowers Advocate*, 30 May, 5.

Toffoletti, K. and Palmer, C. (2019) 'Women and Sport in Australia – New Times?' *Journal of Australian Studies*, 43(1), 1–6.

Tuckerman, M. (2019) 'The Death of Active Support Will Be the Death of the A-League', *The Roar*, available: https://www.theroar.com.au/2019/12/02/the-death-of-active-support-will-be-the-death-of-the-a-league/ [accessed December 2 2019].

Walseth, K. (2006) 'Young Muslim Women and Sport: The Impact of Identity Work', *Leisure Studies*, 25(1), 7594.

Williams, J. (2007) *A Beautiful Game: International Perspectives on Women's Football*, Oxford: Berg.

Wrack, S. (2019) 'Reporting on the 2019 Women's World Cup: "It Was a Turning Point"', *The Guardian*, 27 July, available: https://www.theguardian.com/membership/2019/jul/27/reporting-on-the-201swomens-world-cup-it-was-a-turning-point [accessed November 26 2019].

Chapter 6

European cinema and the football film

'Play for the people who've accepted you'

Seán Crosson

On the day that the UK officially left the EU (31 January 2020), the Leigh Film Society organised a special screening of *The Keeper* (2018) – the biopic of legendary Manchester City goalkeeper Bert Trautmann – to mark the occasion. As noted by Owen Evans and Graeme Harper:

> It wasn't just the footballer's symbolism as a figure of international reconciliation that affected the audience in Leigh that night ... That an Anglo-German production should be screened on the very day Britain was leaving the European Union also seemed deeply symbolic.
>
> (2020, pp. 1–2)

The Keeper, in common with a considerable number of contemporary depictions of football on film, is a co-production between several European countries and in its content and thematic concerns, it reflects and responds to broader European anxieties within the period in which the film was made and released. The film also provides an intriguing link to the earliest footage of football on film. While ostensibly set in Lancashire and Manchester, most of *The Keeper*'s filming was actually done in Northern Ireland and Germany. The scenes depicting Manchester City's home games were shot at The Oval, Belfast club Glentoran's ground. Recent research suggests that it is at this site in 1897 that the story of football on film began, when footage was shot of an encounter between Glentoran and fellow Belfast-based team Cliftonville, most likely by French cameraman Alexandre Promio, then working for film pioneers Auguste and Louis Lumière.[1] While some 120 years may separate the production of these two films, they are connected by the international genesis of their creation and the interconnected nature of the European experience of football on film, the central focus of this chapter, which has emerged from ongoing research examining the phenomenon of sport cinema in the European context. Sport cinema has been among the most enduring, popular, and critically acclaimed of genres within American cinema; however, limited research has been undertaken as yet of the European experience.

As evident in an ongoing quantitative survey being undertaken as part of this research, football is by far the most commonly featured sport. Indeed, a single chapter could not possibly account appropriately for the very large number of relevant productions. In the British context alone, Stephen Glynn's comprehensive 2018 study *The British Football Film* identifies over 90 relevant films pointing 'to the importance of football not only in the quotidian rhythms of national life but also, and especially, its immutable place in Britain's social and cultural *imaginary* landscape' (2018, p. 10, emphasis original). Therefore, a brief overview of the historical development of the sub-genre is provided in this chapter in light of the initial findings of the quantitative survey, with particular attention paid to the impact of a number of representative films in a variety of European contexts. This is preceded by a short survey of considerations of European cinema and the sports film genre.

European cinema and the sports film

On 17 June 2008, the American Film Institute (AFI) presented as part of a CBS television special the 'AFIs 10 Top 10', a listing of the ten greatest American films in ten classic film genres (Anonymous 2011). Among the genres chosen was the sports genre, which the AFI defined as involving 'films with protagonists who play athletics or other games of competition' (Anonymous 2008). The inclusion of this genre as among the most important in American film history was recognition of the enduring popularity and considerable critical acclaim accorded to films featuring sport. While the genre is well established in the American context – including such seminal works as *Rocky* (1976), *Raging Bull* (1980), and more recent Academy Award winners *The Blind Side* (2009), *The Fighter* (2010), and *Ford v Ferrari* (2019) – less research has been undertaken of the place of sport within European cinema.

Since the mid-1990s and through the 21st century, there has been an increasing engagement with the concept of European cinema, evident in film studies in a range of publications from Petrie (1992) to the work of Konstantarakos (2000), Wayne (2002), Mazierska and Rascaroli (2003), Forbes and Fowler (2002), Elsaesser (2005), Everett (2005), Galt (2006), Loshitzky (2010), and Harrod, Liz, and Timoshkina (2014) as well as the many academic articles published on the topic (see, for example, Eleftheriotis 2000 or Halle 2006). The concept of a popular European cinema has also attracted increasing research, particularly following the publication of Richard Dyer's and Ginette Vincendeau's influential collection *Popular European Cinema* (1992), which as Tim Bergfelder notes, 'triggered a thriving academic interest in the topic in the 1990s and early 2000s, at least in the Anglophone context' (2014, p. 34), apparent in subsequent studies including Dimitris Eleftheriotis's *Popular Cinemas of Europe: Studies of Texts, Contexts and Frameworks* (2001) and Tytti Soilas's collection *Stellar Encounters: Stardom in Popular European Cinema* (2009). A recurring issue across all of these works is the challenge in defining European cinema given the diverse and distinct cultures (and cinemas) that Europe encompasses, evident in the title of one of Wendy Everett's interventions: 'Dinosaur, Shipwreck or Museum Piece? The Unstable Identity of European Cinema' (2007). Nonetheless, the European context constitutes an important dimension of film production and reception across the continent, if only in terms of the transnational funding models that now predominate in European film production and the peripatetic and transnational character of the European film festival circuit. In addition, as Everett (2005) remarks in a further study of the topic, the discourse concerning European cinema is vital:

> not only because cinema provides us with a vivid illustration of the vulnerability of the national and regional to the relentless dynamic of globalisation specifically, in this case, to the dominant discourse of Hollywood in a way that raises wider issues of European identity, but also because it exploits the fundamental relationship between seeing and understanding, and recognises the centrality of visual images to the formation of identity, whether personal, regional, national or European.
>
> (Everett 2005, p. 8)

As one of the most distinctive and popular features of European culture, sport may offer a further means of defining European cinema today. Europe was a crucial location for the development of modern sport, both in the spirit of the Olympics but also in the first codifications of various sports – including football, cricket, rugby, and tennis – in nineteenth-century Britain and France. Furthermore, sport constitutes a crucial aspect of many European citizens' everyday identities. No matter what aspect of sport citizens may be involved with, it brings an important sense of belonging, a sense of pride, a sense of being more than just an individual lost in daily routines (Bairner and Shirlow 1999, p. 152). Therefore, when depicted in cinema, sport offers a further significant feature in defining a distinctive European film culture.

While underdeveloped, important analyses have been undertaken of individual European sports films as part of this broader engagement with European cinema (see, for example, Boyle and Haynes 2000; King and Leonard 2006; Briley, Schoenecke, and Carmichael 2008; Poulton and Roderick 2009; Ingle and Sutera 2013a, 2013b), though there are specific challenges in researching the area on a large scale, including the linguistic variations involved. As is evident in relevant studies to date, most research on European sports films has focused on individual case studies of exemplary films – e.g. *Olympia* (Germany 1938); *Chariots of Fire* (UK 1981); *Les Triplettes de Belleville* (The Triplets of Belleville, France 2003) – or the development of sport cinema within specific national contexts – e.g. Jones's (2005) work on the British sports film; Romaguera and Ramió (2003), Rodríguez Díaz (2010), and Ashton (2013) on the Spanish sports film; Cunningham (2004) and Fodor (2017) on Hungarian football films; and McDougall (2017) on East German football films. Though more narrowly focused, these studies have nonetheless revealed the distinctiveness of sport cinema as it has emerged in the European context. European sport cinema provides a unique historical moving image record of the development of a range of distinctive sporting practices across the continent, from traditional sports like

Basque pelota in Spain, to the evolution of the continent's most popular team sport, association football.

This chapter is an initial attempt to identify some distinctive aspects of the sports film genre as manifested in the European context, with a particular focus on how football has featured. By football, I am of course referring to association football rather than the American (or indeed, Irish or Australian) variety. This distinction is important to make at the outset, as in cinematic terms, American football has featured much more prominently, including in some of the most commercially successful films in the sports cinema genre – e.g. *Any Given Sunday* (1999), *Remember the Titans* (2000), *The Blind Side* (2009). Hollywood's considerable power and influence has been an important factor here, though the nature of association football itself has presented particular challenges to directors despite the fact that this sport may seem on one level to offer an obvious parallel with the feature film; the average length of the feature film and a football match, at 90 minutes, is about the same. However, football is also characterised by often long periods in which very little happens, something conventional narrative film seeks to avoid. As Ian Nathan has noted, 'choreographed soccer looks preposterous and totally unbelievable on screen. It is a sport too sustained and random to hold up to artificiality' (Nathan 2000). Directors have responded to these challenges in a number of ways, including incorporating actual players into their films and basing their productions on actual events or individuals (as is the case with *The Keeper*). These responses have met with limited success and presented further challenges, as discussed later. As a consequence, fiction films featuring football, in common with the sports film genre as a whole, have tended to focus as much on issues off the field as on it.

Sport and film

Modern sport and the cinema both emerged contemporaneously towards the end of the nineteenth century. The first modern Olympic Games were held in Athens in April 1896, only four months after the Lumière brothers gave the first public screening to a paying Paris audience of their new invention, the 'cinématographe'. It is significant that these two pivotal events in modern cultural history occurred in the space of less than half a year. The beginnings of the art form that would eventually become popularly known as 'film', 'the movies', or 'the cinema' is inextricably linked with sport. Indeed, sport, as a widespread cultural practice with a considerable following internationally, had a vital role in popularising the new medium of film, including in the European context (McKernan 1996, p. 109). Among the first programme of Lumière films screened in December 1895 were several that had sporting associations. Furthermore, the website catalogue-lumiere.com includes 62 films featuring sporting activities, including boxing, cycling, horseracing, gymnastics, various martial arts, tennis, wrestling, athletics, skiing, and football, including the early film referred to at the opening of this chapter.

As I have noted previously of the earliest film footage of hurling (Crosson 2019, pp. 31–35), early football footage also indicates the challenges of capturing a team sport such as association football in the early years of cinema, particularly with the rudimentary film camera available to early pioneers, limited with regard to movement and lens possibilities at the time.[2] The rather unsatisfactory footage speaks to what would be an ongoing challenge for filmmakers wishing to include football in their work (and the often poor reception of these films): the difficulty of credibly and convincingly depicting this sport. As Andrew Sarris has noted, 'Sports are now. Movies are then. Sports are news. Movies are fables' (Sarris 1980, p. 50). British director Ken Loach has also commented on this aspect, noting that 'the real enjoyment of football is to be there' while for the screenwriter of Loach's football-themed film *Looking for Eric* (2009), Paul Laverty, 'A film can never match the excitement of football. Unfortunately we can normally guess in 95% of cases how a film is going to end but the beauty of football is that you just never quite know'.[3] If people seek a representation of football (apart from attending a match itself), film cannot hope to match the immediacy and versatility of live television, or the various related live streaming possibilities that the internet age has facilitated. As a consequence, as Glen Jones has noted, the more accomplished films that have featured football have been those that have analysed and looked 'at issues surrounding soccer' (Jones 2005, p. 33) rather than being focused primarily on the sport itself or on sporting sequences.

In one of the most persuasive studies of sport cinema, David Rowe (1998) recognised the changing and evolving nature of the genre and argued that 'to claim that sports films may constitute a genre (perhaps with a range of subgenres) it would be necessary to establish the existence of some shifting yet patterned relationships within or between subject matter, presentation, narrative, and affect'. Taking this as his starting point, Rowe suggests a

> common basis to nondocumentary or instruction-based sports films as a genre (or, more cautiously, as a 'complex of sub genres'), underpinning a panoply of formal, substantive, and stylistic variations: that all films that deal centrally with sports are at some level allegorical, that they address the question of the dual existence of the social and sporting worlds as problematic, and that they are preoccupied with the extent to which (idealized) sports can transcend or are bound by existing (and corrupting) social relations.
>
> (Rowe 1998, pp. 351–352)

My own approach to sport cinema, including depictions of football in fiction film, is indebted to Rowe's analysis. While we may define a sports film as works in which a sport, sporting event, athlete (and their sport), or follower of sport (and the sport they follow) are prominently featured, and which depend on sport to a significant degree for their plot motivation or resolution, sport is ultimately rarely the central concern of such films. Rather, sport (as well as providing a seductive and popular point of engagement for audiences) performs primarily an allegorical role in the sports film genre, including within the sub-genre dedicated to depictions of football.

The football film in European cinema: a quantitative survey

In compiling my own database of sport cinema in Europe, the first challenge I encountered was the lack of an entirely comprehensive database of European cinema; those databases that do exist – including the European film directory[4] – don't currently provide the facility to search by sport or sport genre. While recognising the importance of non-fiction sports films in Europe (both as influential film texts and important historical records of specific sports), due to the sheer number of relevant films involved, I have focused for the purposes of this initial survey on fictional and theatrically released works produced or co-produced by or with a European company that feature sport, sports people, or followers of sport prominently and in which sport is an important aspect of the plot development or motivation. However, the challenge in this exercise was not just deciding what films qualify as sports films (and how we define that term) but equally the linguistic challenges we encounter in attempting to undertake a pan-European study of a popular cinema genre. For the purposes of this initial enquiry, I have begun with perhaps the most well-known and comprehensive database of international cinema, the Internet Movie Database or IMDb.[5] In deciding to start here, I am entirely conscious of the limitations of this resource, including the gaps that exist regarding international cinema but also the issues with how films are classified there, with not all relevant films categorised with regard to sport. What IMDb does offer, however, is the possibility to identify sport, feature film, and country as categories, allowing us to examine what is classified in this way and then to extrapolate from there. In total I found relevant sports films listed in 32 European countries (including no longer existing states the Soviet Union, Czechoslovakia, Yugoslavia, and West Germany). While this is an imperfect measure and one that needs to be interrogated at each point, it does nonetheless provide a useful initial resource to undertake a quantitative survey of European sport cinema. As well as giving us an initial understanding of the extent of films that could be classified in this manner within the European context, IMDb can elucidate a number of further useful aspects, including: how many of these films are co-productions between several European (and non-European) countries; and what the trend has been in terms of the increase (or decrease) of the production of sports films over more than 100 years, and the specific sports featured, including the prevalence of depictions of football.

The first striking feature to emerge from the survey is the sheer number of relevant films, even focusing only on theatrically released fiction work – approximately 692 between 1911 and 2018. A further pattern evident from my analysis is the increasing number of sports featured in film from the 1970s onwards, more than doubling from 25 sports up to the 1960s to 58 sports represented by 2018. A further feature evident is the very significant increase in

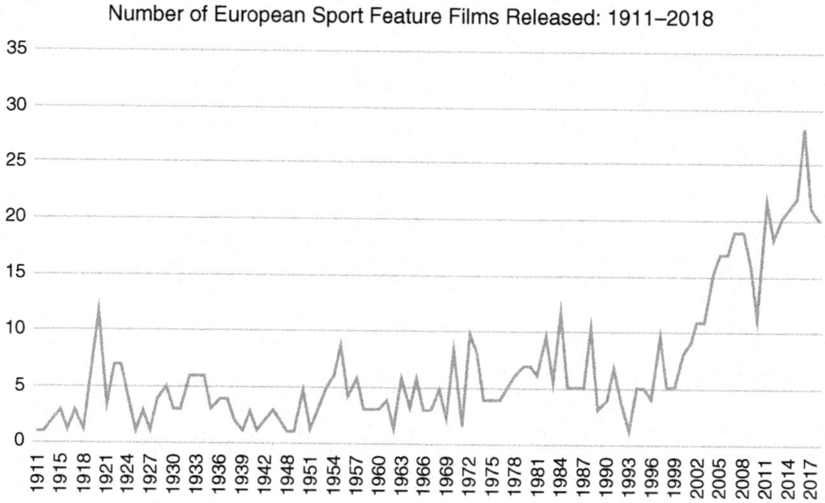

Figure 6.1 Number of European Sport Feature Films Released 1911–1918 *Source*: IMDb.

production of sports films in Europe over the past 20 years, with over 45% of all films produced in that period (Figure 6.1).

As Figure 6.2 indicates, by far the most prolific country to produce or co-produce sport cinema is the UK, followed by Germany, France, the Soviet Union, Spain, Italy, and Russia. The high number of British produced or co-produced sports films (224) reflects on one level the prominence of sport in the UK (particularly football, evident in the high number of football films produced there). However, the fact that the UK also shares a language and strong cultural ties

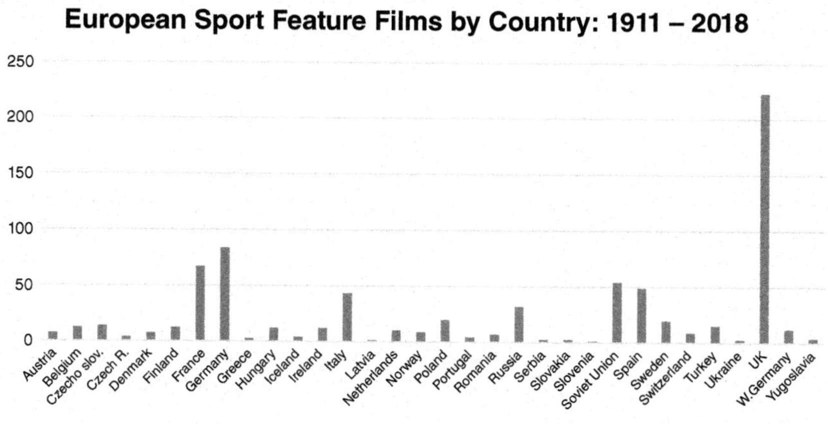

Figure 6.2 European Sport Feature Films by Country: 1911–2018 *Source*: IMDb.

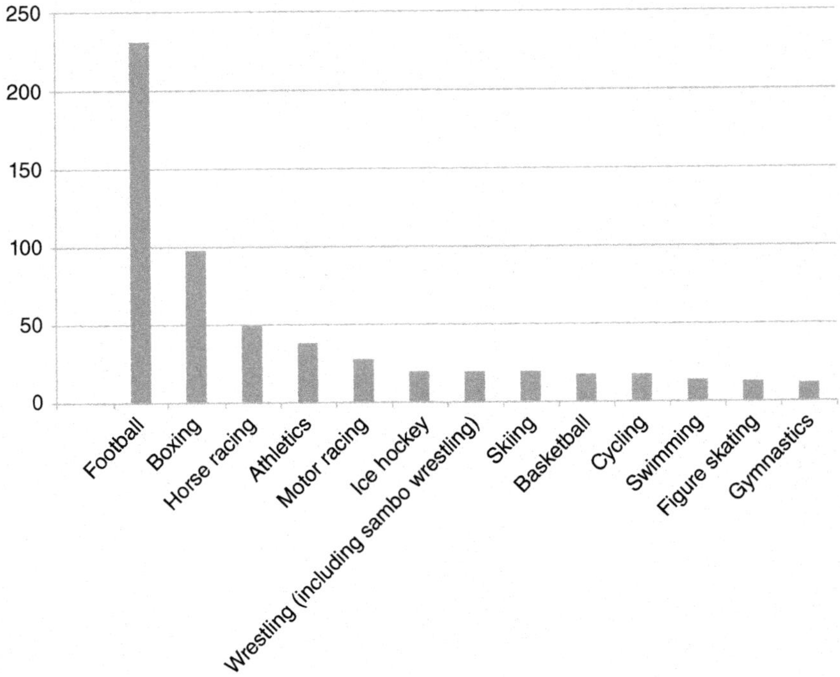

Figure 6.3 Prevalence of Specific Sports Featured in European Cinema *Source*: IMDb.

with the United States (the producer of most sports films) has also contributed to the large number of sports films produced by the UK. This is evident in the high number of US/UK co-produced sports films, with 13% of UK produced sports films having an American co-producer.

With regard to sports featured, perhaps unsurprisingly, football is by far the most popular sport featured in European sport cinema, featuring in almost one third (228) of all films produced followed by boxing, horseracing, and athletics (Figure 6.3).

The first football films

Indeed, the first European sports fiction release was a football-themed production, *Harry the Footballer*, directed in 1911 by Lewin Fitzhamon, one of the most popular directors of the early silent film era in Britain. The film concerns the kidnapping of super-striker Harry by the opposition team, the Bestham Vampires, and his subsequent rescue by his girlfriend and race to the match, making it just in time for the kick-off. The plot was repeated three years later when Maurice Elvey directed *The Cup Final Mystery* (1914), though this time it was the goal-keeper, rather than the striker, that was kidnapped just before the Cup Final at Crystal Palace. Fitzhamon directed a further football-themed film in 1914,

A Footballer's Honour, a work considered to be the first commercially successful film devoted to football (Seddon 1999, p. 365). Two years previous, the first animated film featuring football appeared, *The Cat's Cup Final*, directed by one of the pioneers of this art form, Arthur Melbourne Cooper. Indeed, the first film directed by Britain's first female director, Ethyle Batley, was a football-themed work, *The Rival Captains* (1916), a film in which a dog rescues a football captain following his kidnapping (Glynn 2018, p. 24). In common with the practice more generally in the industry in this period, all these early films were less than 20 minutes in length; the first feature-length (that is, of approximately 90 minutes or more in length) British football film to enjoy considerable commercial success was Hugh Croise's *The Ball of Fortune* (1926), based on a novel by Sydney Horler. Contributing to the film's success no doubt was its featuring the legendary Welsh striker Billy Meredith, star of cup-winning teams for Manchester City and Manchester United, with whom he also won the League championship in the 1907–1908 and 1910–1911 seasons. Meredith played himself in the film in the lead role as a football coach, and the football sequences of the film were played at Leeds United's Elland Road ground (Seddon 1999, p. 635).

While football would continue to feature in fiction film throughout the interwar period, the most frequent encounter with professional football on film in this period was via highlights of major games featured in cinema newsreels. Films of football were generally uncontroversial, and their short and exciting nature made them very suitable for cinema showings, and thus football featured prominently. Indeed, football was one of the most popular newsreel items in Britain and across Europe in the 1920s and 1930s, with sales of individual newsreels increasing where football was included (Huggins 2007, p. 84).

The importance of newsreels was evident in Thorold Dickinson's 1939 football-themed feature *The Arsenal Stadium Mystery*, a murder mystery film concerning the investigation of the murder of a football player, John Doyce, during a charity match. The film begins with a Gaumont British newsreel detailing the upcoming game between professional side Arsenal and the fictional touring amateur club Trojans. Indeed, the game featured in the film is itself commented on by legendary Gaumont commentator E.V.H. Emmett, ably assisted by the Arsenal manager at the time George Allison, also a former journalist. The foregrounding of the media here would anticipate what is now a staple of the sports film: the focus on the media and their role in relaying the action on screen. This is also a feature of *The Keeper*, which uses contemporaneous newsreel coverage of its subject to add additional realism and authenticity to the production.

Furthermore, in common with *The Ball of Fortune*, *The Arsenal Stadium Mystery* relies heavily on featuring leading players, and personnel, as well as media figures associated with football in the period. This includes many of the then Arsenal team – one of the most successful teams in English football in the 1930s – as well as members of fellow London team Brentford, which was also a Division 1 side at the time.[6] However, the film enjoyed limited audience or critical success on release, with Charles Barr remarking, conscious of earlier films featuring professional players, that 'Even in 1939, the centring of *The Arsenal Stadium*

Mystery on a match between professional and amateur sides seemed tame and anachronistic', while for Barr the acting of the 'authentic footballers ... is stilted, and the action into which the film incorporates them is ... unconvincing' (Barr 2003, p. 630). This includes the remarkable reserve exhibited by players from both sides when they discover that one of the players has just died during a game. However, the film was responding to the challenges that faced filmmakers trying to combine depictions of football with a fictional scenario when people's engagement with this sport was primarily through attendance at games, or via newspaper reports, radio broadcast, or newsreels. *The Arsenal Stadium Mystery*, as many subsequent films would do (including, as discussed later, *Escape to Victory* (1981)), falls awkwardly between two stools where the need to instil realism in the work involves including non-actors whose performances leave much to be desired while the actual sporting sequences are less than compelling themselves, combining close shots of unconvincing staged runs past peculiarly immobile defenders with more convincing long shot sequences taken from the actual Arsenal-Brentford game.

However, while football takes up a small percentage of *The Arsenal Stadium Mystery*, it does serve a larger allegorical role, a role bound up with affirming aspects of British (and particularly English) culture in the period. As noted by Huggins of newsreels (featured prominently within the film) in the period concerned:

> The regular projection of screen soccer helped move it from being publicly perceived as largely a working-class sport (although there were always middleclass supporters too) to being a widely accepted part of popular culture. Newsreels further embedded the sport within the fabric of the British way of life as an apparently unproblematic, innocently pleasurable experience which perhaps helped audiences face the social and economic difficulties of the period more cheerfully.
>
> (2007, p. 97)

Huggins's remarks are also relevant to the depiction of football on film across Europe as the twentieth century developed, particularly with regard to its role in affirming prevailing structures and values within the broader society concerned.

Football on film beyond the UK

While the first depictions of football in fiction film emerged in the British context, other European countries followed soon after. Peter Dahlén has identified Per-Axel Branner's football-themed *Hans livs match* (*The Match of His Life*) (1932) as the 'final breakthrough for a broad, popular and 'completely Swedish' sports film'. As Dahlén continues:

> Here, the storyline is based entirely on football and the fate of the football hero, Gunnar 'Nicken' Gawell (Björn Berglund) – the nickname 'Nicken'

> alludes to 'nick the ball' ... the film showcases the great and increasing popularity of football and sports heroes in the early 1930s.
>
> (2021, p. 136)

Dahlén also notes the important ideological role of this film, as with other European depictions of football in the period and subsequently, particularly evident in the 'symbolic reconciliation between the social classes that takes place at the end of the film' (2021, p. 136).

The use of football films to bolster hegemonic culture and shore up prevailing conceptions of national identity was evident across European cinema, particularly in the years during and in the immediate aftermath of World War II. In Germany, the filming of the Berlin Olympics in 1936 (in which football features prominently) by Leni Riefenstahl in her aesthetically groundbreaking (if politically controversial) documentary *Olympia* (1938) was also connected with the wider national cultural and ongoing state project, in particular concerned with celebrating the achievements of Nazi Germany and affirming the German nation (Downing 1992). Football also featured in German cinema in the war years, including within Robert Adolf Stemmle's innovative 1942 release *Das große Spiel* (*The Big Game*). Focused on a fictitious German team, Gloria 03, the film follows the tensions and competition between the team's star forward, Werner Fehling, and fan favourite, goalkeeper Jupp Jäger, with each player seeking the affections of the leading lady, Grete. Though not explicitly employing Nazi rhetoric, Rebeccah Dawson has contended that Stemmle's production nonetheless employs football 'to circumvent the obvious, direct self-glorification' evident in Nazi propaganda of the period while simultaneously and more subtly 'replaying and illuminating the everyday expectations of Nazi citizens', including German moral strength and character, 'as well as the glorious splendour of The German Reich, its government, and its people' (2021, pp. 160–161).

In some European contexts football films have been sufficiently popular – both in terms of numbers produced and audience engagement – to constitute a distinctive national sub-genre; a case in point being the phenomenon of the Spanish 'kick-flicks'. These works were an important part of the larger popular context (of which sport was a key component) that affirmed and popularised government control in the challenging post-World War II period of Franco's initially largely isolated fascist regime. As noted by Marañón:

> The abundance of films like *The Pelegrin System* (1951), *The Aces Search for Peace* (1954), *Eleven Pairs of Boots* (1954), *Blond Dart* (1956), *The Phenomenon* (1956), *The Fan* (1957), *The Angel is on the Summit* (1959), *The Soccer Pool* (1959), *The Economically Weak* (1960), *The Red Cross Three* (1961) and *Sunday's Battle* (1963) couldn't be the fruit of mere coincidence. And so soccer converted itself into one of the country's cinematographic genres. Films in which the popular side of soccer served to divert into

> comedies of local customs and manners, to indoctrinate into sporting dramas, or even to expose the best essences of the country.
>
> (Quoted and translated in Ashton 2013, p. 173)

These Spanish 'Kick-Flicks' enjoyed immense popularity as their production coincided with a period in which major international football stars began to emerge at Spanish clubs, including Real Madrid's legendary Argentine striker Alfredo Di Stéfano who featured prominently in several films in this period, including *Blond Dart* (*Saeta rubia*) (1956) and *Sunday's Battle* (*La batalla del domingo*) (1963). These films focused above all on defending morals, defining masculinity, and asserting values in line with the ruling Franco regime (Ashton, 2013, pp. 173–174). A relevant example is the 1954 production *The Aces Search for Peace* (*Los ases buscan la paz*) – a film described by Ashton as 'designed to draw the soccer fans to the box office and at the same time glorify the Franco regime' (2013, p. 172). Focused on the life story (and hardships) of FC Barcelona's Hungarian striker Ladislao Kubala (who also starred) in escaping his socialist homeland (and contrasting that with the opportunities Franco's Spain provided), the film has been described by Marañón as 'an enormous propagandist triumph for the Franco regime' (Quoted and translated in Ashton 2013, p. 173).

In Kubala's home country, Peter Fodor has also identified a similar pattern in Hungarian football-themed films from the 1950s, noting how the legendary 'Golden Team' of footballers from that period (that featured such acclaimed players as Ferenc Puskás, Sándor Kocsis, Nándor Hidegkuti, Zoltán Czibor, József Bozsik, and Gyula Grosics) 'was at least in part an instrument of [the communist dictatorial] Rákosi regime, which sought to profit from the team's victories and prowess on the field in order to legitimise the regime's hold on political power' (2017, p. 329). Hungarian football films produced in that era attempted to build on this popular sporting success while simultaneously supporting the ruling regime. Indeed for Fodor, 'Like the daily press, the schematic film productions of the era were also characterised by the ideological utilization of sports' (Fodor 2017, p. 328). A relevant example of this approach is the 1951 production *Civil a Pályán* (*Try and Win*) directed by Márton Keleti, which employs classical comedy elements to combine the factory life with the world of football. As Fodor continues, 'Keleti's film was intended to popularize a centralized mass sports movement of Soviet origins called "Ready to work and fight" and to communicate the party's message to professional sportsmen who were considering emigration' (2017, p. 328).

European co-productions

Football has continued to feature in European fiction work since the 1950s, though productions have met with very mixed responses from both audiences and critics. Perhaps one of the most famous examples is Irish-American director John Huston's British/US/Italian co-production *Escape to Victory* (1981) (very loosely based on an actual football game played between PoWs and their German captors during World War II) described by Ellis Cashmore as 'Soccer's filmic nadir' (Cashmore 2000, p. 134). Glen Jones has also criticised this film for the 'poor sporting skills of Sylvester Stallone, Michael Caine and the poor acting skills of Pelé, Bobby Moore et al' not to mention the unconvincing scenario which is as insulting to war veterans as it is to the general public's naivety (Jones 2005, p. 33). Apart from *Escape to Victory*, football fanatic and novelist Nick Hornby has described the football-themed film *Yesterday's Hero* (1979), a UK/Australian co-production written by popular fiction writer Jackie Collins, as 'probably the worst British film since the war', including its 'breathtakingly daft' attempt to combine real footage of football celebrities with the film's narrative (Hornby, quoted in Jones 2005, p. 33). However, critical lambasting does not necessarily mean that football films have not had significant impacts on audiences. Since its first release, *Escape to Victory* in particular (perhaps due to its inclusion of legendary figures in the game) has had an enduring popularity with football fans and film audiences evident in several dedicated websites to the film and its repeated selection in audience polls as among the best football films ever.[7] *Escape to Victory* and *Yesterday's Hero* also share a feature increasingly found in European football films: a co-production genesis involving partners in differing European and international contexts. Indeed, as Figure 6.4 indicates, almost 20% of football-themed films produced in Europe, since the first football-themed co-production – the Spanish/Italian co-production *Volver a vivir* – was released in 1968, now involve multiple international producers. The advent of the European Economic Community in 1957 (incorporated as the European Community into the European Union (EU) in 1993) and the establishment of a range of European international co-production and film funding initiatives – including Eurimages (established 1989) and MEDIA (1991) – has encouraged this development. As Figure 6.4 also indicates, depictions of football in European cinema has also increased considerably since the early 1990s, a period of huge growth more generally in the media coverage of football in Europe.

Some of the most acclaimed football-themed films produced in that period have been the product of international co-productions, including the Iceland/Finland/UK co-production *Strákarnir okkar* (*Eleven Men Out*) (2005), the France/UK co-production *Sixty Six* (2006), Ken Loach's *Looking for Eric* (2009) (a co-production between five European countries), and Gurinder Chadha's UK/German/USA co-production *Bend It Like Beckham* (2002), the most commercially successful football film released to date.[8] While more research is needed of these productions and the phenomenon more generally of European co-productions, it is evident that in contrast to the more nationalistic sentiments apparent in earlier football-themed productions noted previously, these European co-productions challenge prejudice and foreground themes of international and intercultural understanding in which sport plays a prominent role. *Bend It Like Beckham* (2002) is focused on the attempts of Jesminder 'Jess' Bhamra, the 18-year-old daughter of Punjabi Sikh immigrants living in London, to play for a girls' soccer team, against the wishes of her conservative parents. At the centre of the film is a conflict between the traditional values of Jess's parents and the

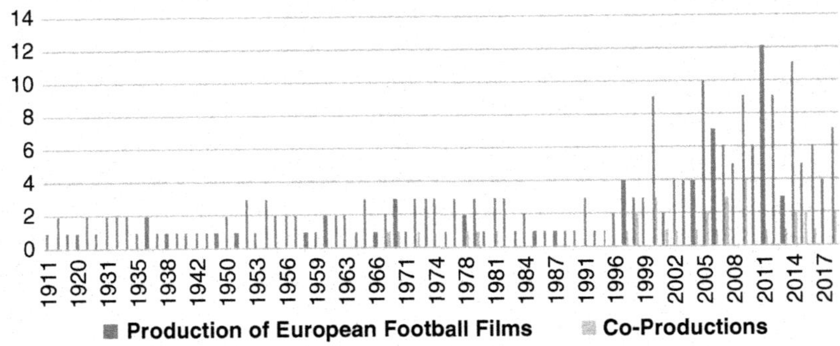

Figure 6.4 Production of European Football Films (1911–1918) *Source*: IMDb.

more progressive impulses of Jess, more interested in embracing aspects of English popular culture – in particular football – than with submitting to the traditions of her parents. While the film depicts aspects of Punjabi Sikh culture, including the wedding of Jess's sister, football functions within the narrative as the means through which Jess finds her own independence separate to her family, who eventually agree to her wish to play football, allow her to accept a scholarship to the US and, indeed, as the last scene of the film suggests, to develop a relationship with her football coach, an Irish 'gora',[9] outside of the arranged marriage traditions of her family and culture. While the overall narrative resolution may not be entirely convincing (and follows the transcending pattern described by Rowe earlier), the film nonetheless suggests in football a forum where differing cultures and ethnicities can interact and find understanding. A further relevant (if less commercially successful) co-production is the film referred to at the outset of this chapter, the UK/German co-production *The Keeper*, to which we now return to conclude.

Conclusion

While dating from the earliest days of European cinema, depictions of football on film have grown considerably to constitute an increasingly important part of Europe's film heritage deserving of increasing academic attention. As these films have responded to larger developments within specific European countries and the continent more broadly, they have served as a barometer of changing cultural values and concerns since the early twentieth century. To return to the film referred to at the beginning of this chapter, *The Keeper* provides a relevant recent exemplar which manifests features found across the European football film sub-genre. Given the challenges of depicting football in fiction film, it is significant that football, as in passages in which the sport is depicted, actually has a very limited presence within the film. Over *The Keeper*'s entire 119 minutes, less than 10 minutes consist of football sequences. Indeed, its British producer Chris

Curling resisted its designation as a sports film, remarking prior to the film's release that,

> For me, it's much more a personal story about a young guy who got caught up in the Nazi movement and was then fighting on the eastern front. He saw terrible things in the war and was eventually captured by the British. When he entered the PoW camp, he was still following Nazi ideology. But he learned to see a different version of the world. He decided to stay in the UK, fell in love and was very successful on the football field. That interests me as much as the football.
>
> (Alberge 2017)

However, though football may only feature briefly in *The Keeper*, its presence nonetheless carries a significance that far outweighs its screen time and draws upon the symbolic resonances of this sport in the European context. The basis of the film on actual events and individuals (or the involvement of familiar and well-known footballers) is also found across many football-themed films, again as a means of responding to the challenge of depicting the sport convincingly in fiction film. These strategies have also responded to distinctive developments within specific European contexts and the recurring practice of moving the focus from the playing field to the challenges faced by protagonists in their everyday life. In some contexts, as in Nazi Germany or Franco's Spain, this has involved the employment of football on film to affirm and promote hegemonic constructions of national identity. However, as European cinema has increasingly relied on international co-production models, a change of emphasis is evident in more recent productions. While *Bend It Like Beckham* stresses intercultural understanding and tolerance, a similar concern is also evident in the extraordinary story of Bert Trautmann, a former German soldier who following his imprisonment in England as a PoW, decided to stay on and play football professionally with Manchester City. As depicted in the film, Manchester City encounter considerable opposition to their decision to sign Trautmann, but he ultimately gains the respect of the club's supporters, including those among the large Jewish community in the city, due to his performances on the field of play. A key aspect of the film is the transformation of central characters – including Trautmann's eventual wife Margaret and the head of his PoW camp Sergeant Smythe – from being initially prejudiced towards and distrusting of Trautmann to being among his strongest supporters. As Smythe remarks when he encounters Trautmann in a graveyard following his son's tragic death, 'Go out there and play, Bert. Play for the people who've accepted you. For those of us … who've lost someone in the wartime. Play for your son. Go out there and give something back'. As the final credits indicate, Trautmann would eventually be awarded both an honorary Officer of the Order of the British Empire (OBE) and the Order of Merit of the Federal Republic of Germany for his contributions to Anglo-German relations and understanding through football. Football in the film therefore (in line with the tendency of sport cinema generally to transcend challenging circumstances) provides a central forum to facilitate understanding and overcome prejudice. However, as is often the case in sport cinema, while the setting may be historical, the concerns are contemporary. As Curling also remarked at the time of the film's production,

> It's a story about reconciliation between people. There was a big campaign against him at Manchester City. So, in the film, we watch a man coming to terms with his past and starting anew … overcoming hostility towards him. These days, that seems particularly relevant as well – how we as British people treat outsiders.
>
> (Alberge 2017)

The period of *The Keeper*'s production and release was marked by huge division in the United Kingdom following the Brexit referendum in June 2016, when those in favour of leaving the EU won a small majority. In the run-up to the referendum and in its aftermath, a prominent concern particularly among those in favour of Brexit was the high levels of immigration to Britain. Indeed, concerns regarding immigration have been described as a 'key driver' among those who voted in favour of leaving the union (see, for example, Goodwin and Milazzo 2017). In this context, *The Keeper* uses the engaging topic of British football and the life story of a legendary player to articulate an appeal to tolerance, reconciliation, and understanding in Britain's relationship with other European countries and nationalities at a time when Britain politically is moving away from the European Union, a feature remarked upon by several reviews at the time of the film's release (see, for example, Alaba 2018; Clarke 2019; Gamble 2019; Hattenstone 2019; GOTP Editorial Team 2019; Solomons 2019; Tyers 2019). In this manner, *The Keeper* suggests the important role depictions of football on film can have in the European context in articulating larger social concerns and contributing to the discourse of how we define European cinema and society today.

Notes

1 This information is further to recent research by Glentoran supporter Sam Robinson (published in his 2016 book *There's a Green Sward Called the Oval – the Life and Times of a Football Stadium*) who identified the teams, particularly from the distinctive white shamrock design evident on the Cliftonville players' shirts, as well as coverage of the game – played on 23 October 1897 – in the Irish press of the time and further coverage of the screening of the film two days later in Belfast. Further information on this discovery is available here: *Who's Who of Victorian Cinema*, June 2016, https://www.victorian-cinema.net/news and in Glynn 2018, p. 15.

2 This footage (though wrongly identified as being shot in London in light of the research referred to earlier) is accessible on YouTube at the following link: https://www.youtube.com/watch?v=qRl56TOinKk.

3 Both Loach and Laverty made these comments in Toby Reiz's documentary *United We Stand* (Feasible Films Production, 2009), included on the DVD edition of *Looking for Eric* (2009).

4 Further information on this directory is available here: http://lumierevod.obs.coe.int/. The directory is also restricted to 'European films available on on-demand services in Europe'.
5 The International Movie Database (IMDb) is accessible at the following link: https://www.imdb.com/.
6 The football footage was shot during the final game of the Division 1 season on 6 May 1939 before World War II broke out. A further poignancy is added to the film today when one considers that nine Arsenal players – some of them featured in the film – died on active service with the British army during the war.
7 See for example the IMDb online poll of best football films, where *Escape to Victory* is listed second: https://www.imdb.com/poll/ETf7js45cDI/results?answer=1&ref_=po_nr.
8 *Bend It Like Beckham* took almost $77 million at the international box office when first released. Box office figures for this film are available at https://www.boxofficemojo.com/release/rl3074721281/.
9 A Gora is a Hindi and Indo-Aryan racial epithet for Europeans or a light-skinned person. The word is used in this respect within the film.

Bibliography

Alaba, R. (2018) '*The Keeper*', cinemusefilms.com, n.d., available: https://cinemusefilms.com/2019/10/03/the-keeper-2018/ [accessed February 10 2020].

Alberge, D. (2017) 'German PoW and hero goalie stars in tale of reconciliation', *The Guardian*, 19 March, available: https://www.theguardian.com/football/2017/mar/19/bert-trautmann-new-film-nazi-past-fa-cup-manchester-city [accessed March 26 2017)].

Anonymous (2011) 'AFI's 10 Top 10', www.cbs.com, available: https://web.archive.org/web/20120624022727/http://www.cbs.com/specials/afi_10_top_10/ [accessed January 20 2020].

Anonymous (2008) 'America's 10 greatest films in 10 classic genres', www.afi.com, available: http://www.afi.com/10top10/ [accessed March 25 2017].

Ashton, T. (2013) *Soccer in Spain: Politics, Literature and Film*, Toronto: The Scarecrow Press.

Baker, A. (2003) *Contesting Identities: Sports in American Film*, Champaign, IL: University of Illinois Press.

Bairner, A. and P. Shirlow (1999) 'The territorial politics of soccer in Northern Ireland', in Armstrong, G. and Giulianotti, R., eds., *Football Cultures and Identities*, London: Macmillan, 152–163.

Barr, C. (2003) 'Sport', in McFarlane, B.,ed., *The Encyclopaedia of British Film*, London: Methuen/BFI, 630–631.

Bergfelder, T. (2014) 'Popular European cinema in the 2000s: Cinephilia, genre and heritage', in Harrod, M., Liz, M., and Timoshkina, A., eds., *The Europeanness of European Cinema: Identity, Meaning, Globalization*, London: IB Tauris, 33–58.

Bordwell, D. and Thompson, K. (1996) *Film Art: An Introduction*, Boston; London: McGraw Hill.

Bowden, M. J. (1994) 'Beach, and Kings Cross: Imagined places as metaphors of the British class struggle in Chariots of Fire and The Loneliness of the Long-Distance Runner', in Aitken, S.C. and Zonn, L.E., eds., *Place, Power, Situation and Spectacle: Geography of Film 1994*, Lanham, MD: Rowman & Littlefield, 69–100.

Boyle, R. & Haynes, R. (2000). *Power Play-Sport, Media and Popular Culture*, London: Longman Press.
Briley, R., Schoenecke, M.K. and Carmichael, D.A. (2008), eds., *All-Stars & Movie Stars: Sports in Film and History*, Lexington, KY: The University Press of Kentucky.
Cashmore, E. (2000) *Sports Culture: An A-Z Guide, London*; New York, NY: Routledge.
Catterall, A. (2010) 'Review of The Firm', film4.com, available: http://www.film4.com/reviews/2009/the-firm [accessed March 24 2016].
Clarke, D. (2019) 'The Keeper: The man who played an FA Cup final with a broken neck', *The Irish Times*, 5 April, available: https://www.irishtimes.com/culture/film/the-keeper-the-man-who-played-an-fa-cup-final-with-a-broken-neck-1.3846942 [accessed March 20 2020].
Coates, P. (1994) *Film at the Intersection of High and Mass Culture*, Cambridge: Cambridge University Press.
Cox, R., Jarvie, G., & Vamplew, W. (2000) *The Encyclopaedia of British Sport*, Oxford: ABC-CLIO.
Crosson, S. (2013) *Sport and Film*, London: Routledge.
Crosson, S. (2019) *Gaelic Games on Film: From Silent Films to Hollywood Hurling, Horror and the Emergence of Irish Cinema, Cork:* Cork University Press.
Crawford, G. (2004) *Consumeing Sport: Fans, Sport and Culture*, London: Routledge.
Cunningham, J. (2004) 'Foci, Fradi and the "Golden Team"', in *Hungarian Cinema: From Coffee House to Multiplex*, London: Wallflower, 183–188.
Dahlén, P. (2021), 'Sport and national culture in Swedish film', in Crosson, S., ed., *Sport, Film, and National Culture*, London: Routledge, 134–156.
Dawson, R. (2021) 'Soccer, film, and the Third Reich: Hunters, cowards, and glory', in Crosson, S., ed., *Sport, Film, and National Culture*, London: Routledge, 157–172.
Downing, T. (1992), *Olympia*, London: BFI Publishing, 1992;
Dyer, R. and Vincendeau, G. (1992) *Popular European Cinemas*, London: Routledge.
Easthope, A., ed., (1993) *Contemporary Film Theory*, London; New York: Longman
Eleftheriotis, D. (2000) 'Cultural difference and exchange: A future for European film', *Screen* 41(1), 92–101.
Eleftheriotis, D. (2001) *Popular Cinemas of Europe: Studies of Texts, Contexts and Frameworks*, London and New York: Continuum.
Elsaesser, T. (2005) *European Cinema: Face to Face with Hollywood*, Amsterdam: Amsterdam University Press.
Evans, O. and Harper, G. (2020) 'So, it has finally happened…', *Studies in European Cinema*, 17(1), 1–3.
Everett, W. (2005) *European Identity in Cinema*, Bristol: Intellect.
Everett, W. (2007) 'Dinosaur, shipwreck or museum piece?: The unstable identity of European cinema', in Demoissier, M., ed., *The European Puzzle*, Oxford, UK: Berghahn Books, 102–118.
Fodor, P. (2017) 'Erasing, Rewriting, and Propaganda in the Hungarian Sport Films of the 1950s', *Hungarian Historical Review*, 6(2), 328–354.
Forbes, J. and Fowler, C., eds., (2002) *The European Cinema Reader*, London: Routledge.
Galt, R. (2006) *The New European Cinema: Redrawing the Map*, New York, NY: Columbia University Press.
Gamble, P. (2019) 'The remarkable reconciliation tale of Bert Trautmann – and why his story is more relevant than ever today', thesetpieces.com available: https://thesetpieces.com/latest-posts/the-remarkable-reconciliation-story-of-bert-trautmann-and-why-his-tale-is-more-relevant-than-ever-today/ [accessed February 15 2020].

GOTP (Game of the People) Editorial Team (2019) 'The Trautmann film – gentle, poignant and authentic', *Game of the People*, 24 April, available: https://gameofthepeople.com/2019/04/24/the-trautmann-film-gentle-poignant-and-authentic/[accessed April 30 2020].

Giardina, M. D. (2003) 'Bending It Like Beckham' in the global popular: Stylish hybridity, performativity, and the politics of representation', *Journal of Sport & Social Issues*, 27(1), 65–82.

Goodwin, M., Milazzo, C. (2017) 'Taking back control? Investigating the role of immigration in the 2016 vote for Brexit', *The British Journal of Politics and International Relations*, 19(3), 450–464.

Graciela Rodríguez, M. (2003) 'Behind Leni's outlook: A perspective on the film Olympia (1938)', *International Review for the Sociology of Sport* 38(1), 109–116.

Grant, B.K. (1986) *Film Genre Reader*, Austin, TX: University of Texas Press.

Glynn, S. (2018) *The British Football Film*, Basingstoke: Palgrave Macmillan.

Halle, R. (2006) 'German film, European film: Transnational production, distribution, and reception', *Screen* 47(2), 251–259.

Harrod, M., Liz, M., and Timoshkina, A., eds., (2014) *The Europeanness of European Cinema: Identity, Meaning, Globalization*, London, IB Tauris.

Hattenstone, S. (2019) 'From Nazi to football hero: The incredible story of Man City's Bert Trautmann', *The Guardian*, 28 March, available: https://www.theguardian.com/film/2019/mar/28/from-nazi-to-football-hero-the-incredible-story-of-man-citys-bert-trautmann [accessed March 20 2020].

Holt, R. (1990) *Sport and the British: A Modern History*, London: Oxford University Press.

Huggins, M. (2007) 'Projecting the visual: British Newsreels, soccer and popular culture, 1918–39', *The International Journal of the History of Sport*, 24(1), 80–102.

Ingle, Z. and Sutera, D.M., eds., (2013a) *Gender and Genre in Sports Documentaries: Critical Essays*, Lanham, MD: Scarecrow Press.

Ingle, Z. and Sutera, D.M., eds., (2013b) *Identity and Myth in Sports Documentaries: Critical Essays*, Lanham, MD: Scarecrow Press.

Jones, G. (2005) '"Down on the floor and give me ten sit-ups": British Sports Feature Film', *Film & History*, 35(2), 29–40.

King, C. R. and Leonard, D. J., eds., (2006) *Visual Economies Of/In Motion: Sport and Film (Cultural Critique)*, Oxford: Peter Lang Publishing.

Konstantarakos, M. (2000) *Spaces in European Cinema*, Bristol: Intellect.

Loshitzky, Y. (2010) *Screening Strangers. Migration and Diaspora in Contemporary European Cinema*. Bloomington, IN: Indiana University Press

Marañón, C. (2005) *Fúetbol y cine. El balompié en la gran pantalla*, Madrid: Ocho y Medio.

Mazierska, E. and Rascaroli, L. (2003) *From Moscow to Madrid: Postmodern Cities European Cinema*, London: I.B. Taurus

McDougall, A. (2017), 'Eyes on the ball: Screening football in East German cinema', *Studies in Eastern European Cinema* 8(1), 4–18.

McKernan, L. (1996). 'Sport and the first films', in Williams, C., ed., *Cinema: The Beginnings and the Future*, London: University of Westminster Press, 107–116.

McKernan, L., (n.d.)'Acres, Birt (1854–1918)', *Screenonline*, available: http://www.screenonline.org.uk/people/id/449777/index.html [accessed March 15 2020].

Miller, T. (1997) *The Avengers*, London: BFI.

Mosher, S. D. (1983) 'The white dreams of God: The mythology of sport films', *Arena Review*, 7(2), 15–19.

Nathan, I. (2000) 'Best review', *Empire*, 1 January, available: http://www.empireonline.com/reviews/ReviewComplete.asp?FID=5825 [accessed May 24 2017].
Neale, S. (1987) *Genre*, London: BFI.
Petrie, D., ed., (1992) *Screening Europe: Image and Identity in Contemporary European Cinema*, London: British Film Institute.
Poulton, E. (2007) '"Fantasy Football Hooliganism" in Popular Media', *Media, Culture & Society* 29(1), 151–164.
Poulton, E. and Roderick, M., eds., (2009) *Sport in Films*, New York, NY: Routledge.
Robinson, S. (2016) *There's a Green Sward Called the Oval: The Life and Times of a Football Stadium*, Belfast: Self-published.
Romaguera, I. Ramió, J. (2003) *Presencia del deporte en el cine español, un primer inventario*, Sevilla, Fundación Andalucía Olímpica y Consejo Superior de Deportes.
Rodríguez Díaz, Á. (2010) 'Spain's cocial values through film: Films about sports', in Dine, P. and Crosson, S., eds., *Sport, Representation and Evolving Identities in Europe*, Peter Lang: Frankfurt am Main, 119–140.
Rowe, D. (1995) *Popular Cultures: Rock Music, Sport and the Politics of Pleasure*, London: Sage Publications.
Rowe, D. (1998) 'If you film it, will they come? Sports on film', *Journal of Sport & Social Issues*, 22(4), 350–359.
Sarris, A. (1980) 'Why sports movies don't work', *Film Comment*, 16(6), 49–53.
Schaub, H. B. (2003) *Riefenstahls Olympia: Körperideale-ethische Verantwortungoder Freiheit des Künstlers?* München: Wilhelm Fink Verlag.
Schulze, L. (1990) 'The Made-for-TV movie: Industrial practice, cultural form, popular reception', in Balio, T., ed., *Hollywood in the Age of Television*, New York, NY: Unwin Hyman, 351–376.
Seddon, P. J. (1999) *A Football Compendium*, London: The British Library.
Soila, T., ed., (2009) *Stellar Encounters: Stardom in Popular European Cinema*, New Barnet, Herts: John Libbey.
Solomons, J. (2019) 'The indestructible goalkeeper', *The New European*, 8 April, available: https://www.theneweuropean.co.uk/top-stories/bert-trautmann-goalkeeper-film-jason-solomons-1-5978336 [accessed March 20 2020].
Street, S. (2003) 'National Cinema', in Mac Farlane, Brian, ed., *The Encyclopedia of British Film*, London: Methuen/BFI.
Tyers, A. (2019) 'Bert Trautmann movie The Keeper: FAO Manchester City fans', *The Telegraph*, 25 March, available: https://www.telegraph.co.uk/football/2019/03/25/bert-trautmann-movie-keeper-fao-manchester-city-fans/[accessed January 10 2020]
Wallenfeldt, J.H. (1989) *Sports Movies*, New York, NY: CineBooks.
Wayne, M. (2002) *The Politics of Contemporary European Cinema: Histories, Borders, Diasporas*, Bristol: Intellect.
Williams, R. (2006) *Sports Cinema – 100 Movies: The Best of Hollywood's Athletic Heroes, Losers, Myths, & Misfits*, New Jersey, USA: Limelight Editions.

Filmography

Avildsen, J.G. (1976) *Rocky*, MGM *Tower, Century City*, Los Angeles: United Artists.
Barfoed, K. (2015) *Sommeren '92*, Denmark/UK: Film i Väst/Meta Film/PeaPie Films.LL
Batley, E. (1916) *The Rival Captains*, UK: British Oak.

Branner, P.-A. (1932) *Hans livs match (The Match of His Life)*, Stockholm: Film AB Minerva.

Camus, M. (1968) *Volver a vivir*, Spain/Italy: Meteor Film S.r.l./Producciones Cinematográficas D.I.A.

Castillo, A. R. (1954) *Aces Search for Peace*, The (Los ases buscan la paz) Spain: Titán Films.

Chadhe G. (2002) *Bend It Like Beckham*, UK/Germany/USA: Kintop Pictures/Film Council/ Filmförderung Hamburg.

Chomet, S. (2003) *Les Triplettes de Belleville (Belleville Rendez-vous)*, Paris: Diaphana Films.

Croise, H. (1926) *The Ball of Fortune*, UK: Mercury Film Service.

Dickinson, T. (1939) *The Arsenal Stadium Mystery*, UK: Greenspan & Seligman Enterprises Ltd.

Douglas, R.I. (2005) Strákarnir okkar (Eleven Men Out), Iceland/Finland/UK: The Icelandic Filmcompany/Solar Films/Film and Music Entertainment (F & ME).

Elvey, M. (1914) *The Cup Final Mystery*, UK: Britannia Films.

Fitzhamon, L. (1911) *Harry the Footballer*, UK: Hepworth.

Fitzhamon, L. (1914) *A Footballer's Honour*, UK: Motograph.

Hudson, H. (1981) *Chariots of Fire*, Los Angeles, CA: Fox Plaza, Century City, 20th Century Fox.

Huston, J. (1981) *Escape to Victory*, UK/USA/Italy: The Pelegrin System Lorimar Film Entertainment/Victory Company/New Gold Entertainment.

Iquino, I.F. (1951) *El sistema Pelegrín* Barcelona: IFISA.

Keleti, M. (1952) *Civil a Pályán (Try and Win)*, Hungary: Magyar Filmgyártó Állami Vállalat.

Lee Hancock, J. (2009) *The Blind Side*, Burbank, CA: Warner Bros.

Leifer, N. (1979) *Yesterday's Hero*, UK/Australia: Packer Organisation/Cinema Seven Productions Ltd.

Loach, K. (2009) Looking for Eric, UK/France/Italy/Belgium/Spain: Sixteen Films/Canto Bros./France 2 Cinéma/Tornasol Films/Les Films du Fleuve/Radio Télévision Belge Francophone (RTBF).

Mangold, J. (2019) *Ford v Ferrari*, Los Angeles, CA: Fox Plaza, Century City, 20th Century Fox.

Marquina, L. (1962) *La batalla del domingo (Sunday's Battle)*, Spain: Cesáreo González Producciones Cinematográficas.

Melbourne Cooper, A. (1912) *The Cat's Cup Final*, UK: Alpha Trading Company.

Rosenmüller, M.H. (2018) *The Keeper*, UK/Germany: Zephyr Films/British Film Company/Lieblingsfilm

Russell, D.O. (2010) *The Fighter*, Hollywood, CA: Paramount Pictures.

Stemmle, R.A. (1942) *Das große Spiel*, Munich: Transit-Filmgesellschaft.

Stone, O. (1999) *Any Given Sunday*, California: Warner Bros.

Riefenstahl, L. (1938) *Olympia*, Berlin: Olympia-Film.

Scorsese, M. (1980) *Raging Bull*, *MGM Tower, Century City*, Los Angeles: United Artists.

Setó, J. (1956) *Saeta rubia (Blond Dart)*, Madrid: Unión Films.

Weiland, P. (2006) *Sixty-Six*, France/UK: Working Title Films/Studio Canal.

Yakin, B. (2000) *Remember the Titans*, Burbank, CA: Walt Disney Pictures.

Chapter 7

Football, fantasy, film

Cinema and the cultural politics of fans' imaginative investments in football stars

Marcus Free

The medium of film offers unique opportunities to explore sports fans' individual and collective imaginative investments in sport. Through the potential for deviation from realist form and aesthetic in both fiction and documentary, film can dramatise and visualise fans' often complex and ambivalent relationships with sport teams and individual sport stars. This chapter explores this theme, primarily through analysis of Ken Loach's (2009) *Looking for Eric*. The film offers a utopian vision of a fan who finds in his fantasy version of former Manchester United star Eric Cantona, a supreme individual talent who also provides a timely reminder of football's moral lesson of collective mutual dependence and solidarity. Rather than seeing its central character as delusional, it depicts his emotional investment in the idealised Cantona as creative 'illusionment' through which he finds a solution to his difficulties. Following the subsequent decade of austerity and widening social inequality in Britain, and the brilliant dramatisation of their devastating impact in Loach's more recent *I, Daniel Blake* (2017) and *Sorry We Missed You* (2019), *Looking for Eric* may seem somewhat dated. However, it is nonetheless a fascinating example of how film as a popular cultural form can imagine and dramatise the complex relationships between fans and football, and the psychic and cultural meanings of football fandom. The chapter draws on concepts and approaches from Freudian and object relations psychoanalysis. It develops earlier work (Free 2014) on the ways in which films featuring fans of Diego Maradona dwelt on the tensions between his status – for them – as a potentially de-contextualised, narcissistic extension of the self, and a symbol of collective identity, solidarity and political resistance. In order to introduce and explain these concepts, the following section revisits this earlier work. While *Looking for Eric* offers a positive reading of football's potential as utopian symbol and vehicle through the indulgence of fictional fantasy, the Maradona films are more ambivalent, or at least ambiguous. In different ways, they depict Maradona as an elusive, frustrating object of fantasy, highlighting the labour of fandom in infusing him with symbolism, but also his shortcomings as a symbol.

Looking for Maradona: an elusive object of fantasy

The earlier article concerned three films variously focused on Diego Maradona as an object of intense psychodynamic investment for his fans. The term 'psychodynamic' refers to how 'unconscious mental activity' and 'conscious thoughts, feelings and behavior' are dynamically interrelated (Cabaniss et al. 2011, p. 4), but in ways only partially or inconsistently consciously accessible.

That Maradona should become the focus of several films is uncoincidental. One of football's greatest talents, he was also highly controversial. His goals against England in the 1986 World Cup – the first from an undetected handball, the second following a sublime dribble past half the England team – encapsulate this duality. In 1991, he was banned for 15 months for taking cocaine while at Napoli, and in his 1994 World Cup comeback he was expelled for using the banned drug ephedrine. He outspokenly criticised FIFA in 1986, so fuelling his status as an icon of resistance to the game's hierarchy, an image further enhanced by his Napoli career. As recently explored in Asif Kapadia's 2019 documentary *Diego Maradona*, Napoli was both a poor relation of the wealthier northern Italian clubs and a geographical representative of Italy's poorer south. Maradona's success there was both geographically and economically symbolic, and it became intertwined with a romantic narrative, in Argentina, of his rise from the impoverished Buenos Aires suburb Villa Fiorito to national hero. While he later supported Fidel Castro and Hugo Chávez, his political beliefs are notoriously inconsistent and often incoherent. He also supported Argentine President Carlos Menem and Domingo Cavallo, Menem's neoliberal economic minister widely blamed for the 2001 economic collapse. Tobin (2002) argues that Maradona's appeal lies in the perception of his being against 'power' in a non-specific sense, however incoherently. Such gestures make him a compelling, populist symbol of resistance to American geopolitical hegemony despite his contradictions.

Maradona's self-described 'hand of God' goal against England was widely celebrated in Argentina as legitimately crafty play, and he claimed that his goals were vengeance for the 1982 Malvinas/Falklands War (Tobin 2002, p. 68). The longer historical context for this dates to football's bifurcation in the Argentine imagination into a quintessentially British, 'industrial' style and a more imaginative '*criollo*' (creole) style described by Archetti (2001, p. 155) as 'restless, individualistic, undisciplined ... agile and skilful'. In Archetti's fieldwork, Maradona's Argentine fans repeatedly stressed his 'liminal', in-between quality (Archetti 1997, p. 38) as an archetypal *pibe*, the perpetual boy who has never submitted to the demands of adult masculinity.

In order to make sense of such football stars' appeal, specifically how they become fantasy figures for fans, psychoanalytic perspectives on sport are helpful. A key reference is Lili Peller's (1954) situating of formal games and sport as the most advanced phase of play in childhood development. Positing that play 'alleviates anxiety' (Peller 1954, p. 179) deriving from internal or external dangers, Peller sees pre-Oedipal play as attempted emulation of maternal control by manipulating objects that the child begins to identify as separate. Oedipal play involves more structured, representational, game-like activities, which enable working through family attachments and fantasies, easing the disappointment of loss (Peller 1954, pp. 187–190). Formally organised games and sports are post-Oedipal, reality-adapted play fostering mutual identification, channelling homosexual urges into teams and observing rules as more significant than victory.

These 'latency games' represent 'independence from external superego figures' (Peller 1954, pp. 191–192). Extending this logic, Barry Richards (1994, p. 33) argues that soccer's handling taboo, forcing the cultivation of the foot, psychologically and socio-historically contributed to more disciplined social behaviour. By making the foot a means of expression rather than violence or forward propulsion, soccer constitutes a sublimated fusion of Freud's libidinal and aggressive drives, 'an image of society … with its rituals, its agonistic encounters and above all its taboos and rules' (Richards 1994, p. 40).

However, as therapeutic observations and analyses of sport and fan biographies have highlighted (Free 2008), involvement in professional sport may facilitate the perpetuation of pre-Oedipal and Oedipal fantasies, especially given sport's systematic reproduction of capitalism's contradiction between promised opportunity and personal development, and alienation and expendability (Ingham et al. 1999, p. 249). The celebration of Maradona's handball goal in Argentina enmeshed both personal and collective Oedipal pleasure: the 'liminal', man-child 'pibe' (Archetti 2001) versus the game's originators.

Archetti (2001, p. 159) highlights another feature of the Maradona myth, his 'capacity to "die," metaphorically', 'and be resurrected', to return through creativity rather than expressing guilt and serving punishment, and so be forgiven for any moral and social transgressions. Established in 1998, the 'Church of Maradona' in Buenos Aires merges this symbolism in profaning the Christian narrative, venerating Maradona's Christ-like suffering with a football crowned with thorns, initiating its members through re-enactment of the 'hand' goal. This profanation of Christian belief is congruent with the 'cultures of devotion' in Argentina to such 'folk saint' martyrs as Gaucho Gil, a 19th-century outlaw brutally executed without trial (Graziano 2007, p. 113).

Maradona-focused films illustrate the refraction and geographical specificity of his symbolism. In each case, the focus on affective – over and above intellectual – investment, and the often visually suggestive, rather than verbally articulated, form of the text lends itself to interpretations variously inspired by Freudian and object relations psychoanalysis. Carlos Sorín's Argentine road movie *El Camino de San Diego* (2006), a seemingly romanticised narrative of a fan's fascination with Maradona, highlights these tensions through the contrast between the fictional fan's pilgrimage to visit his deified idol and the impoverished and fractured national geographical and cultural space through which he passes. In the 2007 British documentary *In the Hands of the Gods*, five 'freestyle' footballers from the UK embark on a pilgrimage to his home. Their geographical movement through North and South America is presented as an opportunity for psychological rebirth and self-realisation.

The 2008 documentary *Maradona by Kusturica*, by Bosnian-born Emir Kusturica, is perhaps most illustrative in that it foregrounds psychoanalytic concepts through Kusturica's own voice-over narrative of his efforts to interpret Maradona's personal and political symbolism. The repetitive structure of this non-narrative film and Kusturica's expressions of frustration with his project are evidence of a reflexive acknowledgement of fan investment as a form of narcissism leading back to himself. The film offers a more optimistic vision of Maradona's notionally Christ-like symbolism as a potentially redemptive, revolutionary figure for the geopolitical South than Sorín's *El Camino de San Diego*, in which Maradona is depicted as a somewhat narcissistic mirror for its fictional protagonist (Free 2014). Kusturica both acknowledges and reflexively explores his own narcissistic identification with Maradona and extends his earlier filmic themes of extremely marginal figures as anti-heroes (Gocic 2001, p. 53), and of harmony in dissonance (Iordanova 2002).

Kusturica establishes Maradona as an enigmatic figure eluding description, interpretation and prediction, embodying irrepressible vitality in his play and seemingly unconscious self-destructiveness in his cocaine abuse. As with the other films, it is in Maradona's representation of pre-Oedipal immaturity that Kusturica is most invested as a fan, mapping a geopolitical fantasy of resistance on to Maradona's body. As his second goal against England is shown in replays, Kusturica comments that 'even God himself got involved' here, as 'a country heavily in debt to the IMF triumphed over one of the rulers of the world'. Verbally referring to the 'hand' goal with the reference to Maradona's 'hand of God' quote as we see the second goal suggests artistic equivalence. Neither hand nor foot acts as expected within the post-Oedipal, paternal, authoritative codification of football. Kusturica's fantasy of pre-Oedipal recovery and Oedipal resistance combined undergoes numerous repetitions, with minor variations, in periodic animated sequences. Here Maradona, his photographed face transposed on to a cartoon body, bamboozles various elite Westerners (including Margaret Thatcher and George W. Bush) while the Sex Pistols' 'God Save the Queen' is played. This is a distinctly corporeal fantasy of refusal of the post-Oedipal rules of global football and global politics alike.

However, for all that he is clearly enthralled by his own fantasy, the film constantly reiterates Maradona's enigma and his frustration of Kusturica's project. It shares the repetitive structure of music, and of football itself, in its multiple cycles of restart, defence and attack, stressing Maradona's transcendence of hierarchical distinctions through his corporeal irreducibility to discursive explanation or translation. Thus, on discovery that Maradona is again seriously ill and cannot be seen, Kusturica witnesses a street performance of Argentina's other famous export, the tango, and verbally indulges a favourite theme of his, finding harmony in dissonance (Iordanova 2002, p. 104). He connects Maradona's vibrant football, revolutionary political alignments, self-destructiveness and miraculous survival with the dance 'most obviously suggest[ing] the union between thanatos and eros', Freud's (2001/1920) death and life instincts.

Kusturica thus suggests that Maradona may be unconsciously masochistic, echoing Freud's (1984/1923) theory of masochism as the eroticisation of the death instinct. He repeatedly shows Church of Maradona processions and ceremonies. Their equation of Maradona's punishment by FIFA with the Crucifixion is evident as a member holds a football that 'represents Diego's sacrifice', followed later by a 'barbed-wire crown' representing 'the pitch, the field, the grounds' where he suffered. Like Jesus's death, Maradona's disastrous return to football in 1994 was voluntary. Combined with his near-death, due to chronic obesity and his cocaine addiction, Maradona's actions are clearly open to the interpretation of unconscious masochism.

While the three films variously address Maradona's symbolism, only *Maradona by Kusturica* engages critically with his contradictions as an Argentine cultural icon, and with his place or places in the imagination of his fans. Kusturica's is a decidedly postmodern documentary, as befits Maradona's contradictions: 'at once the imaginary and the symbolic, he was marginal and he was central, he was strong and he was weak, he was popular and he was the elite' (Bilbija 1995, p. 205). Unable to establish exactly who Maradona is as a person and what he 'means' as a cultural phenomenon, Kusturica conveys his ambivalent relationship to Maradona's rather contradictory celebrity persona.

Looking for Eric: from the delusional and elusive to the fantasy film

While the Maradona films feature fan fantasies, and *Maradona by Kusturica* explores their limitations due to Maradona's actual limitations, *Looking for Eric* is a borderline 'fantasy film' in its central ambiguity, made all the more surprising by its director Ken Loach's association with 'social realism'. As a fantasy film, it eschews any clear distinction between fantasy and reality. Rather, its blurring this distinction enables an exploration of its central character's 'inner world' and the ways in which football as a metaphorical space of play can facilitate a utopian vision, irrespective of contemporary elite football's commercial reality.

The director of such films as *Riff Raff* (1990), *Raining Stones* (1992), *My Name Is Joe* (1998), *It's a Free World* (2006), *I, Daniel Blake* (2017) and *Sorry We Missed You* (2019), Ken Loach is renowned as a key exponent of 'social realist' film and television, whose aim is to 'show the effects of environmental factors on the development of character through depictions that emphasise the relationship between location and identity' (Hallam and Marshment 2000, p. 184). Loach has focused predominantly on the plight of the British industrial working class following progressive de-industrialisation and worsening economic and working conditions under neoliberal policies pursued by successive Conservative and Labour governments since 1979. His avowed aim is to get 'insights into personal relationships and experiences that you can get through fiction, and yet to set them in a firm, concrete context' (quoted in Fuller 1998, p. 10). Leigh (2002, p. 151) has traced a progressive move from the overt didacticism of such earlier work as the television series chronicling the 1926 General Strike, *Days of Hope* (1974) towards a more episodic structural form, mixing moods with a more melodramatic character focus, with humour often intertwining with the mutual support of friends, work colleagues and family as coping resources. Since the 1990s his films often conclude with the potential for positive outcomes to struggle with overwhelmingly difficult material conditions.

Written by regular collaborator Paul Laverty, *Looking for Eric* addresses social and familial disintegration and incipient mental illness, focusing on the psychological consequences of its protagonist Eric's abandonment of his wife and child. Despite oddly echoing the contemporary neoliberal discourse of the refusal of individual responsibility as the source of social ills, in Loach's vision Eric's despair and recovery derive from failure of trust in collective working-class solidarity, a moral lesson learned by imagining a famous ex-footballer's (Eric Cantona) reminder of football's team game as a symbol of mutual interdependency. Hence his recovery of belief in collective solidarity by fantasised recovery of the symbolic potential of team sport, despite its seeming embodiment of the neoliberal logic of capital accumulation, through marketisation and stock market flotation, and the financial enrichment and media projection of individual athletes as celebrities.

Although Cantona plays himself, the film focuses on his role as an *imagined* hero. Thus Loach's customary social realism mingles with 'magical realism'. A somewhat slippery term, literary magical realism is defined as a 'modern fiction in which fabulous and fantastical events are included in a narrative that otherwise maintains the "reliable" tone of objective realistic report'. It draws on 'the energies of fable, folk tale, and myth while maintaining a strong contemporary social relevance' (Baldick 2008, p. 194). Distinct from the Hollywood 'fantasy film' whose promise of a potentially 'happy ending' through wish fulfilment is sustained by willing suspension of disbelief, it nonetheless shares the latter's tendency towards 'ambiguity, paradox, and contradiction' (Fowkes 2010, p. 54). Here, fantasy facilitates Loach's vision of a social reality obscured by Eric's sense of social atomisation and personal isolation. The fantasies whose hallucinatory status is made ambiguous through their material realisation and visible narrative efficacy enable his recovery. The ambiguity of Cantona's presence is conveyed through his periodically speaking French – if he is imaginary, how is this possible, given that Eric apparently cannot understand French?

An established actor in France by 2009, Cantona was the outstanding player in Manchester United's 1990s renaissance, winning the English Premiership in four of his five seasons there. He was as notorious for his ban for dropkicking a Crystal Palace supporter – who verbally abused him in January 1995 (Gardiner 1998) – and for his ensuing, cryptic press conference remark (perhaps a metaphor for the tabloids' relationship with elite football) that 'when the seagulls follow a trawler, it's because they think sardines will be thrown into the sea' (see Auclair 2009, p. 392; Storey, 2019, p. 57) as for his stylish play. Indeed Cantona's persistently breaking boundaries made him the perfect transgressor of the boundary between the real and fan fantasy. The film's heightening of his enigmatic public persona may also have inspired the 2017 publication of his ambiguous drawings and playful idle thoughts, *my notebook* (Cantona 2017). The 1990s Premiership's 'king of endorsements' (Auclair 2009, p. 415), as John Hill argues (2011, p. 198), Cantona was thus a source of 'unresolved tension' as the film's 'symbol of anti-corporate sentiment'. Philippe Auclair (2009, p. 351) maintains, though, that Cantona's repeated insistence on fans' centrality to football made him a (Jock) 'Steinian', repeatedly echoing, in his sentiments, the legendary Celtic manager's maxim: 'football is nothing without its fans'. It was Cantona's friendship with a real fan (probably Gary King, featured in the film's DVD extra, the documentary *United We Stand*), who followed him from Leeds United to Manchester United when he departed the club on poor terms in 1992, that led to Cantona's initial invitation to Loach to work together. However, Loach and Laverty opted for the 'freedom' and 'enormous pull' (Laverty 2009, p. 9) of a fictional story rather than documentary as a way of exploring this 'Steinian' quality as an inspiration for collective solidarity.

In the film Eric, a postman involved in an opening car accident, and who seems to be suffering from some earlier psychic trauma, fantasises that his hero Cantona appears as he stares at his bedroom wall poster. Smoking marijuana, he asks, 'Have you ever done anything that you're ashamed of?' Cantona, materialising behind him replies 'Well, have you?' Quickly developing as an uncompromising conscience as much as an auxiliary ego, Cantona confirms his intimate knowledge of Eric's mind (where 'he' resides), remarking 'it's Lily, n'est-ce pas?' He instructs him to open a trunk of personal belongings (evidently, given Eric's fearful reaction, having remained shut for some time) 'without danger'. Finding an old photograph of himself with a teenage Lily (the ex-wife he has later abandoned following the birth of their daughter Sam), Eric relates the story of their winning a dance competition some 30 years previously. His accident has followed Sam's request that he and Lily share their granddaughter's childcare while she prepares for her final college exams. Parodying his public image, Cantona utters a series of proverb-like statements – 'he that forecasts all perils will never sail the seas', etc. – and persuades Eric to face Lily again.

The Lily plot intersects with Eric's inept single parenting of stepsons Ryan and Jess from a failed second marriage, his efforts thwarted by Ryan's involvement with a dangerous criminal, Zac, and by Eric's depleted self-worth. Having failed as a biological father, Eric has masochistically adopted a submissive maternal-feminine position at home. Ryan even stores Zac's illegal gun for him in Eric's house. Eric experiences the worst of maternity, having forsaken the opportunity to grow into parenthood with his daughter. But while trying to confront Zac directly, he is humiliated when threatened with a Rottweiler and the recorded footage is uploaded to YouTube.

Cantona inspires an alternative to masochistic feminine submission and Zac's narcissistic masculinity, revealed to be fragile when ultimately exposed. The result, a violent solution that avoids actually inflicting retributive personal violence on Zac, combines 'masculine' hardness with feminine pragmatism and problem-solving, employing a strategy that ensures Zac's weakness defeats him. By attacking his house wearing Cantona masks, forcing him to acknowledge his gun before destroying it, and threatening to upload their recording to YouTube, they reverse Eric's earlier humiliation. In a Foucauldian outcome, they can be sure that he will stay away for fear of 'losing face'.

This solution also validates their public servant status and otherwise socially devalued masculinity, and it avoids police involvement. When Eric's friend Meatballs warns Zac that if he disappears he'll find him ''cause I'm a fucking postman', he is invoking a sub-State potential network of worker surveillance made possible by collective solidarity. This cements the direct connection between Cantona's vision of football as a team game and the cooperative teamwork of public sector workers. Earlier in the film, Eric invites Cantona to recall his favourite career moment. After Eric describes many brilliant goals as we witness their replay, Cantona then remarks that 'it was a pass ... you have to trust your teammates, always. If not, we are lost' – prompting the replay of an exquisite and selfless pass from Cantona which led to teammate Denis Irwin's goal. Apparently inspired by Cantona's conversations with writer Paul Laverty (2009, p. 13), Cantona's 'trust your teammates' becomes the principle that leads to their successful collective assault on Zac's narcissism.

Gender and fantasy in *Looking for Eric*

Released towards the end of the 'New Labour' government (1997–2010) and a year after the 2008 financial crisis, *Looking for Eric* shares with many British films from that time a problematic displacement of an established 'social realist' theme of class and social inequality onto one of threatened masculine identity (Hill 2011, p. 199). However, while Eric's restoration of self-respect occurs through a quasi-re-masculinisation of sorts, some complications playfully suggest a homoerotic undercurrent in football fandom that is not necessarily fanciful. Anthony King (1995, p. 15) suggested that, prior to departure for Manchester United and becoming a hate figure at Leeds, Cantona's Leeds fans 'loved him in the way that someone might love their partner'. Philippe Auclair (2009, p. 263) cites Gary King's confession that he 'felt less pain' when his wife left him than when Cantona was sold to Manchester United.

In an early scene, inspired by 'self-help' therapy, Meatballs encourages his postal co-workers to imagine their mirror reflection through the eyes of someone they admire. Eric's choice of Cantona leads to his later fantasy vision in which Cantona appears in person. However, when Cantona materialises, he sarcastically greets Eric's suicidal thoughts with 'so I suggest a jump off the nearest block of flats'. Effectively, Eric is challenging himself here. As James Walters (2011, p. 30) comments, in fantasy 'we discover not only fragments of our world, but fragments of ourselves'. Cantona represents the healthy part of Eric's psyche, the 'good object' representing life, creativity and imagination, thus creatively challenging a move towards death, lifelessness, disintegration.

Interestingly, the latter are prompted by re-encountering Lily, suggesting her representation of a harsh maternal superego in his imagination so terrifying that he cannot face her. Thus, Eric's gendered psychic economy is such that uncompromising but creative masculinity and masculine solidarity vie with a construction of femininity associated with death – either Lily as a feared destructive object or the failing maternal role he has now masochistically adopted.

Here, though, the film differs from the sometimes reactionary gender politics of the post-industrial cycle of 1990s British films. Cantona's surprising provocations include translating Lily's indifference when he tries to explain to her his abandonment as 'the noblest vengeance is to forgive'. Earlier he describes to

Cantona his shock, on first seeing her again with their granddaughter, a vision of (grand)maternal perfection that seems to have precipitated his crisis. He later describes to her his initial panic attack at Sam's christening, brought about by the image of Lily feeding Sam (suggesting an unconscious sense of sibling privation rather than paternal responsibility), while we witness in flashback his father's bullying: 'you've made your bed now, son, you can lie on it'. Hence a double blow to his psychic and masculine integrity.

Cantona's intervention brings something approximating a Kleinian 'depressive position' in Eric. Melanie Klein's psychoanalysis derived from the study of the pre-Oedipal infant's ambivalent relationship with the mother or primary carer, and the individuation of identity and capacity for empathy and sociality via the working through of this ambivalence. The 'depressive position' was her term for the progression from psychic splitting of the mother into 'good' and 'bad' 'part-objects' towards the experience of guilt and desire for 'reparation' (Klein 1975/1935, pp. 262–289). Eric must accept Lily as Other, a whole being rather than his own fantasy extension. Cantona, as the 'introjected' 'good object' with which Eric identifies, summons a capacity for guilt and reparation, acknowledging Lily's achievements without the paranoid fear of reprisal and envious destructiveness – albeit masculinising her in the process. Cantona's remark – 'I like this woman a lot. She has big balls!' – ironically confirms Eric's sense of 'feminine' diminution. Lily, it emerges, has also preserved Eric's youthful creativity, handing him his blue suede shoes following their reconciliation, a visual and narrative pun (Elvis's 'you can do anything but stay off of my blue suede shoes'). The imagined Cantona recovers the memory of their dancing, by inviting him to dance with him (therefore dance both with himself and the imagined Cantona-as-Lily) helping to recover the 'healthy' narcissism of their initial dancing encounter when, following a flashback showing Eric lifting and catching her, he intimates: 'it was like she fucking trusted me, you know what I mean?' 'Healthy' narcissism entails a self-regard facilitated by the recognition and validation of the Other.

The film thus shows Eric's move from abandoning Lily through the implied abandonment *by* his second wife Chrissie and the masochism of caring for the boys as a quasi-mother, towards a 'good enough masculinity' (Yates 2015, p. 104). Rather than fetishising athletic masculinity, Cantona is an enabling 'good object', restoring Eric's dancing as a vehicle for creative expression and love of the other. Eric actually describes Cantona's playing as 'balletic'; but beautiful football, like dance, interlinks bodies in a seamless chain, enabling individual and collective creativity without retreat into defensive, destructive and fragile narcissism or fearful submission to a castrating, bullying paternal ideal.

The film is unbalanced in that Lily is still relatively minor. Eric's recovery is an intrapsychic, all-male affair. While ultimately accepted as an enabling father figure by Ryan, Jess and Sam, there is no romantic reunion with Lily, or indication that this might happen. Yet, despite Lily's relative marginality, there is a progressive sexual politics of sorts. By reshaping himself as a *social* being, fathering the adopted sons, trusting in himself and friends through football as metaphor, being a carer (with Lily) for his granddaughter (so enabling his daughter's educational progression), and recovering a childlike creativity and playfulness, Eric's masculinity is flawed but 'good enough'.

The film also plays with the generally unacknowledged homoeroticism of same-sex sports fandom. Eric's healthy narcissism is enabled by introjecting a masculine ideal with which he identifies. However, this is not the same as Judith Butler's (1997) reading of performativity in heterosexual gender identification. She reads the acquisition of gender as a performed identification with the same-sex parent that signifies the repudiation of a proto-homosexual love for this parent in infancy. Butler maintains that the heteronormativity of the culture into which children are inducted is such that this is a love that cannot be grieved because it cannot be acknowledged. The object that cannot be a love object is instead introjected as an object of identification. Eric's rediscovery of dancing is enabled by the fantasised Cantona's invitation to dance ('I'm the girl, come on'), which Eric initially resists ('that's just a step too far now!') before relenting. Here, Eric dances with an introjected object that he identifies with and loves as an Other object. Even though we go into fantasy shots of the older Eric dancing with the younger Lily, then Eric with the older Lily, these are interspersed with shots of Eric dancing with Cantona to 'Blue Suede Shoes'. This plays with a quasi-Freudian reading of the denial of homosexual desire by projection of it onto the other ('I do not love him. He loves me'; Freud 1911, p. 63), and thus with sports fandom's homoeroticism. The play is not cancelled by the return to 'reality'. Indeed Eric's slightly disconcerted look when Cantona speaks admiringly of Lily's 'big balls' humorously extends the theme. On the film's DVD, in a post-screening discussion, the actor who plays Eric, Steve Evets, also references this subtext, joking that 'sometimes I make my girlfriend wear' his souvenir signed Cantona mask from the film.

Insufficiently 'Loachian'?

While the film's unsteady focus and shifting moods provoked a mixed critical reception (Rickards 2018), its venture into more familiar 'social realist' territory is humorous but critically pointed. It features fictional fans of FC United, a football club formed in opposition to Manchester United's rampant commercialism, particularly since the American Glazer family's 2005 takeover. The club became heavily indebted in order to cover the huge loans the Glazers used to purchase it (Conn 2013). However, these fans' nonetheless ambivalent feelings are depicted through Spleen, one of Eric's mates. Spleen is accused by a Manchester United supporter of having 'run away' from the club when seen sporting a FC United shirt in a pub as a televised Manchester United game is about to commence. He leaves in anger but rushes back when the others pretend to cheer a goal. Just as Cantona is an enduring symbol for Eric because Eric has a sense of 'ownership' of him through years of financial, intellectual, emotional and symbolic investment in his club, Manchester United embodies years of investment by Spleen and the others. Commercialism and highly dubious financial practices cannot entirely cancel its 'authenticity'. However, the fantasy of Eric's return on his psychic investment in Cantona is not matched by the supporters' relationship to the club. This scene highlights sport fandom's 'cultural contradictions' (Free and Hughson 2006): supporter loyalty rooted in popular culture exposes those supporters to the most ruthless exploitation by 'investors' seeking to profit from the club's accumulated economic and symbolic capital.

That this is dealt with humorously arguably reflects the film's failure to be sufficiently 'Loachian'. Perhaps also it may be seen retrospectively as a missed opportunity given the actual impact of, and worker resistance against moves towards, 'modernisation' and privatisation in the UK postal service at the time. The eventual, much-contested Royal Mail 2013 privatisation had predictably deleterious consequences for working conditions following failed privatisation attempts in 2003 and 2009–2010. That those attempts failed and that the Communications Workers Union secured a participatory role in the Royal Mail's 'restructuring', a role extended in the 2014 agreement, reflect the 'enduring capacity of organised labour to disrupt, influence and apply pressure' (Mustchin 2017, p. 308). Loach's *Sorry We Missed You* (2019) depicts the dehumanising impact of current 'gig economy' working conditions, exemplified by services like Deliveroo. Here the central character struggles to sustain a meaningful life, family relationships and health given the perpetual surveillance that tracks and quantifies his every move in this unregulated sector where workers are demanding re-classification from 'self-employed' to employees with entitlements (Cant 2019). *Looking for Eric* now seems slightly dated in its seeming disinterest in the debilitating impact of neoliberalism, and in its search for solutions in a reconstructed masculinity.

Yet, like *I, Daniel Blake* (2017) (Lebeau 2019) it highlights the necessity for the understanding – and *feeling* – of mutual dependency and relatedness. Its intra-psychic focus and use of football as metaphor allow it to explore the affective dimensions of this theme in ways unique and quite distinct from Loach's more readily identifiable, empirically grounded social realist films.

Conclusions

As these examples demonstrate, the medium of film can highlight football's potential facilitation of social, cultural and political exploration in ways that exceed the limitations of live television broadcast, especially in an increasingly corporatised and commodified media environment. In particular it can facilitate exploration of the intra-psychic aspects of fans' engagement with the game and their paradoxes.

Like the Maradona films, *Looking for Eric* explores the football supporter's intra-psychic world and the playing out of fantasy resolutions to real-life predicaments through symbolic investment in football heroes. It is an unusual, creative intersection of football and popular film, eschewing dramatised on-field action in favour of exploration of the 'star' as meaningful object of investment: a narcissistic self-extension, an independent, unpredictable being, a 'teammate' whose interconnectedness in football reminds the protagonist of his own complex, gendered, social interconnectedness. Its recourse to an imagined version of a real hero thus sustains football as a field of imaginative, hopeful 'illusionment' of the potential for collective solidarity and thus both symbolic and material transformation – illusionment in Donald Winnicott's (1971) sense that at the heart of imaginative potential is the early childhood illusion that what is a found object has actually been created, given symbolic meaning by the infant. Hence 'a growing capacity to tolerate the continual and increasingly sophisticated illusionment-disillusionment-re-illusionment process throughout the life cycle' (Phillips 2007/1988, p. 121).

And yet, fascination with celebrity footballers in ways that do not address their implication in football's corporatised world is limited in the extent to which it can facilitate critical reflexivity. While Emir Kusturica acknowledges his only partly met aspirations for Maradona as political symbol, neither his nor the other Maradona films address the power dynamics within professional and international football and Maradona's mobilisation as a commodified symbol through the course of his career. This is also curiously marginalised within *Looking for Eric*, a film that turns a blind eye to the commodified Cantona's association with Manchester United and the English Premiership's movement of football beyond the economic accessibility of local working-class supporters. Quoting the club administration's aim to 'leverage the global brand' and 'convert' more global 'fans into customers', David Andrews (2004, p. 2) highlights how the 'emergence of the emblematic Manchester United plc' from the 1990s onwards illustrated 'broader societal shifts within which the boundaries between cultural and commercial spheres' became 'increasingly indivisible'.

However, this shortcoming is consistent with the 'cultural contradictions' of football (Free and Hughson 2006). Supporters' intense affective investment in this commodified cultural form contributes to its *making* as it unfolds in each iteration. Because sport as commodity is 'produced' while in progress, and because sporting contests unfold unpredictably and are influenced to unquantifiable degrees by vocally and corporeally expressed emotional support, there is a sense that it somehow contains part of the self as a supporter. Yet corporatisation and commodification are largely accepted as immutable givens. The imaginative investment in football's utopian symbolism dramatised in *Looking for Eric* co-exists with a sense of the inevitability of the commercial exploitation of supporters.

References

Andrews, D.L. (2004) 'Introduction: Situating Manchester United plc'. In Andrews, D.L. (ed.), *Manchester United: A Thematic Study*, Abingdon, Oxon: Routledge, 1–10.

Archetti, E.P. (1997) '"And Give Joy to My Heart." Ideology and Emotions in the Argentinian Cult of Maradona'. In Armstrong, G. and Giulianotti, R. (eds.), *Entering the Field: New Perspectives on World Football*, Oxford: Berg, 31–51.

Archetti, E.P. (2001) 'The Spectacle of a Heroic Life: The Case of Diego Maradona'. In Andrews, D.L. and Jackson, S.J. (eds.), *Sport Stars: The Cultural Politics of Sporting Celebrity*. London: Routledge, 151–163.

Auclair, P. (2009) *Cantona: The Rebel Who Would Be King*. London: Macmillan.

Baldick, C. (2008) *The Concise Oxford Dictionary of Literary Terms*, 3rd ed. London: Oxford University Press.

Bilbija, K. (1995) 'Maradona's Left: Postmodernity and National Identity in Argentina'. *Studies in Latin American Popular Culture*, 14, 199–208.

Butler, J. (1997) *The Psychic Life of Power: Theories in Subjection*. Stanford, CA: Stanford University Press.

Cabaniss, D.L., Cherry, S., Douglas, C.J. and Schwartz, A.R. (2011) *Psychodynamic Psychotherapy: A Clinical Manual*. Oxford: Wiley-Blackwell.

Cant, C. (2019) *Riding for Deliveroo: Resistance in the New Economy*. Cambridge: Polity.

Cantona, E. (2017) *My Notebook*. London: Weidenfeld & Nicolson.

Conn, D. (2013) 'Manchester United Title Triumph Shows How the Glazers Have Won in the End'. *The Guardian*, 23 April. Accessed July 5 2020: https://www.theguardian.com/football/blog/2013/apr/23/manchester-united-glazers-finance.

Fowkes, K. (2010) *The Fantasy Film*. Chichester: Wiley-Blackwell.

Free, M. (2008) 'Psychoanalytic Perspectives on Sport: A Critical Review'. *International Journal of Applied Psychoanalytic Studies* 5(4), 273–296.

Free, M. (2014) 'Diego Maradona and the Psychodynamics of Football Fandom in International Cinema'. *Celebrity Studies* 5(1–2), 197–212.

Free, M. and Hughson, J. (2006) 'Common Culture, Commodity Fetishism and the Cultural Contradictions of Sport'. *International Journal of Cultural Studies* 9(1), 83–104.

Freud, S. (1911) 'Psycho-Analytic Notes on an Autobiographical Account of a Case of Paranoia (Dementia Paranoides)'. In Strachey, J. (ed.), *Standard Edition of the Complete Psychological Works of Sigmund Freud*Vol XII. London: Vintage, 1–82.

Freud, S. (1984/1923) 'The Economic Problem of Masochism'. In Richards, A. (ed.), *Penguin Freud Library*, Vol. 11, London: Penguin, 409–434.

Freud, S. (2001/1920) 'Beyond the Pleasure Principle'. In Strachey, J. (ed.), *Standard Edition of the Complete Psychological Works of Sigmund Freud* Vol. XVIII. London: Vintage, 3–64.

Fuller, G. (ed., 1998) *Loach on Loach*. London: Faber & Faber.

Gardiner, S. (1998) 'The Law and Hate Speech: "Ooh Aah Cantona" and the Demonization of "the Other"'. In Brown, A. (ed.), *Fanatics! Power, Identity and Fandom in Football*, London: Routledge, 249–264.

Gocic, G. (2001) *Notes from The Underground: The Cinema of Emir Kusturica*, London: Wallflower.

Graziano, F. (2007) *Cultures of Devotion: Folk Saints of Spanish America*. Oxford: Oxford University Press.

Hallam, J. & Marshment, M. (2000) *Realism and Popular Cinema*. Manchester: Manchester University Press.

Hill, J. (2011) *Ken Loach: the Politics of Film and Television*. Basingstoke: Palgrave Macmillan.

Ingham, A.G., Blissmer, B.J. and Davidson, K.W. (1999) 'The Expendable Prolympic Self: Going Beyond the Boundaries of the Sociology and Psychology of Sport'. *Sociology of Sport Journal* 16, 236–268.

Iordanova, D. (2002) *Emir Kusturica*. London: British Film Institute.

King, A. (1995) 'The Problem of Identity and the Cult of Cantona'. *Salford Papers in Sociology*. Manchester: Salford University.

Klein, M. (1975/1935) 'A Contribution to the Psychogenesis of Manic-Depressive States'. In Money-Kyrle, R.E. (ed.), *Love, Guilt and Reparation, and Other Works*. New York, NY: The Free Press, 262–289.

Laverty, P. (2009), 'Introduction'. In Laverty, P., *Looking for Eric*, Pontefract: Route.

Lebeau, V. (2019) 'Feeling Poor: D.W. Winnicott and Daniel Blake'. *New Formations*, 96–97, 160–175. doi: 10.3898/NEWF:96/97.07.2019.

Leigh, J. (2002) The Cinema of Ken Loach: Art in the Service of the People. London: Wallflower.

Mustchin, S. (2017) 'Public Sector Restructuring and the Re-regulation of Industrial Relations: The Three-Decade Project of Privatisation, Liberalisation and Marketisation in Royal Mail'. *Industrial Relations Journal*, 48(4), 294–309.

Peller, L.E. (1954) 'Libidinal Phases, Ego Development, and Play'. *Psychoanalytic Study of the Child* 91, 178–198.

Phillips, A. (2007/1988) *Winnicott*. London: Penguin.

Richards, B. (1994) *Disciplines of Delight: The Psychoanalysis of Popular Culture*. London: Free Association Books.

Rickards, C. (2018) 'An Ordinary Spectacle: Critical Responses to Fantasy and Whimsy in Looking for Eric and The Angels' Share'. *Journal of British Cinema and Television*, 15(4), 553–570.

Storey, D. (2019) *250 Days: Cantona's Kung Fu and the Making of Manchester United*. London: HarperCollins.

Tobin, J. (2002) 'Soccer Conspiracies: Maradona, the CIA, and Popular Critique'. Arbena, J.L. and LaFrance, D.G. (eds.), *Sport in Latin America and the Caribbean*. Wilmington, DE: Scholarly Resources, 51–73.

Walters, J. (2011) *Fantasy Film: A Critical Introduction*. Oxford: Berg.

Winnicott, D.W. (1971) *Playing and Reality*. London: Tavistock.

Yates, C. (2015) *The Play of Political Culture, Emotion and Identity*. Basingstoke: Palgrave Macmillan.

Part III

Football and/as cultural identity

Chapter 8

Yugoslav football and British popular culture 1975–1991

From Petar Borota to 'Sexton's Lions'

Dejan Zec and Miloš Paunović

Introduction

This chapter investigates the role of football and football-related culture during the final years of the Socialist Federal Republic of Yugoslavia. During this period, Yugoslavian society, and its large urban centres in particular, experienced an influx of contemporary British cultural products (TV series, music records, radio programmes, films), and a growing fascination with British football. This strengthening of British influence across the different areas of popular culture influenced not only the way Yugoslav football fans experienced their favourite game, but also their lives.

Yugoslavs and British popular culture

World views and tastes of the Yugoslav population have always been heavily influenced by foreign cultural patterns. Some parts of Yugoslavia had stronger connections with Europe, historically being a part of the Habsburg Empire, but other areas were connected with the modern Western world only after liberation from the Ottomans in the early and mid-19th century (Čalić 2004; Stojanović 2008). By the beginning of the 20th century, a large part of the population, certainly most of the bourgeoisie and urban dwellers, were familiar with what was going on in major cities of Europe and the world (Gašić 2005). Until the Second World War, the Yugoslav bourgeoisie was heavily influenced by continental cultural patterns and ways of life, trying to mimic life in major capitals of continental Europe, such as Paris, Vienna, Budapest or Prague. Yet British culture was distant and unfamiliar.

Few people understood the English language, very few literary works were translated into Serbo-Croatian, and British art and music were absent from the public scene (Momčilović 1990; Toševa 2007). This gradually began to change during the late 1930s, especially with the rise of the radio (a contributing factor was the fact that the Belgrade radio station was owned by the British *Marconi* company) (Marković 1979; Nikolić 2006). By the time Yugoslavia was attacked by the Axis forces in 1941, the rise of British cultural influence in Yugoslavia coincided with the growth of the antifascist and anti-German sentiment of the people (Hoptner 1972; Lampe 2000; Radić 2012).

There were indications that in the immediate post-World War II period, the new cultural orientation of the country would very much be in alignment with the political preferences and loyalties of the new communist authorities and that it would mostly rely on the Soviet Union. In a very short time span, supported by the government, Soviet movies, books and songs became dominant in Yugoslav public discourse (Dimić 1988; Petranović 1988). Western cultural influences were not completely rejected, but they were severely limited and scrutinised for potential politically subversive content (Dobrivojević 2012). However, the political turbulence of the late 1940s and confrontation between Yugoslavia and Cominform[1] put a halt to this trend. The need for Yugoslav authorities to distance themselves from Stalin and the USSR, and the willingness of the western powers to aid Yugoslavia in those efforts without insisting on major internal political reforms, created an atmosphere in which the Yugoslav communist government was able to relax its guard and allow the gradual reintroduction of British, French and American movies, literature and music into Yugoslav public space (Dimitrijević 2016). British politics played an important role in supporting Yugoslavia during the period of confrontation with Cominform, and ties between representatives of the Labour Party and leading Yugoslav politicians grew particularly strong (Unkovski-Korica 2014).[2]

A shift towards the Anglo-American cultural sphere began in the 1930s, mostly visible in the popularity of Hollywood movies and the rising popularity of jazz, but it was only during the 1960s and 1970s when Anglo-American popular culture became undoubtedly dominant in Yugoslavia (Marković 1992; Vučetić 2009; Blam 2011; Vučetić 2015). By the mid-1960s, almost all major American and British movies were distributed in Yugoslavia, novels were translated and published, comics were printed in Yugoslav papers and the– new sound of rock 'n' roll, however strange it may have sounded to older audiences, was capturing the hearts and minds of Yugoslav youth, being broadcasted by government-owned radio stations and syndicated by government-owned record labels (Raković 2012). It is fair to say that while the lion's share of the Anglo-American cultural influence was actually American, bands like the Beatles and the Rolling Stones were among the most popular in the country, British movies, such as *To Sir, with Love* and *A Clockwork Orange*, defined a whole generation, and British TV shows, such as *Monty Python's Flying Circus*, *The Dave Allen Show*, and *The Benny Hill Show* had a huge impact on the Yugoslav public (Kostić 1975; Dragićević-Šešić 2007; Raković 2012). Moreover, a significant element of this Anglo-American cultural influence in Yugoslavia was seen in sports – and by the late 1960s, two of the most popular sports in the country were football and basketball (Perica 2003; Todić 2006).

Yugoslav football

Yugoslavs always acknowledged that the British Isles were the cradle of football, which strongly influenced and nurtured a certain relationship of respect and admiration, which is not a very common feature of Yugoslav footballing discourse (Todorović 1996). However, Britain was not the place of origin of football in Yugoslav lands – Yugoslav footballing pioneers learned about the game in the cities and universities of Central Europe (Zec 2010). Before the First World War, football as a British game was an exotic concept and few Yugoslavs were able to witness 'Brits' playing it. However, things changed during World War I. In the battlefields of Macedonia and field hospitals of the Ionian isles, Serbian and British soldiers shared both the trenches and leisure time, which inevitably led to friendly football matches and tournaments. This contact was profoundly important for the development of football in post-war Yugoslavia, as most of the Serbian soldiers were simple peasants who had not previously had the opportunity to see or play the game, as it was essentially limited to a small group of young and urban protagonists (Zec, Baljkas & Paunović, 2015).

With such modest beginnings, few could foresee how rapidly the game would develop in the interwar period. Yet, by the 1930s, Yugoslavia was a globally respected footballing nation. The Yugoslav national football team participated in the first ever FIFA World Cup in Uruguay in 1930, reaching the semi-finals (Stanišić 1969). Several Yugoslav football clubs, such as *Jugoslavija*, *BSK*, *Građanski*, *HAŠK*, *Concordia* and *Hajduk*, attracted crowds numbering tens of thousands of people and were quite respectable in European football circles, participating in the Mitropa Cup and beating the best teams in continental Europe. In the second half of the 1930s, several Yugoslav footballers signed for prominent French, Swiss, Hungarian and Romanian clubs. Many consider the peak of Yugoslavian football during the interwar period to be the match played between Yugoslavia and England, in 1939, in which the Yugoslavs defeated the team they saw as undoubtedly the best in the world (Zec 2019).

Glocalisation of the British football experience

One has to question what the actions and processes were which paved the way for British football to become an important part of the Yugoslav footballing experience. Roughly, these processes could be marked by three different labels: (1) *promoting* – where British football in general, British clubs and players, famous matches and footballing accomplishments were given more space in the media (in the sporting press, on the radio and TV, as well as in the sporting literature); (2) *familiarising* – where players, fans and audiences learned about each other as a result of matches played between the clubs from both counties (or national teams); (3) *colonising* – where footballers and coaches who were engaged by the clubs from both countries served as a nexus between the two audiences (in particular, popular Yugoslav footballers who played for English clubs during the late 1970s and 1980s).[3] These processes fit with the notion of *glocalisation*, a process of tailoring of global and universal products and services to suit particular cultural tastes (Giulianotti and Robertson 2007, p. 134; Robertson 1992, pp. 173–174). However, in this particular case, glocalisation is seen as a set of actions or mechanisms by which local agents adapt to global pop-cultural forms (Đorđević 2009). The mixing of local and global thus creates specific hybrid identities, which have the power to reconcile and incorporate all the opposing or contradictory elements (Beck 2000).

The process of *promoting* British football in Yugoslavia started as late as the 1920s and 1930s. The first generation of Yugoslav football enthusiasts, some of whom were lucky enough to travel across Europe and watch British clubs perform, wrote about what they saw and published their experiences in the Yugoslav sporting press (Jakopić 1937). This interest in British football grew and was subsequently transformed into publications of weekly digests of what was happening in the English and Scottish football leagues, usually syndicated from German, Swiss or Hungarian papers but occasionally containing original eyewitness accounts by Yugoslav sports journalists. Still, the distance was great, and because so very few people had the opportunity to watch it, British football was portrayed as a mythical game, essential and pure, and on a completely different level from football played at home (Zec 2019).

After the Second World War, and the implementation of communism, a certain level of political and ideological alignment was visible in sports. Yet the Yugoslav public was still keen to learn about what was happening in UK football. The communist authorities did not suppress such enthusiasm – on the contrary, more information became available, especially during the early 1950s and after football tournaments during the Festival of Britain, in which Yugoslav football clubs took part (Stojković 1951).[4] In the early 1950s, *Engleska futbalska škola* (Anonymous 1952) was a huge success among football audiences and sold tens of thousands of copies in Yugoslavia. The book presented a short history of the English national team and leagues from the 1920s to the late 1940s, biographies of the most prominent players and descriptions of the tactics most widely used, such as the notorious Herbert Chapman's WM.[5]

The biggest breakthrough in *promoting* the game came during the 1960s and 1970s. By the mid-1960s, Yugoslav football connoisseurs could enjoy reading several quality weekly sporting magazines, such as *Tempo* and *Sportske novosti*, and all of them reported regularly on what was happening in top English and Scottish leagues (Brentin and Zec 2017). In addition, by the late 1960s and early 1970s, TV sets were no longer exotic items; the majority of Yugoslav households could watch TV programmes and by that time, the Eurovision network enabled Yugoslavs to watch major global sporting events, including European club competitions in football (Mihelj 2014).

During the 1980s, another form of promotion became dominant, one which was more suitable to the sub-cultural level of the game and which was more appealing to the younger generation of football fans. Roaming through the flea markets of the larger Yugoslav cities, such as Belgrade, Zagreb, Sarajevo or Split, one could find and buy British football scarfs, caps and T-shirts. They were sold for a hefty price by people who had smuggled them into the country, either directly from the UK, or from other countries where they were available, such as Italy or Greece (M Šaranović 2014, pers. comm. 12 May). Such items were usually pre-ordered and if someone travelled abroad, they would buy it and bring it back to the country. By the end of the 1980s, foreign footballing accessories became widely available, not just at flea markets and independent boutiques, but also through small ads in the sporting and regular press. Driven by entrepreneurial motives, some of the Yugoslav aficionados of British football started making and distributing their own merchandise without acquiring permission – or paying – the clubs.

Until the late 1970s, football in Yugoslavia was much more part of dominant and parents' culture than a youth sub-culture. Generational change challenged the existing rules and norms and questioned the very core of football fandom. The new goal of supporters and their groups was to forge their own identity, which was rooted in hooliganism and the creation of a spectacle at football matches. They desired to be actively involved, to be subjects and creators of spectacle, rather than passive observers. Therefore, new identities and roles required new symbols and colours. One prominent Yugoslav fan of this period recounted how, sometime in the mid-1980s, he was given a scarf of the English national football team and that he wore it all the time, which made him extremely happy and proud (exx 2010). Examining old photographs of the Yugoslav terraces during the 1980s, one can see a dissonant patchwork – with scarfs of Manchester United, Liverpool, Tottenham Hotspur, Leeds United, Derby County, Newcastle United and many other teams prevalent. There are even pictures in which one could spot Celtic and Rangers scarves next to one another.

During the 1980s, British and Yugoslav replica kits were very rare. Replica kits were simply not part of Yugoslav football culture, for many reasons, but mostly because they were expensive and they were not available for fans to buy. If somebody owned and wore a proper football jersey, it was usually acquired from somebody who was part of the club, either a player or member of the coaching staff. Indeed, Yugoslav football clubs were not organised on a commercial basis and so did not consider selling club merchandise to fans. Moreover, replica kits were not fully accepted as a part of British football culture, at least by adult fans, until the late 1970s and early 1980s (Stride, Williams, Moor and Catley 2015).

Familiarising between Yugoslav football supporters and British clubs began only after European club competitions commenced in the late 1950s – and after England's national football team decided to compete in tournaments organised by FIFA and UEFA. Prior to World War II, contacts between clubs and players from two countries were rare and sporadic. During the 1930s, two prominent Yugoslav football clubs toured the British Isles, with Jugoslavija from Belgrade playing against the team of the Irish Free State and Građanski from Zagreb playing against several British clubs, including Hearts, Wolverhampton Wanderers and Charlton Athletic (Jakopić 1937; Jovanović and Vukadinović 1939). These tours drew the attention of Yugoslav football fans, yet they were not able to learn much about British football because they could only rely on written reports by the few Yugoslav journalists who accompanied the clubs on their journeys. The first proper clash happened in Belgrade in 1939, when the English national team visited Yugoslavia to play a match to celebrate the 20th anniversary of the Yugoslav Football Association (Zec 2019). The game had huge implications, both sporting and political. Yugoslav football fans were excited to see their squad hosting what was considered to be the best national team in the world. At the same time, the match between the two countries was also seen as confirmation of the political friendship that existed between the two countries – an important symbolic gesture when Europe was on the brink of war. Yugoslavia's narrow victory left the football fans ecstatic, and the match itself is still regarded as one of the greatest successes in the history of the Yugoslav national team.

After the war, the encounters became rather more common. Between 1945 and 1991, the Yugoslav senior national football team played 13 matches against England, winning three, drawing five and losing five. Furthermore, eight matches were played against Scotland, with Yugoslavia winning one, drawing five and losing two; eight matches were played against Wales, Yugoslavia winning five and drawing three, and seven matches were played against Northern Ireland, with Yugoslavia winning five, drawing one and losing one (Anonymous 2019). Apart from these clashes, Yugoslavia also played against a Great Britain side in the semi-finals of the 1948 Olympic Games in London, winning 3–1 at Wembley (Stanišić 1969). The most important competitive match played between Yugoslavia and England was the 1968 European Championship semi-finals in Italy, which the Yugoslavs won 1–0.

Regarding the notion of *familiarising*, one game worth mentioning was the European Championship qualifying match between Yugoslavia and England, played in Belgrade in November 1987. Despite a heavy 4–1 defeat, the match was important because for the first time several thousand English supporters travelled to Yugoslavia (Stojković and Konstantinović, 1988). Despite their notoriety, the English fans experienced a friendly greeting in Belgrade, with fans of both teams mingling before and during the match. Scarfs, hats and T-shirts were exchanged, and there was a lot of joint drinking and singing in Belgrade's pubs and streets (N Senić 2012, pers. comm., 5 November; Ćata 1996).

Colonising also represents an interesting phenomenon, especially considering the limitations imposed on Yugoslav footballers by their national Football Association and their government. By law, a Yugoslav footballer could not leave the country and sign for a foreign club before the age of 29 and also not before he finished his compulsory military service, which originally lasted two years, but was reduced to one year in 1980 (Abram 2017). These limitations severely disadvantaged footballers as they allowed them to play abroad only after their prime playing years had passed. Thus, it was very difficult for Yugoslav footballers to find good and lucrative arrangements in European football leagues after leaving their Yugoslav clubs. However, beginning in the 1960s, footballers from Yugoslavia who fulfilled these statutory requirements did go abroad, usually to Germany and France. If they were unable to find employment in the top European leagues, they went to the Netherlands, Belgium, Greece or Sweden. However, it was only in the late 1970s that Yugoslav footballers started to sign for British clubs. Between the first Yugoslav signing in 1978 and 1991, when Yugoslavia collapsed, there were 14 Yugoslav footballers who played for English clubs.[6]

Some of these footballers made great careers in England and, because of their immense popularity in Yugoslavia, Yugoslav football fans started to support clubs they were playing for. For example, many supporters of Partizan from Belgrade adopted Chelsea as their second favourite club because of the fact that flamboyant goalkeeper Petar Borota, who was an idol of many Partizan fans during the second half of the 1970s, especially the younger ones, signed for the London club in 1979 (Anonymous 1996; Gudžević 2010; Mladenovic 2013). Those Yugoslav footballers acted not just as Yugoslav sporting ambassadors in the UK, but also as mediators who explained the British way of life and culture to a wider Yugoslav audience. They were frequently interviewed by the Yugoslav media, and the press wanted to know not just about the state of football in the UK, but also how ordinary people were living, what were they eating, what the prices in the supermarkets were, what kind of TV shows people were watching and what kind of music were they listening to (Sekulić 2017). Despite the rise of television and the general accessibility of information, the role of these Yugoslav sporting ambassadors in the UK cannot be overemphasised.

Brutishness – colours of rebellious youth

The necessary preconditions for British footballing and cultural influences to become the kernel of new footballing and subcultural developments in Yugoslavia were all in existence by the mid-1980s. However, the late 1970s and early 1980s brought new developments which, combined with political, cultural, economic and social dynamics in Yugoslavia itself, determined ways in which the British influence would be understood and accommodated in Yugoslavia. Firstly, the revolution happening within the British musical scene was immediately noticed, and it wasn't long before it was accepted and reproduced (Pavlović 2016; Trifunović 2013). Mainstream pop and rock music of the late 1960s and 1970s was being challenged by new genres, which emphasised a more aggressive sound and socially and politically engaged lyrics, supporting discontent with the existing status quo and calling for radical changes in society. Punk rock and its derivatives such as street punk or Oi! became genres which many young people in Yugoslavia heartily accepted, finding both their style and message appealing (Pavlov and Šunjka 1990). The early 1980s saw the punk and new wave revolution sweep across Yugoslavia, and in a very short period of time numerous bands were making and playing loud and socially engaging music, spreading edgy messages; fanzines were being made and distributed all over the country and copious records were being made and sold, reaching astonishing circulation (Božilović 2013).

It is interesting to see how quickly this revolution was accepted by both the major record labels and the political and governing structures in Yugoslavia. Record labels had acted cautiously during the 1960s surge of rock 'n' roll, because they were not convinced that the new genre would be popular and also because they were still scared that the ruling communist party would eventually find it subversive. Yet, by the 1980s, the situation had drastically changed. For various reasons, the state's grip on artistic expression was not as strong as before and, free from the ideological scrutiny of the government, record labels functioned on a much more commercial basis (Bousfield 2020). The new wave of rebellious sound emerging in Yugoslavia in the 1980s was not uniform, and one could see that the influences shaping it were various. However, it is clear that the most important incentives came from Britain, in the forms of punk and new wave. This music was distinctly for a young and urban population. It reflected their way of life, their frustrations and their interests (Pavlov and Šunjka 1990; Janjatović 2007). Unlike the exalted and esoteric music of the 1970s, the sound of the 1980s probed poverty, poor living conditions, lack of employment opportunities, inherent injustices and political and ideological rigidity, but also sexuality, alcoholism and drug abuse, violence and, of course, football. Indeed, never before in the history of Yugoslav popular music was football seen as such an important issue. Several Yugoslav bands of the 1980s sang about football in general, the clubs they were supporting and their heroes on the pitch. A few bands from the city of Sarajevo, closely connected by participating in the subcultural movement, which they called New Primitivism, were especially interested in football topics. Indeed, the band *Bombaj štampa* (Bombay Press) had a song about *Željezničar*, a popular Sarajevan football club, and a band *Zabranjeno pušenje* (No Smoking) recorded a beautiful and moving song, *Nedjelja kad je otiš'o Hase* (Sunday When Hase Left), about the very last match played by Sarajevo football legend Asim Ferhatović Hase. The common denominator in all these songs was the fact that football and football fandom were recognised, not only as an important part of urban life but as a defining factor in self-identification and local and national pride (Fanuko, Magdalenić, Radin and Žugić 1991).

Another important development during the 1980s was the gradual rise in the importance of British terrace culture (Vrcan 1990; Lalić and Pilić 2011). Reports on football and fans' related violence throughout Europe, and especially in the UK, were a common feature both in the media and in social science research (Perasović 1989). The 1985 Heysel stadium tragedy, for example, was covered extensively. In Yugoslavia, both scholars and politicians approached the subject from a typically Marxist perspective, viewing the rise of fans' violence and extremism as symptomatic of the decay of capitalist societies and the subsequent radicalisation of the alienated youth (Koković 1990; Vrcan 1990). However, they also warned the authorities and policymakers that many of the symptoms of 'decaying capitalism' were also present in Yugoslav socialism. Indeed, they noted that a history of sport-related violence already existed in the country that was usually related to regional, ethnic or religious confrontations; that the modern world was unavoidably connected and intertwined; and that the Yugoslav football fans would undoubtedly be affected by different football cultures. They predicted that Yugoslavian football culture was fertile ground for such negative, destructive and anti-socialist activities (Kovačević 1987) and urged for vigilance and decisive action (Vrcan 1990). Yet, contrary to the official position, Yugoslav football fans, especially those younger fans already influenced by Anglo-American films and music, enthusiastically embraced this new and violent subculture (Previšić and Mlinarić, 2020).

Organised groups of football fans existed in Yugoslavia since the 1950s, and even in those early days, they were very much influenced by the scene abroad.[7] However, during the 1980s new groups formed, usually representing a small or mid-sized loose organisation of fans of the particular football club in certain neighbourhoods or smaller towns (Kovačević 1987). Many of these groups had English names and banners – Heroes (Crvena zvezda), Gravediggers, Untouchables (Partizan), Maniacs (Željezničar), Bad Blue Boys (Dinamo), Red Firm (Vojvodina), Blue Marines (Spartak), Red Army (Velež), Vultures (Borac), etc. Some of them even referred to already existing hooligan groups in England – Red Devils, Zulu Warriors (Crvena zvezda) or Sexton's Lions (Partizan) (Anonymous 1990a; Anonymous 1995). Their organisation and actions were somewhere in between the Italian *ultras* style (with flags and banners in club's colours, scarves and massive utilisation of pyrotechnics) and British casual style. Despite their failure to completely establish themselves as British-style casual and hooligan groups, partially because of the already existing terrace customs and practices, and partially because they did not fully understand the circumstances and whereabouts that the British casual subculture came from (e.g. urban decay, deindustrialisation, racism), Yugoslav organised football fans nevertheless declared the British as their ideal and something to strive to (exx 2010; Ćata 1996).

One of the most important symbols used by football fans in Yugoslavia during the 1980s and early 1990s was the Union Jack. Almost all the fan groups, regardless of the club, city, region or nation, used to carry and display Union Jacks on their terraces. Sometimes those British flags were ornamented with club emblems or inscriptions, such as the name of the group, town or a football club, in a similar fashion to British fans when travelling away. Sometimes those Union Jacks contained other graphic material, such as the bulldog's head or Eddie, the mascot of the band Iron Maiden (Anonymous 1990b).

Examining the testimonies of the people who were involved in Yugoslav football subculture during the 1980s and 1990s reveals several reasons why the Union Jack was so popular. Firstly, the Union Jack was seen as a symbol of 'Britishness', a vague and illusive quality, which meant different things to different people. However, in the context of Yugoslav football fandom, it was mostly related to music (punk, streetpunk, Oi! and new wave), fondness of British football and football culture (pubs, chants, banter, travelling for away games). Secondly, the Union Jack was seen as a symbol of rebellion and resistance. Some of the fans displayed Union Jacks as a sign that they were ready to confront the oppressors (the police or magistrates), the same way British hooligans did. Interestingly, apart from the Union Jack, the most popular flag on Yugoslav terraces during the 1980s was the Confederate battle flag, which also symbolised rebellion and opposition (before it became a fully racist symbol during the 1990s). Thirdly, the Union Jack was clearly seen as an anti-communist symbol, especially in the final days of Yugoslavia and the dissolution of its communist government (Ž Tomić 2013, pers. comm. 21 January). From the early stages of football fans' organising in Yugoslavia, the authorities were very concerned about the display of foreign flags, seeing it either as a provocation or as an act of treason. By the mid-1980s foreign flags were becoming more and more common in Yugoslav stadiums, but still on occasion, fans who displayed them would be arrested for causing disturbances and endangering law and order (Kačić Movrić 1989).

In the sense of its political symbolism, the Union Jack was perceived in two different ways, both of which were strictly anti-communist. Many who displayed the Union Jack on the terraces, especially in Serbia, considered it to be a of symbol of monarchy and the old order that existed prior to World War II, embodied by the *Chetniks* – nationalist and monarchist Serbian forces that were supported by the British during the Second World War and which were eventually defeated by the communists in 1945 (Marković 1990). For Serbian nationalists, who comprised a striking majority among organised fans on the terraces by 1991, the British flag, in a political sense, represented a sharp declaration of disloyalty and discontinuity to the existing (although crumbling) socialist order and ruling ideology. On the other hand, in other parts of Yugoslavia, especially in Croatia, displaying the Union Jack was connected to the far right; as in the UK, where the national flag was tainted by organisations such as the National Front during the 1970s and 1980s (Gray 2013).

Conclusion

In their attempts to challenge everything, which was 'Yugoslav' in nature, some Yugoslav football fans wanted to completely transform Yugoslav football culture, into a British football culture. During the late 1980s Union Jacks became standard on the terraces in Yugoslavia, which particularly frustrated the communist authorities. Fans wore the scarves and shirts of British football clubs, particularly those with notorious or infamous fans, such as Chelsea, Liverpool or Millwall, and club songs were being sung to the tunes of British pop or punk standards, such as Cock Sparrer's 'We're Coming Back'. The popularity of football in Yugoslavia during the late 1980s and the possibility to express otherwise suppressed sentiments at football matches caused football sub-culture to become an increasingly integral part of the wider popular culture of the 1980s and early 1990s. During Yugoslavia's twilight years, this culture was recognised as a part of a wider social movement which articulated a general sense of discontent with the country, its economic troubles and political and ideological oppression.

In the period between 1975 and 1991, organised Yugoslav football fans carried out a revolution, suppressing the existing football culture which was conformist and non-confrontational, and creating a sub-culture which was deeply rebellious, violent and political. Yet, in order to do so, they needed role models, symbols and soundtracks. Due to the nature of the previously dominant Yugoslav football culture and the oppressive governmental apparatus, it was difficult to find preformed, indigenous material. As such, Yugoslav football fans resorted to a process of cultural appropriation and glocalisation – not by any plan or intention, but because they had an appreciation for, and were familiar with, British cultural products. Thus, British popular culture became the clay from which the Yugoslav youth modelled their own football culture, music and humour. Such patterns, themes and symbols were copied but attributed different meanings and interpretations, closer to Yugoslav social, economic and political reality. Yet, in their form, if not their orientation, they remained close to the original source material, the core which constituted their very Britishness.

This chapter aimed to provide an insight and consideration of a process which is widespread in the modern, connected world, where adoption, interpretation and appropriation of a foreign but globally enjoyed cultural phenomenon become building blocks for new identities and patterns of behaviour. Soundly grounded in historiographical methodology and by experimenting with certain sociological concepts such as glocalisation, this research on how British popular culture, and British football in particular, influenced self-identification of Yugoslav football fans and modelled their subculture not only provides a valuable empirical case study for the researchers, but also allows them to re-examine and re-think issues like cultural transfer, cultural appropriation and soft power from a theoretical perspective.

Notes

1 Cominform (The Information Bureau of the Communist and Workers' Parties), was the official central organisation of the International Communist Movement from 1947 to 1956. Cominform was a supranational alliance of Marxist-Leninist communist parties in Europe, created to coordinate their activity under the direction of the USSR during the early Cold War. In 1948 Yugoslavia was expelled from Cominform and accused of betraying the international communist movement, despite being one of the founders. This confrontation had deeper political precedents and it had a decisive influence on the history of post-war Yugoslavia.

2 Apart from the Labour Party, Yugoslavs had very influential friends among certain Conservative politicians as well, mostly among those who spent some time in Yugoslavia during the war, such as Randolph Churchill or Sir Fitzroy Maclean.

3 Players such as Ivan Golac, Radomir Antić or Petar Borota.

4 Football tournaments during the 1951 Festival of Britain represented a very important event in the history of Yugoslav football. Post-World War II ideological scrutiny forced Yugoslav football teams to seek contacts and create connections with teams from ideologically similar countries, such as the USSR, Czechoslovakia, Hungary and Bulgaria. This ideological alignment left Yugoslavs quite isolated after 1948, when all the connections with Cominform countries were severed because of the Tito-Stalin rift. The invitation the Yugoslav clubs received to visit Britain in 1951 actually represented a sort of reaching out to Yugoslavia, not just in the context of sports cooperation, but a political one also.

5 The WM system, known for the shapes described by the positions of the players, was created in the mid-1920s by Herbert Chapman of Arsenal, and proved to be so successful that by late 1930s almost all English clubs had adopted it. Outside of Britain, this formation was considered as one of the cornerstones of the British approach to the game.

6 They were: Ivan Golac (Southampton), Božidar Janković (Middlesbrough), Petar Borota (Chelsea), Radojko Raddy Avramović (Notts County, Coventry City), Dragoslav Stepanović (Manchester City), Nikola Jovanović (Manchester United), Džemal Hadžiabdić (Swansea City), Anto Rajković (Swansea City), Dražen Mužinić (Norwich City), Ivan Katalinić (Southampton), Dušan Nikolić (Bolton Wanderers), Ante Miročević (Sheffield Wednesday), Radomir Raddy Antić (Luton Town) and Vladimir Petrović (Arsenal) (Mrkalj 2019). There were also several active British footballers, who were of Yugoslav origin, such as Steve Ogrizovic, John Lukic and Mike Pejic.

7 In the very early stages of organised football fandom, Yugoslavs were heavily influenced by Italians and the Latin Americans. See Vojnović (2006).

References

Abram, Sandi 2017, '"To smo fantje": Genealogija (re)produciranja dominantne socialistične moškosti skozi dispozitiv JLA na Slovenskem', *Časopis za kritiko znanosti*, vol. 267, pp. 62–80.

Anonymous 1952, *Engleska futbalska škola*, IP Novi Sad, Novi Sad.

Anonymous 1990a, 'Dinamo: To je naša politika!', *Ćao Tifo*, iss. 1, April 1990, pp. 9–14.

Anonymous 1990b, 'Grlo, dlan i fajt!', *Ćao Tifo*, iss. 4, August-September, p. 36.

Anonymous 1995, 'Crazy South', *Daj gol*, iss. 1, November 1995, p. 12.

Anonymous 1996, 'Chelsea are back', *Daj gol, iss*. 2, February, pp. 14–15.

Beck, U 2000, *What is Globalization?*, Polity Press, Cambridge.

Blam, M 2011, *Jazz u Srbiji 1927–1944*, Stubovi kulture, Belgrade.

Bousfield, J 2020, '*Jugoton*', *inyourpocket*, 7 January, https://www.inyourpocket.com/zagreb/Jugoton_74070f

Božilović, J 2013, 'New Wave in Yugoslavia: Socio-Political Context', *Facta Universitatis*, vol. 12, no. 1, pp. 69–83.

Brentin, D & Zec, D 2017, 'From the Concept of the Communist 'New Man' to Nationalist Hooliganism: Research Perspectives on Sport in Socialist Yugoslavia' in D Brentin & D Zec (eds.), *Special issue: The History and Social Role of Sport in Socialist Yugoslavia, The International Journal of the History of Sport*, vol. 34 9, pp. 713–728.

Čalić, M-Ž 2004, *Socijalna istorija Srbije 1815–1941: Usporeni napredak u industrijalizaciji*, Clio, Belgrade.

Ćata 1996, 'Pisma', *Daj gol*, iss. 3, April 1996, p. 17.

Dimić, Lj 1988, *Agitprop kultura: Agitpropovska faza kulturne politike u Srbiji: 1945–1952*, Rad, Belgrade.

Dimitrijević, B 2016, *Potrošeni socijalizam: Kultura, konzumerizam i društvena imaginacija u Jugoslaviji (1950–1974)*, Fabrika knjiga-Peščanik, Belgrade.

Dobrivojević, I 2012, 'Pod budnim okom partije. Kulturni i zabavni život u srpskim gradovima 1945–1955', *Tokovi istorije*, vol. 3, pp. 134–158.

Đorđević, I 2009, 'Umeju li antropolozi da igraju fudbal? *Sport i identitet u savremenoj Srbiji*', *Antropologija*, vol. 9, pp. 89–103.

Dragićević-Šešić, M 2007, 'Privatni život u vremenu televizije' in M Ristović (ed.), *Privatni život kod Srba u dvadesetom veku*, Clio, Belgrade, pp. 733–770.

exx, 2010, 'Interview with Zoran Puvača – Klokan', forum post, 24 November 2010, Forum hrvatskih integralista, viewed June 25 2017 http://www.hrhb.info/showthread.php?t=7

Fanuko, N, Magdalenić, I, Radin, F & Žugić, Z 1991, '*Zagrebački nogometni navijači: Grupni portret s BBB u središtu*', *Institut za društvena istraživanja Sveučilišta u* Zagrebu, Zagreb.

Gašić, R 2005, *Beograd u hodu ka Evropi: Kulturni uticaji Britanije i Nemačke na beogradsku elitu 1918–1941*, Institut za savremenu istoriju, Belgrade.

Giulianotti, R & Robertson, R 2007, 'Forms of Glocalization: Globalization and the Migration Strategies of Scottish Football Fans in North America', *Sociology*, vol. 41, iss. 1, pp. 133–152.

Gray, D 2013, *Hatters, Railwaymen and Knitters: Travels through England's Football Provinces*, Bloomsbury, London.

Gudžević, S 2010, 'Petar Borota, prezren i obožavan, '*Portal Novosti*, February 21 2010, http://arhiva.portalnovosti.com/2010/02/petar-borota-prezren-i-obozavan/

Hoptner, J 1972, *Jugoslavija u krizi 1934–1941*, Otokar Keršovani, Rijeka.

Istorija fudbalske reprezentacije, 2019 Utakmice, viewed December 29 2019, https://www.reprezentacija.rs/#

Jakopić, J 1937, *Hrvatski nogometni šport: 1911–1938: u spomenici I. hrvatskog građanskog športskog kluba*, Jozo Jakopić, Zagreb.

Janjatović, P 2007, *Ex YU rock enciklopedija*: 1960–2006, P. Janjatović, Belgrade.

Jovanović, B & Vukadinović, Lj 1939, *Četvrt veka S.k. "Jugoslavije"*, Jugoslovenska sportska revija, Belgrade.

Kačić Movrić, Z 1989, 'Sve boje navijačke mržnje', Top, unknown issue (published on http://www.yugopapir.com/2019/05/kraci-istorijat-divljanja-na-fudbalskim.html)

Koković, D 1990, *Doba nasilja i sport*, OKO, Novi Sad.

Kostić, A 1975, *Kako je "Leteći cirkus Montija Pajtona" prihvaćen u Jugoslaviji*, *RTV Revija*, unknown issue (published on http://www.yugopapir.com/2019/10/kako-je-leteci-cirkus-montija-pajtona.html)

Kovačević, I 1987, 'Fudbalski ritual', *Gledišta*, iss. 5–6, pp. 71–82.

Lalić, D & Pilić, D 2011, *Torcida: pogled iznutra*, Profil, Zagreb.

Lampe, J 2000, *Yugoslavia as History: Twice there was a country*, 2nd edition, Cambridge University Press, Cambridge.

Marković, M (series producer) 1990, 'Maksimir', Sportska emisija Indirekt, television program, Radio-televizija Beograd, 14 May.

Marković, P 1992, *Beograd i Evropa 1918–1941*, Savremena administracija, Belgrade.

Marković, R 1979, 'Prve godine' in M Bulatović, R Marković, M Milenković & S Džunić (eds.), *Ovde Radio-Beograd*, Radio-Beograd, Belgade, pp. 11–27.

Mihelj, S 2014, 'Televizija i modernizacija svakodnevnog života' in A Panić (ed.), *Nikad im bolje nije bilo? Modernizacija svakodnevnog života u socijalističkoj Jugoslaviji*, Muzej istorije Jugoslavije, Belgrade, pp. 68–70.

Mladenovic, I 2013, 'A hero of his time: Petar Borota', *In Bed With Maradona*, February 16 2013, http://inbedwithmaradona.com/journal/2013/2/16/a-hero-of-his-time-petar-borota

Momčilović, B 1990, *Iz istorije jugoslovensko-britanskih kulturnih veza od 1650. godine do II svetskog rata*, Filozofski fakultet, Novi Sad.

Mrkalj, I 2019, 'Jugoslavenski nogometaši u Engleskoj,' *Portal Novosti*, May 27 2019, https://www.portalnovosti.com/jugoslavenski-nogometasi-u-engleskoj?fbclid=IwAR22dyWpd04JL0_ZhZGfDvnvsZ2CS_ED_hXZDIM58YewjLcTx3idl0kKYxU

Nikolić, M 2006, *Radio u Srbiji (1924–1941)*, Zadužbina Andrejević, Belgrade.

Pavlov, D & Šunjka, D 1990, *Punk u YU 1980–90*, IGP Dedalus, Belgrade.

Pavlović, N 2016, 'Nastanak Jugoslovenske Pank scene – "Nije punk bio nikakav simptom dezintegracije... Punk je bio muzika.."', *Solidarnost*, 18 November, http://www.solidarnost.rs/kultura/nije-punk-bio-nikakav-simptom-dezintegracije-punk-je-bio-muzika-nastanak-jugoslovenske-pank-scene/

Perasović, B 1989, 'Nogometni navijači kao dio omladinske subkulture', *Podkulture: Zbornik tekstova*, iss. 4, pp. 57–64.

Perica, V 2003, 'Genetika ili revolucija? O fenomenu južnoslavenske škole košarke', *Reč*, vol. 70, iss. 16, pp. 171–194.

Petranović, B 1988, *Istorija Jugoslavije: 1918–1988. Knjiga 3, Socijalistička Jugoslavija*: 1945–1988, Nolit, Belgrade.

Previšić, M & Mlinarić, I 2020, ' Služba državne sigurnosti Hrvatske protiv nogometnih navijača 1989–1991.', *Istorija 20. veka*, vol. 1, pp. 163–184.

Radić, R 2012, 'Prilog istraživanju mreže anglofilskih organizacija u Srbiji tokom prve polovine 20. veka', *Tokovi istorije*, vol. 3, pp. 278–323.

Raković, A 2012, *Rokenrol u Jugoslaviji 1956–1968: Izazov socijalističkom društvu*, Arhipelag, Belgrade.

Robertson, R 1992, *Globalization: Social Theory and Global Culture*, Sage, London.

Sekulić, J 2017, '*Ivan Golac: Ja sam fudbalski lord*', *Novosti*, 2 April, https://www.novosti.rs/vesti/sport.294.html:658208-Ivan-Golac-Ja-sam-fudbalski-lord

Stanišić, B 1969, *Plavi, plavi!*, Borba, Belgrade.

Stojanović, D 2008, *Kaldrma i asfalt: urbanizacija i evropeizacija Beograda: 1890–1914*, Udruženje za društvenu istoriju, Belgrade.

Stojković, V & Konstantinović, A 1988, *Almanah Yu fudbal 87–88*, Politika, Belgrade.

Stojković, V (ed.) 1951, *Futbalski godišnjak 1951*, Sportska knjiga, Belgrade.

Stride, C, Williams, J, Moor, D & Catley, N 2015, 'From Sportswear to Leisurewear: The Evolution of English Football League Shirt Design in the Replica Kit Era', *Sport in History*, vol. 35, iss. 1, pp. 156–194.

Todić, M 2006, *110 godina fudbala u Srbiji*, Fudbalski savez Srbije, Belgrade.

Todorović, S 1996, *Fudbal u Srbiji 1896–1918*, SOFK Zvezdara, Belgrade.

Toševa, S 2007, *Serbia and Britain: Cultural contacts at the beginning of 20th century, Museum of Science and Technology-Gallery of Science and Technology* SASA, Belgrade.

Trifunović, V 2013, '*Kontrolisana pobuna (Pank u Jugoslaviji)*', *AkuzatiV*, 25 June, http://akuzativ.com/teme/385-kontrolisana-pobuna-pank-u-jugoslaviji

Unkovski-Korica, V 2014, 'The Yugoslav Communists' Special Relationship with the British Labour Party 1950–1956', *Cold War History*, vol. 14, pp. 23–46.

Vojnović, B (ed.) 2006, *Zapisnici Politbiroa Centralnog komiteta Komunističke partije Hrvatske, sveska 2, 1949–1952*, Hrvatski državni arhiv, Zagreb.

Vrcan, S 1990, *Sport i nasilje danas u nas: I druge studije iz sociologije sporta*, Naprijed, Zagreb.
Vučetić, R 2009, Džez je sloboda (Džez kao američko propagandno oružje u Jugoslaviji), *Godišnjak za društvenu istoriju*, vol. 3, pp. 81–101.
Vučetić, R 2015, *Koka-kola socijalizam: amerikanizacija jugoslovenske popularne kulture šezdesetih godina XX veka*, Službeni glasnik, Belgrade.
Zec, D 2010, 'The origin of soccer in Serbia', *Serbian Studies*, vol. 24, iss. 1–2, pp. 137–159.
Zec, D 2019, "White Eagles', 'Proud Albion' and Spicy Garlic Food - The English National Football Team's Visit to Yugoslavia in May 1939' in N Piercey & S-J Oldfield (eds.), *Sporting Cultures: Global Perspectives*, MMU Sport and Leisure History, Manchester, pp. 106–127.
Zec, D, Baljkas, F & Paunović M 2015, *Sport pamti: srpsko-britanski sportski kontakti u vreme Prvog svetskog rata*, Centar za sportsko nasleđe Jugoistočne Evrope, Belgrade.

Chapter 9

Unwrapped

Football fans and *The Anfield Wrap*

Ciarán Ryan

Introduction

Since the commencement of the English Premier League (EPL) in August 1992, the global demand for English club football's marquee division has continued to grow. The extent of this progression is evident by the fact that the EPL is considered the biggest football league in the world, not just in terms of revenue generated (Deloitte, 2019), but also in terms of numbers viewing its matches internationally (Cleland, 2017). Such an increased globalisation of the league (Millward, 2011) has created new opportunities for various parties, from the players who have made the EPL a transnational league (Maguire and Stead, 1998) to the new global directors that seek ways of making significant profits from football (Millward, 2013).

There are other ways in which EPL clubs have actively sought to capitalise on such interest, through various measures including merchandising, global partnerships, and pre-season tours to various new and potentially lucrative territories. The clamour to attain as much global revenue as possible has extended to how media platforms can be utilised to attract both investors[1] and international fans. As Rowe and Gilmour (2009, 173–174) note:

> the restless expansionism of the EPL and its major clubs has led to the aggressive pursuit of fan support that exists far beyond the geographic bounds of their immediate regions. The trans-national scope and proliferation of media technologies, combined with increasingly pervasive merchandizing activities, have fostered fan cultures and viewerships that eschew the norms, rituals and 'rules' that still inform much domestic English football fandom.

The major (or so-called 'big six' in a contemporary context) English football clubs pursue international fan bases through their own official media channels, with an increasing reliance on social media. This, coupled with around-the-clock mediated television coverage, would suggest that football fans at home and abroad are suitably catered for through a plethora of outlets. As Galily (2014) suggests, sports spectatorship is no longer just about what happens at stadia, but instead, a more complex juxtaposition of traditional and new media through increasing reliance on 'second screen' viewing experiences. However, pockets of football fans are adopting contemporary modes – namely YouTube channels, blogs, podcasts and social media accounts – to interact with other fans. These spaces are all providing uncensored and subjective accounts of the travails of football fandom to both local and global audiences. This chapter considers the position of fan-produced media in an era of 24/7 global football news, by specifically focusing on one such example – *The Anfield Wrap* (TAW). It investigates this through a combination of textual analysis, interviews with TAW contributors and users, and data collected through surveying conducted with a significant cohort (530 respondents) of its listeners. Initially launched as a podcast and corresponding website, and later incorporating increasing amounts of video content, *The Anfield Wrap* has been delivering content specifically aimed at fans of Liverpool Football Club since 2011.

Football fan media

In the UK, alternative options to mainstream sports media emerged from the 1970s onwards, as football fans started to provide their own accounts on the clubs that they supported. Somewhat influenced by the spread of punk music fanzines, the football fanzine was a clear example of supporter resistance to an increasingly commercialised game. Haynes (1995) notes that it was in the 1980s in particular – a time when English club football was arguably at its lowest ebb off the field, with a public discourse centred on football and hooliganism – that fanzine culture became a significant part of football fandom. They were a space where supporters could be critical of their club, players, the mainstream media and even the tone of match-day programmes. In essence, they provided column inches for football fans to vent their frustrations. However, one of the drawbacks was that fanzines by their amateur nature were somewhat haphazard in terms of their publication; the opportunity to express one's dissatisfaction was not instantaneous. Drawing on correspondence between Peter Millward (2008) and Steven Kelly, the editor of former Liverpool fanzine *Through the Wind and Rain*, it is evident that the fanzine became somewhat peripheral by the early 21st century:

> Before the Internet, fanzines were the only outlet for fans to 'mouth off' in any way they chose. The 'web' gave people the chance to do it at that very moment and not have to wait to months for a new issue [of the paper fanzine].
>
> (Kelly, cited in Millward, 2008, 303)

As with other forms of culture, football fans started to move online to engage in a more interactive type of fandom. Initially, spaces such as bulletin boards provided fertile grounds for the generation of debate and gossip around one's favourite team. The ability for fans to interact with each other is much more heightened than it ever was in football fanzine culture, but that is not necessarily a positive, according to one respondent to this study: "I used to spend hours on the forums but there was too much noise. Everybody was arguing and there was very little insight into the football" (Martin, Interview 2018). For the likes of this participant, there was an opening for a more curated form of football fandom.

Somewhat influenced by the spirit of the printed fanzine, *The Anfield Wrap* initially appeared on the radar of fans of Liverpool Football Club as a podcast in 2011. The early podcasts were recorded in a room above a Liverpool bar, with the presenter and contributors audibly nervous, whereas now TAW is a multi-award-winning multimedia operation, with offices in the heart of the city's centre. It is not just the output of TAW that has changed in the intervening years, with the ownership structure appearing to have altered somewhat. In 2013, it was announced that Red Touch Media, a software technology company with headquarters in Salt Lake City, Utah, would become a partner. This was originally through sponsoring various events that TAW hosted and providing some content. It is not clear the extent to which Red Touch Media is currently involved in the day-to-day running of TAW, but two of the current six directors of The Anfield Wrap Magazine Limited are the Chief Executive Officer (Wayne Scholes, himself a Liverpool supporter) and the Chief Operating Officer of Red Touch Media. The involvement of Red Touch Media is interesting as it demonstrates a move away from a purely grassroots supporter production to a full-fledged business. It also parallels with the English game itself at the highest level, where there has been an increasing amount of overseas investment (Millward, 2011).

While the company's output now encompasses audio, video and text, the primary focus of this study is very much on its podcast content, through the collection of interview and survey data with TAW contributors and listeners, as well as textual analysis. The success of the podcast has surprised even its creators. According to TAW's main presenter Neil Atkinson, there were no major aspirations beyond creating something different:

> Gareth [Roberts, Editor] and Andy [Heaton, Producer] went for a pint and worked out that you could change the way in which Liverpool supporter media worked, with the rise of podcasts and simultaneously with the idea of doing a written website. I don't think there were targets or anything, but it was the idea that it would change things quite quickly. When we launched, it was with the podcast with sixty pieces of writing … It was more the idea to shake things up.
>
> (Interview, 2017)

Authentic fan voices?

While the contributors started to sound more assured, listenership and website visitor figures steadily rose, and TAW generated a reputation as "essential listening for Liverpool fans" (Glendenning, 2016). It would appear that the investment of time and money into *The Anfield Wrap* had made it a more attractive prospect for Liverpool FC fans globally. A significant part of the appeal clearly is their ability to represent fans in a way that traditional media outlets cannot do. However, their creators believe that this needs to be balanced with quality standards. As such, presenter John Gibbons believes that TAW occupies a middle ground somewhere between genuine fan voice and professional media entity:

> In one way, you want to be professional and want to seem professional, but at the same time you got to be a fan's voice. You don't want to be journalists but you want to aspire to similar standards, so it is dead hard. We are someway between the two I would say now. It's a proper business so it's not like what it was at the start, but then also it's authentic fan voices, from the terraces or whatever you want to put it, and it's people going [to] the ground … It's important that you approach it from a fan's point of view … we're not trying to be objective. Why the fuck would you want to do that? It's your football team. I'm as fucking biased as you like.
>
> (Interview, 2017)

Gibbons, like Atkinson, is a TAW director, and one of twelve employees of the company. They are joined by a rotating cast of somewhere in the region of fifty contributors that participate in the suite of *Anfield Wrap* media outputs – podcasts, videos, writing. Their ability to get paid for their fan labour is primarily due to their subscription service. Early download figures for the weekly podcast were at 20,000 per week (Norman, 2016). The weekly *The Anfield Wrap* podcast is generally released on a Monday after the weekend fixtures and remains free to all. However, a range of new specialised shows was introduced with the establishment of the aforementioned subscription service TAW Player. These cater for everything from transfer gossip (*The Gutter Show*) to in-depth tactical match analysis (*The Review*) to the immediate post-match reaction (*The Post-Match Show*). Initially launched at £5 per month in 2015, a tiered pricing system up to £10 was introduced in 2019 to cater for the growing video content that TAW produce. By 2017, there were a reported 200,000 downloads per week (Cooney, 2017), and as of 2019, there were more than 12,000 subscribers to TAW Player (Kelly, 2019).

This revenue from TAW Player is supplemented by income that is generated through TAW live shows, merchandise and most recently, advertising. Negotiating the boundaries between fandom and commerce can be tricky for an enterprise such as TAW, especially when new elements of the commercial wing of the business are introduced to listeners. During the 2018–2019 Premier League season, the free weekly TAW podcasts were sponsored by RedsBet, a betting operation specifically targeted at Liverpool fans. This follows a similar trend to that seen in traditional sports media (Lopez-Gonazlez and Tulloch, 2015) and in the EPL itself, where there has been an increased 'gamblification' (Lopez-Gonazlez and Griffiths, 2018) of the game. While this sponsorship changed for the 2019–2020 season with *The Athletic*, the US-based subscription-based sports journalism website, coming on board, RedsBet parent company FansBet are still listed as a partner of *The Anfield Wrap* on their website. Of the eight partners listed, there is a distinctly transnational flavour, with corporate behemoths like Levi's and Unilever amongst those. Only one company – Liverpool Gin – has its company's headquarters in Liverpool. *The Athletic* is an interesting choice of sponsor. While it contains extensive coverage of Liverpool FC, this organisation has received extensive venture capital funding to date, with figures in 2020 showing funds raised of almost $140 million (Fischer, 2020). Amongst those who have invested in *The Athletic* are Comcast Ventures, whose parent company Comcast is one of the largest telecommunications conglomerates in the world.

By dipping their toes into various commercial ventures, and by following the trail of their partners, TAW's position as an independent voice from the mainstream commercial football media is a somewhat difficult one to maintain. Furthermore, while they may attempt to sustain a sense of outsiderness, *The Anfield Wrap* relies on the same circuit of news and information as the mainstream press, which now includes its free podcast's primary sponsor. To an extent, there are elements of 'produsage' (Bruns, 2008) to TAW, with users of various types of media (podcasts, videos, websites) increasingly turning into content producers. Cleland (2010) points to how football clubs developed more inclusive relationships with football fans through the building of relationships with supporter groups and fanzines, thus demonstrating a move from the passive to active fan. This can be mirrored in the access that Liverpool FC grants *The Anfield Wrap*. Numerous Liverpool players past and present have featured on TAW, and the podcast has clearly created a strong rapport with some of them, notably Jamie Carragher who has appeared regularly. Furthermore, the podcast has also spoken to all of the club's managers of the past fifteen years, with the exception of Roy Hodgson, a figure widely derided on numerous episodes. They also get invited to club events and press conferences and regularly feature well-known football writers as guests on the show, which further blurs any binary positions of 'us' and 'them'. However, their approach to dealing with famous sporting figures marks them out as being different to their counterparts working for UK broadcasters or daily newspapers. From a technical perspective, they admit to sacrificing sound quality to ensure that they can get usually guarded professional footballers to act more informally. This was evident in an interview with former Liverpool player Xabi Alonso:

> He wanted to do it outside so it's Xabi Alonso, so you do it outside. There was quite a lot of background noise because we did it at the Bayern Munich training ground, so the sound quality wasn't great but the interview was brilliant and he was brilliant and he really enjoyed it. We ended up getting twice as long as we were promised … we actually ended the interview because we felt that we had taken enough of his time … we could have said to him that we want to go inside, but then they would have found us a media room and they would have subconsciously be thinking about [how] he acts in that media room … It's a balance for us but we'd rather that the player was more relaxed. Jordan Henderson said 'that was different'.
>
> (John Gibbons, Interview, 2017)

The differences that the players notice are also part of the reason why fans download the podcasts – they seek something other than the standard press conference answers and want to get to know the players. However, this should not indicate that TAW contributors are not media savvy or literate, with many of their staff receiving a third-level media education and previous work in the media industries. For example, former TAW editor Gareth Roberts spent many years writing for various national and regional publications and holds a degree in journalism. Neil Atkinson, the articulate and erudite main presenter for TAW, has had his written work published in a plethora of national newspapers and is also a film screenwriter. Roberts and Atkinson clearly understand the rudiments of conducting professional audio interviews, but Atkinson believes that their interviewing technique has a role to play in garnering the responses that other media outlets might not necessarily get:

> The thing I always say when we're doing an interview with anybody is that 'I'm going to press record, and then I'm going to press stop, and in the gap, that is what is going to go out. We're not going to mess about with it'. This is something that journalists don't do ever. They want to restructure it to make it more interesting … In the case of Jordan Henderson, Gareth and John are two Liverpool fans who love Liverpool and have thirty minutes with the Liverpool captain and here's what that thirty minutes was. That's quite liberating … The player tends to warm.
>
> (Interview, 2017)

It could be argued that such approaches move away from the reification of celebrity; Jordan Henderson seems more 'ordinary' because of his association with *The Anfield Wrap*, and by extension with other fans. In turn, such informal conversations between TAW and fans' favourite Liverpool FC players satisfy the desires of fans to gain some level of insider knowledge. To an extent, football fan media producers like TAW could be considered what John Tulloch (1995) termed 'executive fans' in his work on science fiction fandom. Tulloch was referring more specifically to those who headed up fan clubs and, as a result, became the voice for other fans in the community.

The Anfield Wrap offers a fan's perspective for those who cannot go to the game, while fulfilling demands for immediate reaction to what happened in the ground. This is most evident in their subscriber podcast *The Post-Match Show*, formerly called *The Pink*, its title a knowing nod to the small post-match newspapers that were once circulated in the hours after a match. These shows are TAW at their most rambunctious and emotional. Following an injury-time winner against their Merseyside rivals Everton in December 2016, Neil Atkinson opened the show with the following exchange with Gareth Roberts:

> Atkinson: What a win! What a gang of reds! What a night! What a fantastic occasion! The Reds have done the decent thing at Goodison Park. They found the most evil, despicable way to beat Everton, and they've done it

> with aplomb. I am absolutely overjoyed! … It is absolutely ridiculous this sort of thing Gareth Roberts, and you know what, fucking cop for that.
>
> Roberts: Oh, absolutely mate. I'm shattered. I'm gone. I'm sweating. Me head's chocka. I've just tried to write something on our Facebook and it's probably absolute nonsense 'cos me head's gone. I mean what better way there to win that … It's left every Liverpool fan in the world absolutely buzzing, on a high, you know Christmas is set up now for the best Christmas ever!

A number of theorists, perhaps starting with Giulianotti (1991), have drawn on Bakhtin's (1984/1968) concept of the carnival in analysing football fandom. In Bakhtin's work, chaos, humour and offensiveness are all central aspects of 'carnivalesque' behaviour, and it is during the post-match shows that TAW is at its most carnivalesque. While some global supporters of Liverpool may determine that Manchester United are the club's most despised rivals, for those who grew up on Merseyside, that title very much falls to Liverpool's nearest neighbours Everton. As such, the most disruptive behaviour and language are saved for what are frequently referred to as the 'blue noses' or the 'blue shite'. Indeed, during a live show that TAW staged in Dublin in 2017, many of the contributors pinpointed goals against Everton as their favourite witnessed as a fan of Liverpool, even if they had limited significance in terms of the club winning trophies. After one particular 3–1 Liverpool victory over Everton, Neil Atkinson was joined by former Liverpool assistant manager Pako Ayestaran to dissect the game. However, as Atkinson outlines, Ayestaran's appearance, detailing tactical nuances of the game, was not what their listeners were in the mood for; essentially, it lacked those elements of carnival:

> Our post-match show after the Merseyside derby when [Sadio] Mané scores in the last minute and we win 1–0 is basically full of Ben Johnson saying appalling things about Evertonians and having a riotous time, and there was a lot of feedback saying that 'we'd rather have Ben Johnson in a room saying rude things about Evertonians and having a riotous time' rather than Pako's frankly brilliant tactical insight into what Liverpool did. It wasn't that they were against Pako doing something but it was like 'all we wanted to hear was youse made up after having beaten Everton 3–1. That's all we wanted to hear. We didn't want to hear a deconstruction of how we did it. We wanted to hear you screaming from the rafters about how we did it' .
>
> (Interview, 2017)

This demonstrates why users engage with *The Anfield Wrap*'s content differently to how they might watch sports television or read the football press. The insights they crave are closer to that of the shared fan experience, a feeling of being at the ground, even if you happen to be living thousands of miles away. Furthermore, it shows that there is an increasing variety of media consumers that are being catered for; some crave in-depth statistical analysis, others prefer expert and punditry opinion, whereas there is also a market for those who seek the carnivalesque.

Global fans and *The Anfield Wrap*

Elsewhere (Ryan, 2020), I have examined at length the role that TAW plays in sustaining fandom for Irish fans of Liverpool. In interview data collected as part of this research, many respondents suggested that TAW helps to support a long-distance love of a football club, based in a city that many of its supporters will rarely or never visit. Without the geographic or familial tradition of following the club, the reasons why these fans from all over the world decided on Liverpool as their favourite team are quite varied. The historic success of Liverpool clearly played a significant role in developing its global fan base; Nash (2000), for instance, explores how the spread of cheaply imported television coverage of English league football to Scandinavian countries from the late 1960s helped heighten a fascination with this league and the establishment of supporters' clubs. Such a visual connection to the clubs and players also coincided with the commencement of an era when Liverpool were utterly dominant in the British game, winning eleven of the league titles between 1972–1973 and 1989–1990, as well as establishing a serious footprint in Europe, winning two UEFA Cups and three European Cups by 1984, with their (and that of other English teams) involvement in European competition prohibited in the years after the Heysel tragedy in 1985. Indeed, tragedy has been another factor in heightening the global awareness of Liverpool FC, and this was never as evident as the Hillsborough (see Scraton, 2016) disaster of 1989. For many of TAW's international users, it was their introduction to a club and their fandom:

> I started to support Liverpool in 1989 after the Hillsborough disaster. I watched the game live on TV and it had an impact on me. When I saw how the Liverpool and Everton fans came together on the [1989 FA Cup] final, I knew there was only one club for me.
>
> (Interview, Thomas, Ireland, 2018)

The lasting legacy of Hillsborough has remained for those who left the city, such as TAW subscriber Pamela, who left Liverpool at eighteen years of age, and is now based in the United States:

> Sad and odd to say, but the appalling coverage of Hillsborough by the gutter press just a year and a half after leaving Liverpool probably helped sustain the relationship too; it felt like Liverpool fans and Liverpudlians needed to stick together in the face of antipathy from the rest of the country.

The Anfield Wrap itself helps maintain the fan discourse around Hillsborough, with numerous podcasts and articles (Atkinson, 2016; Barrett, 2016; Cope, 2016) appearing, and providing an education for those from outside the city.

However, sometimes it can be something as arbitrary as the colour red being a favourite colour, and therefore its association with 'The Reds' leads to selection and intensive fandom over many decades. Chris, a Liverpool fan from Ohio, recalls that his first proper exposure to football was during the 2006 FIFA World Cup, which was hosted by Germany. It was the figures of Peter Crouch and Steven Gerrard, both Liverpool FC players at the time, that led him to the club. After investing time in finding out about Liverpool FC's history, he became a fan and has been one since. Football fandom, according to Porat, "is a permanent component in the fan's identity profile" (2010, 280). This can be difficult for fans like Chris; his friends and colleagues in America's Midwest do not share his passion:

> I don't have anyone to talk Liverpool with and I obviously can't go to the match living in America, so I rely on media in a lot of ways. TAW has emerged as my go to and I have been listening since probably 2011 or 2012. Other sources – ESPN as an example – are too general and broad ... TAW represents the closest I can get to following Liverpool first hand. I may not be able to get to the stadium and watch those mighty boys in red, but I know that I can at least be a part of the conversation surrounding the club with real people who go to the match.
>
> (Interview, 2018)

Aside from getting a sufficient amount of information about the club, Chris expands that *The Anfield Wrap* enables him to get a real sense of what is happening, particularly when the club is going through a difficult patch:

> There have been times over the past 10+ years of following Liverpool where I almost packed it in. I'm an American who chose this team but haven't been to the stadium or the city, so I need to have good voices connecting me to the club and culture. Some of the seasons post [20]13–14 were very frustrating and depressing and it can be hard to see how the next big string of wins will come. If not for TAW I think it would have been easy to let go and follow another sport or only catch an occasional match. TAW helps me better cope with losses, celebrate wins and get a broader picture of things.
>
> (Interview, 2018)

A language of loss appears regularly in this research. The sense of loss regularly contrasting with the therapeutic nature of podcasts was discussed by a number of the respondents. For most, it was in the aftermath of a defeat, but for others it provided a form of solace from aspects of their personal lives.

> TAW re-ignited my love for L.F.C. After the Gillett and Hicks nightmare, I supported from afar, not engaging with the club but thanks to TAW, I'm now far more active, going to games and was out in Dublin pre-season. It's no exaggeration to say that TAW has been a huge influence in my life and has even helped get me through some dark times after my Dad died.
>
> (Irish survey respondent, 2017)

The success of the podcast has resulted in a phenomenon where there are now fans of a fan-generated media text – fans of fans, if you will. International fans of TAW cling to the service's localised contexts at a time when major football clubs have become globalised brands. Out of the 530 surveys completed as part of this study, over 98% of the responded identified themselves as fans of *The Anfield Wrap*. Many of these participants were sourced through a TAW Subscribers Group on Facebook, a group that has an element of exclusivity as only those who are paid-up TAW Player subscribers can participate. Within the group, there are often discussions about the content and tone of the podcast, just as fans may debate tactical decisions or transfer gossip in groups related specifically to the football club. Some of the posters vehemently defend any criticism of the podcast, with a handful of participants terming themselves 'TAW Ultras'.

TAW actively shapes the football fandom and identity of many Liverpool fans, such as Sarah. Like Chris, Sarah is an American fan of the club who came to watching EPL football in the aftermath of the 2006 FIFA World Cup. It took her a year to decide that Liverpool was her team, partially inspired by her memories of singing 'You'll Never Walk Alone' with her family over five decades earlier. After sending TAW's Neil Atkinson a Tweet about how she was watching Liverpool games on her own at 5 a.m. on her birthday, Atkinson reached out and put her in contact with a supporters' club in Seattle, starting new relationships for Sarah:

> Before long I was making the early morning drive down to the LFC pub and making all sorts of new friends. At my age you get used to losing friends and making new – especially young – ones is a gift. I never miss a game at the pub and I have been the Membership Chair for the last three years … In many ways, listening to TAW is what gave me the courage, at the age of 71, to spend six weeks in Liverpool mostly on my own. I felt I knew the politics of the city and its people. I wasn't wrong … Leaving my hotel one evening to catch my Uber to Anfield, three men came bustling around the corner onto Castle Street and I recognised one of them as Neil [Atkinson]. I jumped out to stop him, introduced myself and was invited to visit the offices. Before I got around to doing that, Gibbo [John Gibbons] put out a tweet looking for out-of-town supporters to be interviewed on the Wrap for the Travelling Kop bit and I almost broke a finger responding as fast as I could. Eventually I did do the interview which made me a celebrity in the supporters group when I got home.
> (Interview, 2018)

What we can see in the interview excerpt from Sarah is that her attachment to TAW has conferred on her a special status within the fan group that she belongs to us, as well as having a pivotal part to play in creating a new social community for her to be part of.

TAW and global awareness of Liverpool

Aside from matters on the pitch, TAW fosters a linguistic and cultural exchange. Non-UK listeners adopt 'Scouse' language and phrases utilised by the contributors to TAW. As Chris notes, it has given him "a whacky lexical range that I can use to baffle my Midwest America friends" (Interview, 2018). Fewer than 1 in 4 of the respondents to an early survey circulated as part of this study are from Liverpool. These users identified the ability that the various TAW platforms had to make them aware of issues that happened away from the football pitch itself, such as the Spirit of Shankly[2] movement, the safe standing debate, ticket price walk-outs, Hillsborough and so on. Furthermore, local popular culture and social issues feature, with the growing reliance on foodbanks in the North-West of England (Trussell Trust, 2019) a topic close to the podcast's heart. This was solidified in the summer of 2019 when TAW commissioned a 26-foot mural, featuring Trent Alexander-Arnold, a Liverpudlian that had just appeared in the Liverpool team that had won the Champions League adorned with the quote 'I'm just a normal lad from Liverpool whose dream has just come true', a comment made by Alexander-Arnold on live television in the immediate aftermath of their Champions League victory in Madrid. Aside from the graffiti artist Akse's inscription at the bottom of the wall, the only other text states 'For Fans Supporting Foodbanks'. TAW has not included their logo, or any symbol that directly links them to this mural. Instead, their focus is on highlighting a fan-led initiative that has collection points at both Anfield and Goodison Park, and a cause that Alexander-Arnold, as well as a number of his teammates, has publicly supported. TAW's attachment to the work magnifies the issue to those global fans that may be travelling to the city, and perhaps encourages them to take direct action to support the initiative.

Upon picking up an award for *The Anfield Wrap* at the Football Supporters' Association Awards in December 2019, Neil Atkinson was quizzed by the host, football broadcaster and journalist James Richardson. It was put to Atkinson that Liverpool would soon be returning to Madrid, the scene of their then recent Champions League victory, as they had been just drawn against Atlético Madrid in the knock-out stages of the 2019–2020 competition. Atkinson's response was: "I'm not going. The Spanish police are awful … It's very important to make that crystal clear". Atkinson was using this quite public opportunity to again be a voice for fan concerns and worries, and his issues with Spanish policing of football supporters dates back to a Liverpool away game over two years previous to that awards night.

Atkinson's stream of consciousness, emotional writing is for many one of the highlights of the TAW cannon, particularly his post-match review articles on the website. However, he will use this column to highlight injustices carried out towards Liverpool FC fans. This was evident early in the 2017–2018 season, when coverage of the Liverpool match against Sevilla in the Champions League did not focus on their bombastic first half, when they cruised into a 3–0 lead, or capitulation in the second, when it finished 3–3. Instead, tweets were sent during the match outlining the difficulties that Liverpool's supporters faced getting into the ground, and in particular it outlined the problems with the treatment those supporters received from the Spanish police – official reporting on the match, this was not. Atkinson's post-match report did not focus on the football, and reminded Liverpool Football Club of its responsibilities to protect its supporters, both home and away. This was the fan's experience, warts and all:

> My point is this – bad decisions have been made under needlessly bad circumstances by people inadequately supported. A mentality was wrong first and foremost. Police visors were down and, it appears from the video I saw, a man was assaulted. I was manhandled when there was no need. I saw no Liverpool stewards anywhere. It was an absolute mess and questions should be asked and answered. My hopes are not up. Reflection is something which authorities are good at without being made to be and I hold out no hope that this will happen here. Liverpool Football Club need to support their supporters as a bare minimum.
>
> (Atkinson, 2017)

It was a different narrative to that found in any of the mainstream media's reporting of the game. This suggests that fan media outlets, such as *The Anfield Wrap*, have the potential to give a more rounded fan experience of the travails of football fandom, despite their own inherent biases.

Conclusion

The first two decades of the 21st century have seen a seismic shift in how football fans source information and communicate about football. While the dominant sports media industries still maintain significant power, they are under threat from new platforms. Football streaming has impacted on those that provide paid subscription services to EPL matches, while traditional sports journalism has had to adapt – now football journalists are often multimedia content producers, writing for print and the web, as well as providing audio, video and social media content. Simultaneously, football fans are communicating and debating with each other all around the world with a far greater ease than ever before through ever-growing means of doing so.

Outlets such as TAW occupy an interesting ground in this battle. It has developed relationships with both the football club and its supporters during its first decade in operation. It relies on the same media formats as the more orthodox sports producers do, and similarly charges sports fans for using most of their products. At the same time, they invoke the spirit of previous fan media forums, most notably through their own usage of the word 'fanzine' on their online masthead. The creators of TAW are self-reflexive in this regard, with Neil Atkinson noting that 'the idea that you are DIY doesn't mean that you can't try and build the best set of shelves that you can possibly build. You can basically be better than anyone else doing it, even if it's you doing it' (Interview, 2017). The suggestion is that the influence of fan media does not mean that new media formats need to exactly replicate what their predecessors did; instead, they need to add something new to provide a more unique and immersive fan attachment. Or, to put it in terms familiar to Liverpool FC supporters, they need to 'pass and move'.

Note: All first names of TAW listeners used are pseudonyms of respondents who took part in this study.

Notes

1 For example, the Netflix fly-on-the-wall documentary series *Sunderland 'Til I Die* was approved by then-owner Ellis Short on the basis that it might attract future investors in Sunderland AFC (*Sunderland Echo*, 2018)
2 Spirit of Shankly is a supporter's union for Liverpool FC fans that originally appeared in 2008 during a period when there was significant disgruntlement towards the then owners of the club, Tom Hicks and George Gillett. It would later turn into a cooperative that would represent supporters on matters such as ticketing, travel and community issues (see Millward, 2012).

Bibliography

Atkinson, N. (2016) 'The Hillsborough verdict isn't about football – the disaster was a national disgrace', *The Anfield Wrap*, 27 April. Available at: https://www.theanfieldwrap.com/2016/04/the-hillsborough-verdict-isnt-about-football-the-disaster-was-a-national-disgrace/ [April 30 2020]

Atkinson, N. (2017) 'Sevilla 3 Liverpool 3: Match Review', *The Anfield Wrap*, 21 November. Available at: https://www.theanfieldwrap.com/2017/11/sevilla-3-liverpool-3-match-review/ [January 28 2020]

Bakhtin, M.M. (1984/1968) *Iswolsky, H. (Trans) Rabelais and His World*. Bloomington, IN: Indiana University Press.

Barrett, T. (2016) 'Hillsborough: The media let the country down for 27 years – and I'm ashamed', *The Anfield Wrap*, 1 May. Available at: https://www.theanfieldwrap.com/2016/05/hillsborough-the-media-let-the-country-down-for-27-years-and-im-ashamed/ [April 30 2020]

Bruns, A. (2008) *Blogs, Wikipedia, Second Life, and Beyond: From Production to Produsage*. New York, NY: Peter Lang Publishing.

Cleland, J.A. (2010) 'From passive to active: the changing relationship between supporters and football clubs', *Soccer & Society*, 11(5), pp. 537–552, DOI: 10.1080/14660970.2010.497348

Cleland, J. (2017) 'The English Premier League in a global context'. In: Elliott, R. (Ed.) *The English Premier League: A Socio-Cultural Analysis*. Oxford: Routledge, pp. 70–83.

Cooney, G. (2017) 'Meet one of Liverpool's biggest success stories – The Anfield Wrap', *Balls.ie*, 4 August. Available at: https://www.balls.ie/football/the-anfield-wrap-370683 [May 1 2020]

Cope, P. (2016), Hillsborough and Norman Bettison: Why isn't there a culture of taking responsibility?, *The Anfield Wrap*, 18 November. Available at: https://www.theanfieldwrap.com/2016/11/hillsborough-and-norman-bettison-why-isnt-there-a-culture-of-taking-responsibility/ [April 30 2020]

Deloitte (2019). *Annual Review of Football Finance*. Manchester: Deloitte.

Fischer, S. (2020) 'Exclusive: The Athletic raises $50 million', *Axios.com*. Available at: https://www.axios.com/the-athletic-fundraising-round-series-d-e7026194-ccc7-4ec2-8415-6b8902c9a11a.html [May 1 2020]

Galily, Y. (2014) 'When the medium becomes "Well Done": Sport, television and technology in the twenty-first century', *Television & New Media*, 15 (8), pp. 717–724.

Giulianotti, R. (1991) 'Scotland's Tartan Army in Italy: The case for the carnivalesque', *Sociological Review*, 39 (3), pp. 503–527.

Glendenning, B. (2016) 'They're all talk, but it seems everyone loves a podcast', *Guardian Sportblog*. Available at: https://www.theguardian.com/football/blog/2016/mar/27/podcasts-football-weekly-barry-glendenning [January 3 2020]

Haynes, R. (1995) *The Football Imagination: The Rise of Football Fanzine Culture*. London: Arena.

Kelly, R. (2019) 'The Art of the Podcast: An Interview with Neil Atkinson, The Anfield Wrap', *Digit*. Available at: https://digit.fyi/the-art-of-the-podcast-an-interview-with-neil-atkinson-the-anfield-wrap/ [April 30 2020]

Lopez-Gonazlez, H. and Griffiths, M.D. (2018) 'Betting, Forex trading, and fantasy gaming sponsorships—A responsible marketing inquiry into the 'Gamblification' of English football', *International Journal of Mental Health Addiction*, 16, pp. 404–419, DOI: 10.1007/s11469-017-9788-1

Lopez-Gonazlez, H. and Tulloch, C.D. (2015), 'Enhancing media sport consumption: Online gambling in European football', *Media International Australia*, 155(1), pp. 130–139, DOI: 10.177/1329878X1515500115

Maguire, J. and Stead, D. (1998) 'Border crossings: Soccer labour migration and the European Union', *International Review for the Sociology of Sport*, 33(1), pp. 59–73.

Millward, P. (2008) 'The rebirth of the football Fanzine: Using E-zines as data source', *Journal of Sport and Social Issues*, 32 (3), pp 299–310, DOI: 10.1177/0193723508319718

Millward, P. (2011) *The global football league*. Basingstoke: Palgrave.

Millward, P. (2012) 'Reclaiming the kop? Analysing Liverpool supporters' 21st century mobilizations, *Sociology*, 46 (4), pp. 633–648.

Millward, P. (2013) 'New football directors in the twenty-first century: profit and revenue in the English Premier League's transnational age', *Leisure Studies*, 32(4), pp. 399–414, : 10.1080/02614367.2012.673130

Norman, J. (2016) 'This UK podcast is making money – and employs 4 people', *Online Journalism Blog.com*. Available at: https://onlinejournalismblog.com/2016/03/11/this-uk-podcast-is-making-money-and-employs-4-people/ [May 1 2020]

Porat, A.B. (2010) 'Football fandom: A bounded identification', *Soccer & Society*, 11(3), pp. 277–290, DOI: 10.1080/14660971003619594

Rowe, D. and Gilmour, C. (2009) Global sport: Where Wembley Way meets Bollywood Boulevard, *Continuum*, 23(2), pp. 171–182, DOI: 10.1080/10304310802710512

Ryan, C. (2020) "Talking broken biscuits' – Irish Liverpool fans and The Anfield Wrap'. In: O'Boyle, N. and Free, M. (Eds) *Sport, the Media and Ireland: Interdisciplinary Perspectives*. Cork: Cork University Press.

Scraton, P. (2016) *Hillsborough – the Truth*. Mainstream Publishing.

Trussell Trust (2019). *End of Year Stats*. Available at: https://www.trusselltrust.org/news-and-blog/latest-stats/end-year-stats/ [January 3 2020]

Tulloch, J. (1995) 'We're only a speck in the ocean: the fans as powerless elite'. In: Tulloch, J. and Jenkins, H. (Eds.) *Watching Doctor Who and Star Trek*. London: Routledge, pp. 144–174.

Chapter 10

The resuscitation of a babe

Interrogating the fan-led virtual dedicatory practices of Duncan Edwards

Gayle Rogers

Within the context of football and popular culture, the examination of virtual fan-led commemorative activity reveals a complex network of amplified devotion through online association and disassociation. Virtual platforms across social media, dedicated websites and online forums have become 'virtual terraces' upon which fans can construct and demonstrate their fandom through shared narratives of devotion. For instance, during a match, fans may be following a game online whilst interacting with others in real time on Twitter or Facebook. This virtual sharing of thoughts and feelings by fans provokes online discussion and debate, and later, the virtual world offers fans an arena to reflect on the event and to make predictions for the future. Post-match, the same dynamics of discourse found on the actual terraces, the pub or club play out online, where fan hierarchy, expressions of fan identity, fan alliances and disassociations come to bear.

Beyond the match and post-match narrative, these virtual tools can be used to express fandom and reinforce it as an important aspect of a person's real-life and virtual identity. Fans can express and reinforce their fandom not only through real-time in-match virtual discourse but also by revisiting and reconstructing the matches, teams and players of the past into a present-day virtual world. These reconstructive commemorative acts are not specific to fans but reflect a wider culture shift towards a greater significant virtual presence of the dead in the realm of the living. For former players such as Busby Babe Duncan Edwards (who lived and died in a time before online profiles and platforms existed) fan-led commemorative activity installs them into the present day as a virtual reconstruction. For the most part those reconstructing the dead (such as Edwards) never knew them as living beings and therefore base their acts on notions of perceived truth, preference and supposition. Subsequent fan-led virtual commemorative constructs are fiercely monitored and mediated by fans self-appointed as gatekeepers of 'decency and appropriateness'. Surveillance of the dedicatory acts by fans acutely demonstrates an inherent hierarchical structure of fandom and the assertion of the 'right' felt by some fans to control the actions of others. Yet such surveillance of the dead is essentially not of the dead, but of the notion of the dead as mediated through commemorative acts of strangers. Fans may resuscitate players of the past through commemorative acts based upon certain memories or remembered narratives of other fans. Such resuscitative acts create complex responsibilities and dilemmas for fans. In order to evidence their own fandom, fans may create their own commemorative acts as well as interacting with the stories, memories and beliefs of others. In this regard, commemoration of the dead can form a significant part of a fan's 'life-long project' (Porat 2010, p. 287).

Introduction

To 'commemorate' is defined as the process of preserving 'in memory by celebration or ceremony … be memorial of' (Elliott 1997, p. 138). The concept of preservation implies an activity whereby something or someone is safeguarded or protected from deterioration. Commemorators as the preservers of memories perform acts of commemoration that respond to death by appropriating or creating material or virtual objects and memorials that are intended for public or private consumption. Acts are undertaken at material sites such as graves but also across virtual sites such as dedicated memorial websites.

The concept of memory preservation implies an activity whereby memories are sustained as they are conceived. Memories are by their very nature 'of the past', yet their preservation bestows them the currency of the present. Beyond the paradoxical nature of memory preservation, memories themselves are complex entities to interrogate:

> 'Memory' is commonly envisaged as both the facility to remember and as the mental representation or trace of that which is remembered, both of which are crucially mediated by a variety of cultural forms. In contemporary Western societies, 'memories' are often conceived as possessions: we 'keep' and 'preserve' our memories almost as though they are objects in a personal museum.
>
> (Hallam and Hockey 2001, p. 3)

Since his death in 1958, fan-led commemoration of former England and Manchester United footballer Duncan Edwards has been a fascinating and significant phenomenon. The virtual aspect of such dedicatory activity is apparent across social media, via video channels, podcasts, virtual periodicals and news articles, websites and online forums; as well as the live and recorded sharing of related commemorative activities and events online. That a former football player is commemorated through such activity by football fans could be regarded as unremarkable. However, the commemoration of Edwards embodies fan-led dedicatory activity of an exceptional nature. Investigation of the content, longevity, frequency and sustained commitment of such activity, and of the motivation for it, reveals the significant role of football fandom in the resuscitation of Edwards. This investigation is made from within a wider commemorative context, after Edwards's death from injuries sustained in the Munich Air Disaster in

1958. The veneration of Edwards, specifically, as a hero is considered as a reoccurring and significant commemorative fan-led concept.

As the cause and manner of Edwards's death relates directly to his Manchester United player status, the main focus of fan-led commemoration is on those activities undertaken by self-identifying Manchester United fans. As Edwards was part of the English national team, dedicatory activity by England football fans is apparent, but to a lesser extent. It is acknowledged that Edwards's status as a commemorated football player is not pervasively a fan-led activity and a wider dedicatory cohort of former friends, sports fans in general, people from his local community and family members (past and present) is also evident and relevant.

Commemorating heroes

The role of fans in constructing a significant heroic status for Edwards is manifest in their commemoration of him. As Womack (2003, p. 20) suggests, 'heroes are bigger than life', and the consideration of them goes beyond the scale of normal daily life. Heroes are defined by their heroic acts or achievements, but they are constructed by the demonstrations of admiration made by others. It is essential that an expression of admiration for an individual is seen and shared by others for them to be installed as a hero.

Edwards's celebrated sporting prowess defines him as a sporting hero. However, his heroism is augmented by his death. Manchester United player Harry Gregg survived the Munich Air Disaster and has continually been revered as 'the' hero of the Disaster. He is heralded for his heroic actions by football fans such as Mike Thomas (creator of www.duncanedwards.co.uk), who, in an interview (Thomas, March 2014), stated that 'I would say people who were more like heroes were people like Bill Foulkes and Harry Gregg of course who ran back into the plane to rescue people'. Although consistent in his rejection of this hero status, Gregg is described as a hero for his efforts to help the injured in the immediate aftermath of the Disaster. Despite Gregg's protestations, his publicly constructed identity as a hero has been installed and sustained by others. Even beyond the grave, Gregg, through obituaries to him in early 2020, is 'hailed as a hero of the Munich air crash' (Glanville 2020); credited for his 'heroic bravery and spirit' (Manchester United 2020); and 'remembered for his heroism as he helped rescue a mother and young baby from the burning wreckage' (Fullerton and Rucki 2020).

In 1958, a news report of the crash showed the team as they are about to board the ill-fated plane. In the context of the team qualifying for the next stage of the European Cup, the voice-over states, 'they were national heroes every man' (Universal International News 1958). This team of heroes was surpassed in their tally of wins and achievements by other Manchester United teams, yet their hero status has remained intact, suspended, like their youth, by the Disaster. These dead players, such as Edwards, remain heroes for their measurable achievements, yet also paradoxically for their inability to fulfil their potential and surpass their own sporting achievements.

> From a modern perspective the elevation of the hero to godlike status is problematic for both the secular humanist and the religious believer. For both, the 'exaggerated veneration' of the hero can lead to the abnegation of human responsibility and, at the very least, profound disappointment for the hero-worshipper once the fallibility of the idol is eventually revealed.
>
> (Hughson 2009, p. 89)

The 'disappointment' that Hughson references is dependent on the shortcomings of a hero, yet for Edwards, his death has made him, or rather the memory of him, flawless. There is no evidence of a significant 'abnegation of human responsibility' or any substantial immoral behaviour to tarnish Edwards's image as an 'idol' (2009, p.89). Although part of the 'heroic collective', Edwards is elevated to a greater heroic status because his extended suffering was transmuted into heroism. Fan-led commemoration corroborates this elevation of Edwards, and the word hero has become synonymous with him.

The commemoration of Edwards is inextricably linked to the Munich Air Disaster of 1958. Twenty-three out of the forty-four people on board the plane died as a result of injuries sustained in the crash, and several others were badly injured. Amongst the dead and injured were a number of players from the Manchester United football team. Predominantly young players known collectively and affectionately as the Busby Babes after their manager Matt Busby (who was badly injured in the crash), the Busby Babes fortified a team that were the British pioneers of European club football by being the first British team to compete in the European Cup. Those 'Babes' who died in the crash were (with their ages in parentheses): Geoff Bent (25), Roger Byrne (28), Eddie Colman (21), Mark Jones (24), David Pegg (22), Tommy Taylor (26) and Billy Whelan (22). Edwards (21) died 15 days later as a result of the injuries he sustained.

The deaths of England players Byrne, Taylor and Edwards were considered a national tragedy for English football. Terry Venables, professional footballer and England manager from 1994 to 1996, revered Edwards as his 'hero and inspiration' (Connor 2007, 125) and predicted that Edwards would have been a significant member of the England team. He asserted a belief, shared by a number of football fans that if Edwards had not died in 1958, he, rather than Bobby Moore, would have captained the World Cup-winning team of 1966, as 'how could you pick Moore, great player though he was, ahead of Duncan?' (2007, p. 125). Moore shared Venables's admiration for Edwards, stating that his 'death was the greatest tragedy of the United air crash' (2007, p. 126). So great was Edwards's stature that he 'touched the psyche of every generation and, seemingly every nationality, often in inexplicable fashion' (2007, p. 129).

Manchester United player Bobby Charlton was and remains a key commemorator of the Munich Air Disaster. He survived the crash, played for the club for twenty years and when 'few professionals remain untarnished, Bobby [Charlton] was one of the few, Pelé perhaps the other' (Dunphy 1991, p. 379). He played for the England squad after a call-up just a few weeks after the crash and he was part of the squad that won the 1966 World Cup. A prominent Manchester United fan, Thomas quotes Charlton eulogising about Edwards' abilities. In an interview, Thomas (March 2014) stated that 'If someone like Bobby Charlton would say that then that tells you what he had as a footballer'. The referencing of Charlton's veneration of Edwards by a fan amplifies Edwards's heroic status as a sporting hero.

In a wider context, the way in which this collective of young players died on foreign soil provoked analogies of the young soldiers who died for their country during wartime. Considering the young war dead of the First World War who were commemorated in a way that concealed 'the grim reality of slow, painful death in the primordial conditions at the front' (Berridge 2002, p. 4), there was a purposeful masking of the truth of a painful death that was underpinned by a prevailing 'glorification of death in youth' (2002, p. 38). The purpose of masking the reality of death during wartime was to bolster morale and dignify the dead. In this context, it is noteworthy that Edwards survived for fifteen days after the crash whilst the majority of the Busby Babe collective had already died from their injuries. Post-crash, Edwards's suffering was described as a 'heroic fight for life' (The Busby Babes n.d.). The black-and-white footage of Edwards on the German hospital ward post-crash can be easily found on the internet. It shows an unsettled Edwards in his hospital bed (British Pathé 1958) with a tube inserted and crudely taped to his nose. It is known that due to his failing internal organs that he suffered 'severe haemorrhages, which the medical staff could not stop' (Leighton 2013, p. 246). Edwards's commemorators rarely detail the extent of his injuries. They revere Edwards for his strength and 'brave fight' (2013, p. 245) and retell the heroic narrative whereby doctors told his family that 'anyone else would be dead by now' (2013, p. 246). Such absence of references to Edwards's pain and catastrophic injuries make accounts of his final days more akin to celebrations of superhuman strength. By removing the degenerative element of dying from a memorialised Edwards, the pre-emption of a resuscitated youthful immortal Edwards is born. When the moment of his actual death comes, he is described as 'the lion-hearted Edwards [who] died peacefully in his sleep with no pain' (2013, p. 248).

Edwards is significantly immortalised as a local sporting hero in his hometown of Dudley through a statue, dedicatory stained-glass windows, road names, his grave and a collection of memorabilia at the Dudley Archives. Edwards's statue inspires commemorators to visit his hometown in a fan-led pilgrimage or as dark tourists;[1] 'Nowadays, it could be argued that Duncan Edwards is Dudley's main tourist attraction' (Connor 2007, p. 131). Yearly, on the anniversary of the Munich Air Disaster, fans make these pilgrimages to Dudley to visit Edwards's memorials.

In 2015, a coloured bronze statue representing Edwards in his England football kit was re-installed in a more prominent position and underpinned an enduring affection for, and veneration of, Edwards, demonstrating how 'Dudley remains so proud of its soccer hero' in the process (*Express and Star* 2015). Edwards is reconstructed in his hometown as an England, not Manchester United, player. However, on the fiftieth anniversary of the Munich Air Disaster, Edwards's statue 'bore a United shirt with the message 'Legend – not forgotten' (*Daily Mail* 2008). A fan (or fans) had reclaimed Edwards the 'legend' into the Manchester United cohort and images of his statue bearing the strip were shared and celebrated online.

Appropriate and decent commemorative acts

The re-appropriation of Edwards into the Manchester United 'family' by the re-dressing of his England strip-clad statue in 2008 was a fan-led commemorative act. Fans often use Manchester United-branded items as part of the commemorative acts they undertake at Edwards's memorials.

Although accessed by numerous commemorators, Edwards's grave has always been tended as a family plot. It is not, as some have suggested, 'Maintained by members of the Manchester United family' (Johnston 2008, p. 14), meaning that it is not tended to by the club or fans. However, such an assumption may be due to the many Manchester United and football-related offerings visible upon Edwards's grave year on year. I made eight visits to the grave over a four-year period, from February 2010 to March 2014 (Rogers 2017), to document the 'offerings' on it. During this period scarves were documented on the grave fifty-six times, with fifty-four scarves attributable to Manchester United. At least six Manchester United football shirts were observed during the documentation period, placed in a way, like so many of the scarves, to show the club logo conspicuous and outwardly to other visitors. This persistent fan-led adornment of the grave means it is almost impossible to photograph and share images of it without sharing the evidence of the fan-made Manchester United emblematic 'shroud' of scarves and shirts.

Offerings were observed that were from family members and friends alongside those of fans. No reference is made to Edwards's Manchester United or England career in his epitaph but, through offerings left by fans, Edwards is subsumed as a member of the Manchester United cohort. By accommodating and caring for the offerings, the family grave tenders are complicit in constructing a memorial to Edwards that is overwhelmingly produced by Manchester United fans.

Not all Disaster victim graves are as well maintained or visited. In 2005, the grave of Geoff Bent (a player killed in the Disaster) was found by a Manchester United fan with 'weeds choking the last resting place' and the discovery was reported locally with the headline 'Forgotten grave of a Busby Babe' (*Manchester Evening News* 2005). The fan suggested that the dilapidated plot was the responsibility of Manchester United, stating, 'I think it is disgusting that his grave should have been allowed to get into this state. It should have been a matter of pride for the club to keep it neat and tidy' (2005). In response to the article, a Manchester United club official stated that they would 'look into the matter and do something to keep the grave tidy on a permanent basis' (2005). Such an inferred commitment implies that the graves of the Disaster's dead are officially viewed as the club's responsibility (should no family relation be able to tend the grave). Thomas, a prominent fan commemorator, suggested in an interview

(March 2014) that fans expect Manchester United to honour those players killed in the Disaster, stating, 'I think that the club should contribute. They gave their lives for the club'. The expectation of fans that their club should be the custodian of former players' graves suggests that being a club player is a lifetime – and beyond – project.[2]

Within Edwards's commemorative network, those who knew and were related to him, or were friends with him, are acknowledged as being the most profoundly affected by his death. Such individuals are bestowed a greater 'right' to being bereaved than individuals with a less immediate connection. Within an assumed hierarchy of 'the bereaved', personal grief is considered as the authentic voice of commemoration. Yet, seeking to define 'the bereaved', Walter suggests 'definitions are being expanded so that "the bereaved" are perceived as potentially more than just the next of kin' (Walter 1994, p. 157). In the modern era, such expansion means the way in which family members are perceived and how they act in commemorative networks has continued to shift (1994, p. 157).

The majority of those who now seek to commemorate Edwards have no first-hand knowledge of Edwards, the Busby Babes or the Munich Air Disaster. At the time of writing, Bobby Charlton is the only player-survivor, and only a handful of Edwards's relatives who knew him personally remain with us. The time is fast approaching when these 'first generation' commemorators will soon be gone. This suggests a new dimension for a commemorative network hierarchy. By their actions, second-generation commemorators become custodians and preservers of certain first-hand accounts and will deconstruct these narratives by reconstructing their own. Although the 'first-generation' commemorators may relate truthful narratives, the role of the second-generation commemorator is to install those truths within the commemorative network in a present-day context using their own methods of transmission and translation. It is a practice of memory creation and simultaneous preservation, and, as Hirsch states, 'If this sounds like a contradiction, it is, indeed, one, and I believe it is inherent to this phenomenon' (Hirsch 2008, p. 106). As a second-generation commemorator, a fan is compelled to reinforce the heroic Edwards of the past within the present, whilst considering who Edwards should 'be' resuscitated into the present day.

Commemorators' backgrounds, life experiences and their religious or spiritual beliefs and interests will all influence their dedicatory activity. If 'anyone' can be affected by grief, and the definition of that grief is as an 'individual concept' (Walter 1994, p. 158), then the proliferation of individual perspectives on the death of Edwards is potentially manifold and infinitely expansive. Being part of the Manchester United cohort appears to unite commemorators as a source of motivation, but how that sense of belonging is expressed is ultimately an individualistic concept. Even survivors of the Disaster attest to the heterogeneous nature of individualistic commemorative acts bound within a Manchester United-related cohort.

Although former player Gregg survived the crash, he publicly preserved the memory of the event in a markedly different way to fellow survivor Charlton. In his autobiography when asked about the Disaster, Gregg 'told the assembled press that I tried not to think about it every day (for the sake of my sanity)' (Gregg 2002, p. 143). Whilst Gregg recalled that when asked the same question, Charlton replied, '"I'm not like Harry", and that every morning in life he thought about the crash and the lads who died' (2002, p.143).

Fan-led commemoration

So profound are the ties between fans and their club that some even seek to cement their connection in death. There is a demand for commemorative space within football grounds to scatter the ashes of fans because of the significance of the club to their lives. One family confirmed that their father's ashes being scattered at the edge of Manchester United's pitch at Old Trafford was his 'his dying wish come true' (Sheerhout 2017). That some football grounds have a formal commemorative dimension whereby they offer onsite memorial services by their dedicated grounds chaplain (Scattering Ashes 2010) reinforces the sense of the ground as a place of focus for their fandom and club 'worship'. The rules for the scattering of ashes at club grounds vary greatly from club to club. Manchester United state that they do consider requests for ashes scattering at their stadium, regarding each request on its own merit (2010). Other clubs intern partial ashes when pitches are dug over at certain times of the year or have a memorial garden in the stadium for the formal scattering of ashes (2010).

In 1999, Manchester United football fan Mike Thomas created the website www.duncanedwards.co.uk, which has since become uniquely associated with, but also definitive in, resuscitating Edwards. Initially, Thomas created www.munich58.co.uk as a tribute website in 'memory of those who died', he stated in an interview (March 2014). He developed his Edwards-specific site soon afterwards. Thomas specifically requested that he be identified within the research as a Manchester United fan and cited his fandom as the reason for creating these websites. In the interview, he alludes to Edwards's elevated commemorative status, saying, 'Duncan was probably the most famous and I would say because of that, there was that aura about [him] … people wanted to know so I put together this site'. Through his commemorative websites Thomas has become established as one of the most significant and accessible fan commemorators in the dedicatory network of the Munich Air Disaster, and specifically of Edwards. He has no personal link to either the crash or Edwards, and his commemorative acts are totally fan-led. There are other commemorators within the network who have established dedicatory websites or Facebook pages (Anon 2012). However, Thomas's websites have acquired an apparent legitimacy demonstrated by their formal referencing by the Manchester United Club official website and several supporters' clubs.

Thomas's fandom is not just expressed online; he attends matches and takes part in an annual fan-led Munich Air Disaster anniversary gathering at the Munich Air Disaster Memorial Plaque, Old Trafford. Each year fans congregate beneath the Plaque in memory of the victims of the crash. He records this fan-led event and shares it online via his commemorative YouTube channel. When asked if he would have accepted an invitation to the club's formal fiftieth memorial service inside the ground in 2008, Thomas replied, 'I'd have turned it down because I wanted to be outside with the fans' (March 2014). Such a response underpins his self-identification as a fan and the significance of his fandom to his identity, as 'to differentiate, to compare himself with others, to be unique, to indicate that football fandom is a critical component of his identity' (Porat 2010, p. 287) places his fandom at the centre of his very being.

Fans as commemorative gatekeepers

On the anniversary of the Disaster in 2014, Thomas recalls, 'there were thousands and thousands of tweets from all around the world even from players like Michael Owen, Gary Neville, Rio Ferdinard, Norman Whiteside, Robbie Fowler' (March 2014). This demonstrates ongoing global commemoration of the Disaster which peaks around the anniversary of the crash date. Social media affords commemorators an opportunity to conspicuously commemorate. In an interview, Thomas recalls his interaction with other commemorators, but having had multiple interactions with many commemorators over the years, Thomas occasionally finds it difficult to distinguish those interactions as being in person or online. When considering Thomas's relationship to a commemorator who regularly tends Edwards's grave, the complexity of their association becomes apparent, 'I know Jan – ... – well I don't know her I never met her. She contacted me a couple of years ago. She posts regularly to Duncan's tribute book'. It is apparent that online associations of closeness between some fan commemorators may be exclusively virtual, yet so profound that they are felt intimately.

An assumed closeness of association between Manchester United Football Club and their fans is also evident through the commemoration of the Disaster. Various memorials and dedicatory events have been created at the club's grounds. However, the installation of a temporary memorial in 2008 to mark the fiftieth anniversary of the Disaster provoked some fans to impede the clubs' dedicatory act.

A large temporary decal was installed on the glazed shop entrance façade of Old Trafford. It combined a photograph of the Busby Babes team at the match played before the Disaster, commonly referenced as 'the last line up', with some related text. It was funded by American International Group (AIG), an American insurance company that was the major sponsor of the club at the time. Some fans expressed concern about the memorial because the sponsor's AIG logo on it was considered 'vulgar' (Taylor 2008) and inappropriate advertising. A number of fans publicly campaigned for the logo's removal, whilst other fans questioned the distaste for the AIG logo, saying, 'If you don't want their advertising then don't take their money. Simple' (Taylor 2008).

Notably, as a mark of respect, all sponsorship logos including the AIG logo were removed from the shirts of both Manchester teams playing in the 2008 memorial match. This seemed to contradict the inclusion of the AIG logo on the memorial, and this was discussed across fan forums and in the comments sections of some online newspapers. Some fans questioned the club's behaviour: 'if the blues [Manchester City players] can wear a shirt without sponsorship as a mark of respect then surely the powers that be at Old Trafford can drop the logo out of respect' (Taylor 2008). The club responded to the call for the logo's removal by officially stating 'It is entirely appropriate that a partner as closely involved with the club as AIG would want to remember that extraordinary team' (Taylor 2008).

On the evening prior to the official opening of the memorial, the AIG logo was paint-balled. Although unsuccessful in obscuring or damaging the logo, it was clear that this area had been the shooter's target. Although the paint was removed before the official opening of the memorial, evidence of the act of paint-balling was recorded in media reports and online. The media almost exclusively reported the paint-balling as inappropriate vandalism of a memorial, and the general response was condemnation of the act. One fan posting on an online forum said, 'I'm more humiliated by the vandalism than I am by the logo' (Jak 2008). Although allied with many in objection to the logo's presence, the paint-ballers lost the support of some due to their actions being seen as disrespectful to the memory of those being commemorated. The paint-balling was seen predominantly as inappropriate as it did not 'maintain the integrity' that it sought to preserve (Star and Griesemer 1989). This demonstrates a complex commemorative network where care must be taken when using blanket, all-subsuming terms like 'fan commemoration' without acknowledging that issues of appropriateness of dedicatory actions may be based on a personal belief, not a wholly fan-led basis of consensus.

When free scarves were distributed by Manchester United at a commemorative match to mark the fiftieth anniversary of the Disaster, some were taken by fans and posted for sale on eBay. All sales were subsequently prohibited by eBay, and offending listings were withdrawn, in response to complaints. This official decision was reportedly said to be 'taken in line with the policy not to allow users to profit from human tragedy' (*Manchester Evening News* 2010). Some fans took direct action and placed bogus bids for thousands of pounds on the scarves on auction. While these commemorators led a campaign against their sale, other commemorators discussed the issue via online forums, and some questioned the sacredness of the scarves 'made in China' (Redcafe 2008) to warrant such a response. Events like this signify that the dedicatory networks of Edwards and the Munich Air Disaster are continually shifting and being carried through time, but significantly, they are being monitored for decency/appropriateness and maintained by fans who are effectively self-appointed commemorative gatekeepers.

Edwards – The fan-led construct

In 1958, Manchester United fans described a collective and individual grief in response to the Munich Air Disaster. By surviving the initial crash, Duncan Edwards became a beacon of hope and, although he succumbed to his injuries, his death has been negated by fans installing his resuscitated player-self into perpetuity. Fandom is apparent, extensive, persistent and authoritative in Edwards's commemoration. Fan commemorators reinforce their commemorative endeavours with their own social and cultural beliefs and their personal experiences of death. Their commemoration is an expression of their devotion to Edwards as a player, and to their club, Manchester United. In the commemorative virtual world, these extensive and cumulative expressions of devotion consistently place fans at the forefront of creating and defining the construct of Edwards's resuscitated self, which is ultimately commemorated as 'the' Duncan Edwards.

Within the context of the last twenty years, the commemorative activity surrounding Edwards reflects a cultural shift wherein 'a society which has for so long averted its gaze from death cannot stop staring at it' (Berridge 2002, p. 255). Virtual commemoration allows the living to 'gaze' upon the dead, and dedicated websites suspend the dead in a technologically assembled memorial. Edwards has become a spectacle of death accessible to those unable to attend his physical memorials. His grave or statue may be inaccessible, but through virtual commemorative acts they can be gazed upon through websites like Thomas's www.duncanedwards.co.uk. Interestingly, while Edwards died before social media and the internet became commonplace, he is resuscitated by this technology. It is not the suspension of his own virtual representations that form his virtual existence, but a construct created by others through the preservation of his memory.

Here, Edwards is described (mostly) by strangers who never knew him personally, yet there is a sense of familiarity created by virtual commemoration. As cremation begets the urn of ashes that allows the remains of a loved one to be transportable and divisible among the bereaved, fan-led virtual commemoration takes Edwards and shares him among the bereaved. Virtual images of the temporary Manchester United-related offerings on his grave are given a virtual permanency by their capturing and sharing through image technology. Fans can accessorise and enhance their social media accounts with imported images of Edwards's commemoration on their social media feed or profile images or names. Through such online acts, Edwards becomes an important facet of fans' own virtual identities. Ultimately, the 'virtual Edwards' becomes a commemorative commodity and visual testimony of Manchester United fandom, and, when shared, the dedicatory acts of devotion amplify the fandom of others and create a collective fan construct. As fandom is a 'life-long project that begins at an early age and ends with the life of the fan' (Porat 2010, p.277), commemoration of Edwards for certain fans is an enduring facet of their devotion to their club. Thomas's fandom (evident through his dedicatory websites) is 'self constructed' (Porat 2010, p. 288). His connection to his club is significantly bonded through his commemoration of the Munich Air Disaster, to what Gerrard refers to as 'the glory of the Busby era' (Andrews 2004, p. 85).

Arguably, Thomas has done more than any other person in the virtual world to create the resuscitated version of Edwards. When his website content is shared, a part of his fandom is simultaneously shared with it. When he shares the commemorative acts of others through tribute posts, or through the uploading of footage from commemorative events, the fandom of others is shared. Thomas sustains a part of the fan-led commemorative network that appears to demonstrate a consensus of how fans are expected to commemorate Edwards, the Munich Air Disaster and the Busby Babes. The website is as fixed a memorial as the stained-glass dedicatory windows in Edwards's former church, but it is easier for most fans to access and interact with. The creation of a fan website may be viewed as unremarkable, yet such mundane activity can be transformed within the network to become a significant commemorative act that raises the profile of the commemorator as well as the commemorated. This is due to the commemorative network being mediated and monitored by gatekeepers, as the memories of the dead are preserved and monitored by a system codified by self-appointed guardians. The prevalent dedicatory practices that persist or are rejected are measured by a series of inferred standards of appropriateness.

Conclusion

Even though commemorators have their own personal perspective on death, when they act as fans, their dedicatory activity is fan-led preservation. Belonging to a specific group, such as a Manchester United fan cohort, any activity undertaken by an individual who self-identifies or is identified as a fan will have their dedicatory acts viewed within this context. Individuals and collectives have created localised physical memorials as well as dedicatory events, and technology has afforded commemorators virtual dedicatory tools with a global reach. The 'personal museums' (Hallam and Hockey 2001, p. 3) of individual commemorators of Edwards have become increasingly virtualised, yet non-virtual memorials and acts remain significant and are frequently referenced in the virtual world. Fandom has emerged as a defining life-giving element in the maintenance of Edwards's immortality. The commemorative role of certain individual fans, fan cohorts and fan-allied groups within Edwards's dedicatory network creates 'a 4-dimensional archaeology – some of the structures it uncovers are stable, some in motion; some evolving, some decaying' (Bowker and Star 2000, p. 7). Since Edwards's biological death, a networked Edwards is 'in motion' and yet simultaneously stable.

The relationship between Edwards and Manchester United are perpetually and inextricably linked, but it is the fans, not the club, that lead, bolster and perpetuate Edwards's player existence. A cohort of disparate fans of Manchester United (and, to a lesser but significant extent, of the English national team) will always be potential commemorators of Edwards. Their role in his commemoration includes actively exerting their notion of appropriateness and decency on the club and other fans. In this regard, these fans have a self-initiated commemorative imperative that goes beyond simply commemorating, extending to influencing and controlling the commemorative acts of others. Potential commemorative acts require commemorators to have a knowledge of who Edwards was and, perhaps more significantly, how he died. As fans are the most prolific and active of commemorators, it is their acts that are referenced and shared the most within the network. In the era of 'fake news', the sharing of second-hand unverified 'facts' as truths, whether wilfully done to mislead or not, can compound the telling of untruths as facts. The motivation for sharing an unverified fact is significant to those sharing and those with whom it is shared.

Within the commemorative network, Edwards's commemorative construct is less formed by acts of truth than acts deemed appropriate, decent and respectful. For example, the myth that Matt Busby drove overnight to sign Edwards (before other clubs could) on the morning of his 16th birthday prevails. The less dramatic truth that Edwards was actually signed to Manchester United as a 15-year-old (and not by Busby in person) is less compelling for the narrative supporting the significance of Edwards's abilities and the keenness of Busby to have him play for Manchester United. That inaccuracies persist or even proliferate in a commemorative narrative suggests that commemorators can seize and corrupt dedicatory activity to create what they see as more fitting tributes. This may lead to disputes and acts of impedance across the network if the authenticity of a commemorative act is challenged. Therefore, what fan gatekeepers deem to be appropriate to preserve Edwards's heroic player status (rather than what is factually correct) becomes the barometer for which acts are allowed to prevail in the commemorative network. Commemoration is not the preservation of truth, but the preservation of the dead.

All commemorators are given their network status not only via self-identification but also through the response of others. As Star and Griesemer (1989, p. 389) state, 'Unless they use coercion, each translator must maintain the integrity of the interests of the other audiences in order to retain them as allies'. The rigour by which the virtual commemorative 'rules' of decency and respectfulness are applied is not matched by the monitoring of truth and factual information. The commemorative imperative for fans is not so much fact based as opinion based. Appropriateness in regard to maintaining the dead of the Munich Air Disaster as heroes is the most contested and allied concept. Whilst Edwards's immediate biological family has died and his direct bloodline connections weaken, his adoption as a 'son of Dudley' and his membership of the Manchester United 'family' mean fans are more elevated in the commemorative hierarchy than ever before.

How and why fans individually and collectively formulate a resuscitated virtual version of Edwards reflects the cultural and social beliefs of the individual and their identity as a fan. Edwards the resuscitated immortal footballer will never play for Manchester United again; yet, preserved in memory by fans, he will never stop playing. Indeed, in the words of Thomas, 'I think as long as there are people like myself and other fans who are there to keep the memory of the Busby Babes alive, even when all the people who are left have died, the fans will be there to remember'.

Notes

1 Dark tourism is a collective term for travel to an event or a place specifically because of its link to death.

2 In some instances, fans have formed action groups like the Celtic Graves Society to identify, maintain and protect the memorials of former Celtic players and significant figures associated with the club (The Celtic Wiki Supporters n.d.).

References

Andrews, D., ed. (2004). *Manchester United; A Thematic Study*. Oxon: Routledge.

Anon (2012) 'Duncan Edwards 1936–1958; The Greatest Footballer Who Ever Lived' [online] available: https://www.facebook.com/pages/DUNCAN-EDWARDS-1936-1958-The-greatest-footballer-who-ever-lived/155959201143520 [accessed Dec 8 2015].

Arthur, M. (2008). *The Busby Babes: Men of Magic*, Edinburgh: Mainstream Publishing.

Berridge, K. (2002). *Vigor Mortis: The End of The Death Taboo*, 2nd ed. London: Profile Books.

Bowker, G. and S.L. Star. (2000). *Sorting Things Out: Classification and Its Consequences*, Cambridge MA: MIT Press.

British Pathé (1958) *'Report From Munich 1958', The Day That Shook The World [video]*, 13 Feb, available: http://www.britishpathe.com/video/report-from-munich [accessed Jul 7 2015].

Connor, J. (2007). *The Lost Babes: Manchester United and the Forgotten Victims of Munich*. London: Harpersport.

Daily Mail. (2008) 'Fans Adorn Statue of Duncan Edwards with a United Shirt', MailOnline, 5 Feb, available: http://www.dailymail.co.uk/sport/football/article-512422/Fans-adorn-statue-Duncan-Edwards-United-shirt.html [accessed Aug 20 2016].

Dewhurst, K. (2009). *When You Put on a Red Shirt: Memories of Matt Busby Jimmy Murphy and Manchester United*. London: Yellow Jersey Press.

Dunphy, E. (1991). *Sir Matt Busby and Manchester United: A Strange Kind of Glory*, London: William Heinemann Ltd.

Elliott, J., ed. (1997). *The Oxford Compact Dictionary and Thesaurus*, Oxford: Oxford University Press.

Express and Star. (2015) 'It Will Become A Pilgrimage Site', *Express and Star*, 2 Oct, available: http://www.expressandstar.com/news/2015/10/02/it-will-become-a-pilgrimage-site-dudleys-duncan-edwards-statue-moved/ [accessed Jan 1 2016].

Fullerton, D. and Rucki, A. (2020) 'Harry Gregg dies aged 87: Tributes to Manchester United goalkeeper and Munich survivor who pulled Bobby Charlton and Sir Matt Busby from wreckage' *Manchester Evening News*, 17 Feb, available: https://www.manchestereveningnews.co.uk/news/greater-manchester-news/tributes-paid-harry-gregg-united-17759841 [accessed May 3 2020].

Glanville, B. (2020) *'Harry Gregg Obituary' The Guardian*, 17 Feb, available at: https://www.theguardian.com/football/2020/feb/17/harry-gregg-obituary [accessed May 3 2020].

Gregg, H. (2002). *Harry's Game: The Autobiography*, Edinburgh: Mainstream Publishing Company.

Hall, D. (2008). *Manchester's Finest: How the Munich Air Disaster Broke the Heart of a Great City*, London: Bantum Press.

Hallam, E. and Hockey, J. (2001). *Death, Memory and Material Culture*, Oxford: Berg.

Hirsch, M. (2008) 'The generation of postmemory', *Poetics Today*, 29 (1), pp. 103–127.

Hughson, J. (2009). *The Making of Sporting Cultures; Sport in the Global Society*, Oxford: Routledge.

Jak. (2008) 'AIG logo' Reply #91, Republik of Mancunia Manchester United Football Club Forum, 31 Jan, available: http://republikofmanc.proboards.com/index.cgi?board=generalunited&action=display&thread=5985&page=7 [accessed Aug 21 2015].

Johnston, G. (2008) 'Duncan Edwards – Dudley's football legend: To commemorate the 50th *Anniversary of Duncan's Death' St Francis Church Booklet*, 21 Feb.

LFCHistory.net (n.d.) 'Bill Shankly' [online], available: http://www.shankly.com/article/2408 [accessed Dec 18 2015].

Leighton, J. (2013). *Duncan Edwards: The Greatest*, London: Simon and Schuster UK Ltd.

Manchester Evening News. (2005) *'Forgotten Grave of a Busby Babe' Manchester Evening News*, 21 Jun, available: https://www.manchestereveningnews.co.uk/news/local-news/forgotten-grave-of-a-busby-babe-1117636 [accessed Dec 18 2015].

Manchester Evening News. (2010) *'eBay Remove Munich Memorabilia' Manchester Evening News*, 18 Apr, available: https://www.manchestereveningnews.co.uk/news/greater-manchester-news/ebay-remove-munich-memorabilia-942985 [accessed Jun 29 2020].

Manchester United (2020) 'Obituary: Harry Gregg OBE', [online] available: https://www.manutd.com/en/news/detail/obituary-harry-gregg-former-man-utd-goalkeeper [accessed May 3 2020].

Porat, A. (2010). 'Football fandom: A bounded identification'. *Soccer and Society*, 11(3), pp. 277–290.

Red Ranter, (2008) "The Glazers' Busby Babes Tribute Madness – Sign the Petition', Red Rants Manchester United Blog' [online], 20 Jan, available at: http://redrants.com/the-glazers-busby-babes-tribute-madness-sign-the-petition/5 [accessed Aug 21 2015].

Redcafe. (2008) 'Man United Munich Memorial Scarfs Ebay', *Redcafe Forum*, 10 Feb, available: http://www.redcafe.net/threads/man-united-munich-memorial-scarfs-ebay-watch.186436/ [accessed Sept 11 2016].

Rogers, G. (2017) *The Commemorative Activity at the Grave of Munich Air Disaster Victim, Duncan Edwards: A Social and Cultural Analysis of the Commemorative Networks of a Local Sporting Hero*. (PhD), University of Central Lancashire.

Rosaaen, K. and Amis, J. (2004) 'From the busby Babes to the theatre of dreams', in Andrews, D., ed. *Manchester United; A Thematic Study*, Oxon: Routledge, 43–61.

Scattering Ashes (2010) 'Football Clubs' [online], available: http://www.scattering-ashes.co.uk/help-advice/law/football-clubs/ [accessed Jun 27 2016].

Sheerhout, J. (2017) 'Life-long United fan's ashes are scattered at Old Trafford after Luke Shaw made his dying wish come true', *Manchester Evening News*, 21 Mar, available: https://www.manchestereveningnews.co.uk/news/greater-manchester-news/life-long-united-fans-ashes-12772932 [accessed June 29 2020].

Sheridan, A. (2000). *Heaven and Hell: And Other Worlds of the Dead*, Edinburgh: NMS Publishing.

Star, S. and Griesemer J. (1989). 'Institutional ecology, 'Translations' and boundary objects: Amateurs and professionals in Berkeley's museum of vertebrate zoology, 1907–39', *Social Studies of Science*, 19 (4), pp. 387–420.

Taylor, P. (2008) 'United drop busby from tribute', *Manchester Evening News*, 1 Feb, available: http://menmedia.co.uk/manchestereveningnews/news/s/1032944_united_drop_busby_from_tribute United drop 'Busby' from Tribute Paul R [accessed Apr 23 2014].

The Busby Babes (n.d.) 'Victims of the 1958 Munich air disaster' [online], available: http://www.thebusbybabes.com/victims/victims.htm [accessed Sep 1 2016].

The Celtic Wiki Supporters (n.d.) 'Celtic graves society' [online] available: http://www.thecelticwiki.com/page/Supporters+-+Celtic+Graves+Society [accessed 01 07 2020].

Universal International News (1958) 'Britain Mourns. Soccer Champs Die In Plane Crash 58/02/10', *Internet Archive [video] Universal International News*, 2 Feb, available: https://archive.org/details/1958-02-10_Britain_Mourns [accessed Sep 2 2015].
Walter, T. (1994). *The Revival of Death*, London and New York: Routledge.
Womack, M. (2003). Sport as symbol: Images of the athlete in art, *Literature and Song*, North Carolina: McFarland and Co Inc.
Young, J.E. (2000). *At Memory's Edge: After-Images of the Holocaust in Contemporary Art and Architecture*, New Haven and London: Yale University Press.

Chapter 11

'What's he know about the Premier League?'

Football media and the perpetuated archetypes of 'Englishness'

Jonathan Cable

Introduction

The 2016–2017 and 2017–2018 Premier League seasons saw several high-profile debates about the employment of English versus foreign managers at top-level football clubs. Two such examples include Paul Merson and Phil Thomson's rant about Hull City appointing the Portuguese manager Marco Silva stating 'What's he know about the Premier League? What's he know?', or former England manager Sam Allardyce saying that English managers were being treated as 'second class citizens' (Nicholson 2017; Tyers 2017). These examples highlight the clear distinction being made between a version of 'Englishness' and a perceived threat of foreigners to English football. It represents a crisis in national identity (Porter 2004; Maguire 2011), which has been brought on by the processes of globalisation (Maguire 1999, 2011). This chapter uses Lule's (2001) arguments around myth and its continued use in journalism. It takes a critical look at how the perpetuated archetype of 'Englishness' is portrayed. Furthermore, it examines the narratives present in football media around what makes a 'proper' football manager, and how this archetype is consistently reproduced and reinforced in football punditry and football journalism. The key arguments made in this chapter are that language such as this creates very distinct in and out groups in football media, and a skewed portrayal of modern football and managers who encapsulates a very particular type of nostalgic, myth-based nationalism.

This chapter takes a critical look at how the mythical archetype of 'Englishness' is represented through the prevalent use of the term 'proper football man' (PFM) and what characteristics this phrase comes to exemplify. Myth in this case is 'not unreality. Myth is not false belief. Myth is not an untrue tale' (Lule 2001, p. 15). This is an archetype which is continuously repeated and reinforced by both football pundits and in opinionated football journalism. The main idea behind this chapter was prompted by the columns of Alan Tyers (*Daily Telegraph* journalist) and John Nicholson (journalist and author) on the independent football opinion website *Football365* entitled 'Eye on the Experts'. In one such article from December 2013, 'Clever and a "Football Man"? Give Him a Job …', Nicholson discusses English manager archetypes which they dubbed the 'Proper

Football Man' in relation to Tottenham Hotspur and rumours of former player Tim Sherwood becoming their next manager (2013). They detail, among other facets of the phrase, the very definition of PFM:

> What the hell is a 'proper football man'? And as opposed to what? Was AVB not a 'proper football man'? No. In this context, 'a proper football man' is code for 'a thicko that we can understand and not someone who is too clever for us'; that's what it really means. It's a cipher. For 'breath of fresh air' read 'not some weird foreigner who can construct a sentence, unlike thems of us what can't'. Sherwood is English. English is good. It means you haven't, in that awkward and distasteful phrase, 'gone foreign'. (ibid)

What can be interpreted from this definition is that the PFM is English, traditional in worldview and approach, and represents a state of nostalgia for the 'good ole days'. The conflict created by English vs the rest provides a story with characters, plot, and a theme. The press plays a key role in these arguments because they provide the platform from which Englishness is shaped and which of its preferred national characteristics are amplified.

Literature review

Football exists as a microcosm for wider societal issues, and to unpack the underlying messages found within the press, this section looks at how Britain's best-selling tabloid, *The Sun* (Tobitt 2018), has treated football over the years. Furthermore, the theories behind this research around myth and identity in relation to sport will be entered into in more detail. Whannel (2002) has argued that sport is a combination of news and entertainment where the athletes/managers are treated like characters in a soap opera. *The Sun* is very much at the centre of these kinds of portrayals and myths around Englishness in pursuit of an archetypal working-class male. To get a sense of why *The Sun* is like this, you need to go back to the 1980s when there was a series of 'behind the scenes' books relating to the paper. One such book, *Sun-Sation* by Grose, talked about how television had driven audience attention to newspapers because the tabloids were the main source for backstage gossip, especially around famous people's private lives (1989; see also Chippendale and Horrie 1990). Fundamentally, it is a paper which deals in celebrity and self-publicity rather than news and sport as vital to its operations. The underlying nature of its views are exemplified by the paper's first Sports Editor in 1969, Frank Nicklin, who was referred to as a master of the nostalgia piece; he's also known to have said that the paper needed 'four rows of teeth' (quoted in ibid). In the late 1980s the Sports Editor David Balmforth went further and said that *The Sun* had 'eight rows of teeth' (quoted in Domeneghetti 2014). This confrontation and biting stance led Wagg (1986) to talk of 'guilty men' where 'negative pressure' is heaped onto players and managers either directly or tangentially via 'readers say'. In footballing terms, this tends to follow attributions of blame when the England national team exit a

World Cup. For example, when England lost to Iceland and exited the World Cup in 2016, *The Sun*'s headline was 'Ice Wallies' and referred to it as England's 'most humiliating defeat ever', laying blame for the defeat with 'Everybody wearing an England shirt' (Ashton 2016). In other words, the 'guilty men'.

This type of coverage originates in the late 1950s early 1960s (ibid, p. 38). This moment in time represented a turning point in how football was covered when the press moved from just reporting on matches and transfer speculation towards a much more personality centred narrative. This change came about because of two specific influences:

i) Outside of sport there was the damaging of national pride brought on by the fall of the British Empire and subsequent fears brought on by the Cold War. On the field in 1953 England were beaten for the first time at Wembley by a side from outside the British Isles. Hungary won, 6–3, and the loss was seen as emblematic of England's fall from grace.
ii) The tabloid press wanted to differentiate themselves from the television coverage that was being served up at the time. (ibid)

Even England's World Cup win on home soil in 1966 did not stop this trend from happening, as Carrington argues the narratives around this triumph are seen through a nostalgic, mythical lens which longs for a perceived purer, simpler time, which is also more white (1998). Furthermore, he argues that sports teams represent the image of national identity because they highlight the positive or negative narratives chosen to discipline said identity (ibid). In addition, the journalist Rory Smith wrote in his book *Mister*, about the people who spread the sport worldwide, that English football stalled for a decade because of the 1966 win because the nation looked inwards rather than following tactical developments on the continent (2016).

Central to the relationship between the press and teams has been the manager. Pre-1966, managers were treated with deference and respect, but post-1966, they became personalities, embodying the ethos of clubs, and celebrities in their own rights (Carter 2007, p. 218). A great example of what the relationship used to be like comes from the day after England won the World Cup in 1966. The journalist Ken Jones approached a victorious England manager Alf Ramsey with a view to conducting an interview, but he famously replied, 'Sorry, it's my day off' and he meant it (quoted in Bowler 1998, p. 228). Newspapers at this point in time were the main source of 'behind the scenes' information for fans about their clubs, players, and managers. The press was central in terms of access to more personalised portrayals and the reproduction of archetypal nationalism. The 'myth of '66' continues to weigh heavily in press narratives around players and the national team which Critcher identified as a more celebrity style of journalism that demonises the banal and disciplines players to fit the mould of a much more traditional, nostalgic style of sports star (1979). For example, here is how the *Daily Mail* described England's captain Harry Kane during the 2018 World Cup: 'How magnanimous, gentlemanly Harry Kane conjures up memories of Bobby Moore rather than his scandal-tainted predecessors as captain' (Jones and Rainey 2018).

How a manager becomes defined by the national press is partially due to the culture outside of football, because the game itself does not exist in perfect isolation (Critcher 1991, p. 82). Furthermore, these representations prioritise personality over sporting prowess and place managers into one of three roles: (1) entertainer; (2) individual personalist; and (3) embodiment of sporting narrative (Critcher 1979, 1991). The third of these traits is of particular importance because it represents so much more than surface-level discussions. Where nation fits into all this is exemplified by *The Guardian* journalist Richard Williams who once said (quoted in Boyle 2006, p. 103), 'A 22-year-old has money and wealth, so there isn't that chance to experience an understanding of their way of life'. It is a famous complaint that players are wrapped in cotton wool, overplayed, and lack passion for the English national team. Taken further, if Critcher's (1979, 1991) topology and the importance of style in football is considered, these are the characteristics footballing heroes have or do not have. There is a press need for players, and by extension managers, to remain in the traditional/located mould, where working-class roots of the game are upheld and there is a core of nostalgic myth in order for readers to identify with them. This narrative is, however, up against the modern reality of the dislocated superstar that represents the majority of contemporary elite footballers.

How a player or manager becomes defined by the national press is partially because of the culture outside of football. To highlight this point, we should again mention player Harry Kane, whose ordinariness was perceived as a virtue, embodied in the phrase 'one of our own'. Sport journalist Jonathan Liew wrote about Kane in 2015 referring to the 'He's one of our own' chant, describing it a lament for lost local heroes and a globalised game changed beyond all recognition (2015). In contrast, a previous England captain, John Terry, was seen to embody nostalgia, for the traditional was found in his style of play and personal background, up against his scandal-ridden and dislocated private life (Ewen 2013). These narratives play out as an exemplifier of what has been highlighted in past research.

The centre of this argument is that the '*news most often tells stories that support and sustain the current state of things*' (Lule 2001, p. 36, emphasis in original). The 'current state of things' has developed from what Porter (2004) talked about as English people who lived through or were born in the post-World War II era became accustomed to the idea that they belonged to an old country that had seen better days, and a national sense of 'declinism' was setting in. The sporting triumphs of especially the English national team are 'somehow symptomatic of the nation's health' (ibid, p. 35). Furthermore, Black's article on press narratives around the London 2012 Olympics and the Queen's Diamond Jubilee were emblematic of an identity which 'oscillated between nostalgia for an English/British past – marred by decline – and a present that, while being represented as both confident and progressive, was beset by latent anxieties' (2016, p. 797). Central to this sense of national identity is a view of culture as having an immutable timelessness, a defined origin, continuity, and tradition (Maguire 1999). However, when this is placed against the backdrop of the processes of economic globalisation, Maguire uses the term 'Little Englander' to describe the 'strong defensive reaction to globalisation processes, European integration, the pluralisation of national culture and the assertiveness of the "Celtic fringe"' (2011, p. 990).

Football in this instance is playing a contradictory role. On the one hand, the global success of the English Premier League (EPL) is an exemplar of the processes of globalisation; on the other hand, clubs are anchored geographically, and this plays into national identity formation. The emergence of the EPL and the riches brought by the billion-pound broadcasting deals led to the movement of foreign players and managers to the EPL. The sheer wealth generated by broadcasting rights has meant that the business of football has moved far beyond old perceptions of 'English' football. These perceptions are fuelled by myth from two different sources. One is journalistic myth which 'upholds some beliefs but degrades others. It celebrates but also excoriates. It affirms but it also denies' (Lule 2001, p. 119). The other is nationalistic collective memory which 'serves to flatten the complexity, the nuance, the performative contradictions of human history; it presents instead a simplistic and often uni-vocal story' (Bell 2003). These myths are propagated by the football media, such as Tolson's research into *Soccer Saturday* on Sky Sports in the UK where pundits discuss issues and commentate on live games (2016). But expertise and authority of Soccer Saturday comes from the experience of the pundits having played and managed in football (ibid). This turns managers and players into actors on the stage, and in the tabloid press the performances are a pantomime where nuance is lost, and the heroes and villains are obvious and visibly different from the general public (Maguire 1999). In this case it is the foreign which has been othered. Journalists and pundits are acting as storytellers who tell and retell myths.

This section has detailed the general background concepts to the research. The following section will lay out how the data was gathered and analysed.

Methodology

In order to uncover how the PFM label was being used in the press, a Lexis Nexis search of all UK national newspapers was conducted using the exact phrase 'proper football man/men'. This resulted in 258 articles from June 2002 to the end of December 2019, as well as prominent examples from broadcast coverage mention in newspapers as part of this debate. This was done to examine the contexts within which the word was used, the narratives it drew upon, and what its key characteristics and uses were. The football media in this case is acting as a 'validator' of viewpoints by defining 'whose views need to be taken seriously' (Gamson and Meyer 1996, p. 290). Media framing in this chapter takes from Boykoff and Laschever's work on the American Tea Party movement, where frames exist as:

> consistent, coherent bundles of information that journalists provide to imbue real-world events with structure and meaning. Media frames organise issues, pointing both backward at what happened and forward, offering interpretive cues for what it all means.
>
> (2011, p. 346)

In the football media this constitutes those with a significant enough publicity platform to talk on an issue; be they the ex-players/managers who, acting as broadcast pundits, supply 'colour', analysis, professional experience, ghost-written columns, or prominent sport journalists who generate opinion and perspectives around events. This plays into Entman's concept of a 'cascading activation model' where the ability to amplify and solidify frames depends on someone's position and power; 'Some actors have more power than others to push ideas along to the news and then to the public' (2004, p. 9). Furthermore, the highlighting of particular issues, in this case the number of English managers, supplies a media context that is created through the 'selection and salience' of certain issues by the football media versus those which are ignored (Entman 1993, p. 52). This provides a set of frames that contain what Entman calls an 'imprint of power' whereby issues are diagnosed, moral judgements passed, and solutions suggested (ibid, p. 55). The moral judgements and issues in this situation are around football managers and their country of origin. The following list of words represent an overview of how PFM is defined. This is taken from the Lexis Nexis newspaper articles where the key words and characteristics attributed to the phrase were examined:

> Hard (as in tough), passionate, English (but not always – British and Irish also), hardworking, traditionalist, no-nonsense, term of endearment between managers, battler, authentic, genuine, respectful, manager (only very occasionally players), feels deserving of more credit, masculine, anti-data analytics, anti-intellectual, lacking self-awareness, generally media friendly, and contradictory.

In each story the term 'proper football man/men' was isolated, and the words around the term were read and recorded to build up an overview of the context within which the phrase was used. To complement Entman's framing, this chapter utilises Lule's seven key enduring myths of journalism:

1. The victim – helps to define 'good and evil'.
2. The scapegoat – ridicules and degrades the individual while explaining away problems, and acts as a warning to others.
3. The hero – embodies lauded social values.
4. The good mother – Reaffirms the current social order and community values are given voice.
5. The trickster – illustrates the necessity for societal rules.
6. The other world – the exotic 'other'.

7. The flood – the unstoppable that creates a sense of helplessness (2001)

If we take these categories and map them onto the most common frames of PFM, the majority are applicable. The most regularly occurring myths are the PFM as a hero/victim, whereas foreign coaches are framed as scapegoats, tricksters, and other worldly. The following section will unpack the term 'proper football man' from the sample and examine how it has been used in press coverage and what this means for its continuing use.

Findings and analysis

The origin and use of the phrase PFM go back to the early 2000s, when it was used to describe what the English FA needed in a new Chief Executive to move the organisation forward. Henry Winter writing in *The Telegraph*, talked about it as follows:

> Meanwhile, damage to the FA is being done by the day and unless a proper football man is installed as chief executive the lights will continue to dim at Soho Square.
>
> (2003)

Just in this quote it is clear to see the formation of a myth, and the suggestion that those who do not fit are an 'other'. The PFM is the hero coming to save English football; on the other hand, the non-PFM is a scapegoat who will bring about the game's destruction. More on these aspects in a moment. The term really rises to prominence in 2007, with its usage becoming popularised around discussions of the English national team and the connotations of its use has a traditionalist form. This has seemingly been prompted by press debates around the nationality of the England national team's manager, because the England FA's managerial appointments in the 2000s went from Swede Sven Goran Ericsson, to Englishman Steve McLaren who failed to qualifying for the European Championships in Austria and Switzerland in 2008, then came Italian Fabio Cappello before he left the job, and Englishman Roy Hodgson took charge (see Griggs and Gibbons 2014 for more on the manager's nationality, national identity, and the English press). The nationality of the English coach has always been at the centre of debates in the British press.

Take the following from Longmore in the *Sunday Times*, for example, who in discussing Harry Redknapp's candidacy for the England job as being 'no-nonsense', a man who 'believes football is a simple game made unnecessarily complicated' and is as 'tactically astute as any manager in the Premier League' (2007). Here, we are getting into an almost hegemonic, natural, common-sense existence of the PFM as English. You do not need to perform a test to find out if someone is a PFM or not; you just know. To use Steve McLaren again, he was said to be thinking of inviting previous England manager Terry Venables onto his coaching staff for reasons relating to PFM because McLaren 'knows a proper football man when he sees one' (Samuel 2006, p. 76). When this is extrapolated further, there is a clear 'cascading activation' taking place which comes as part of a community of practice, in this case football. In punditry the people used are traditionally drawn from ex-players and managers and therefore they possess common experiences and a common system of beliefs. Equally, there is a sense that pundits know each other as demonstrated by their familiarity and friendliness towards their colleagues (Tolson 2016). This community of practice is then projected onto what Anderson (1983) referred to as an imagined community, in this case football fans who are assumed to share the same belief systems as the pundit. Football journalism exists in this same world where there is shared language, culture, and narrative construction.

But for every in-group, the PFMs, there is an out-group, and it is strictly hierarchical. If you do not have the same background or shared interests as these pundits, you are dubbed a Non-Football man. For example when the ex-Director General of the BBC, Greg Dyke, was in charge of the English Football League, sport journalist Paul Hayward in the *Daily Telegraph* commented that Dyke had tried 'convincing people he is a proper football man' going on to define PFM as 'that strange brotherhood you know you are a member of only when one of the greats of the game refers to you as such. Non-proper football men are a lowly breed' (2013). This fits neatly into Lule's hero archetype and places those deemed fit to wear the PFM badge as above reproach. The ultimate non-PFM, however, are the foreign managers who are othered and placed firmly into the category of outsiders. This is something which has happened consistently with foreign players, Millward's (2007, p. 618) research on the topic speaks about 'Outsiders, such as foreign players are easy targets for criticism because they are "different"'. One such incident which took place on the Sky Sports programme *Soccer Saturday* in January 2017 featured the pundits Paul Merson and Phil Thompson criticising Hull City's hiring of Portuguese coach Marco Silva who they turn into a scapegoat for all the ills of English football:

> Paul Merson: 'What's he know about the Premier League? What's he know?'
> Phil Thompson: 'It's totally astonishing that they have plumped for someone like this. It's baffling. When there are a lot of people out there who know about the Premier League, about what's required to dig in. He's not got a clue' (quoted on *Football365* 2017a)

These types of attitudes, however, exist in a kind of echo chamber of amplification because they are often supported and repeated in the press. Take the following from Martin Samuel in the *Daily Mail*:

> And yes, it is easy to mock observers such as Paul Merson and Phil Thompson, who both expressed surprise when Silva got the job in January. Yet those who questioned the appointment were making a wider point than the suitability of one man. It was about the opportunity afforded to British coaches. (2017)

The targeting of Silva did not stop there. When he later moved from Hull City to Watford following Hull's relegation, Paul Merson again commented that 'No, they [Watford] will get relegated ... To have a manager who has enhanced their reputation by being relegated is remarkable' (Redmond 2017). Non-English League accomplishments either do not matter or do not count as much, and this view is surely aided by Sky's 'Best league in the world' mantra. The validity of claims around British coaches not getting chances to manage at the highest level was examined by one of the originators of the PFM term as a negative when Alan Tyers, writing in 2017 in the *Daily Telegraph*, looked at the statistics behind quotes like Merson's.

Tyers charted the nationalities of English Premier League managers between 2007 and 2017 and found that British and Irish managers do get jobs in the top division, but their roles tend to be lower down the league. For instance, over the 10-year period in which Tyers examined, there were 30 relegations featuring 49 full-time managers, constituting of 43 different individuals, including six managers who had been relegated twice (2017). Of these managers, 82% were of British or Irish descent, and the names often featured were David Moyes, Tony Pulis, Mark Hughes, Sam Allardyce, Harry Redknapp, and Roy Hodgson (ibid). Taking the first name on that list David Moyes and Merson's quote about relegation, Moyes was hired to the West Ham United job in November 2017 following a stint at Sunderland where he recorded an 18.6% win ratio and the club were relegated (ibid). Similarly, and without a sense of contradiction, noted PFM Harry Redknapp has talked about English coaches not getting a chance to manage at a higher level because elite clubs 'keep going foreign, foreign, foreign' (quoted in Davies 2015). But in a separate anecdote, he has also spoken how he helped Englishman Frank Lampard (who is also his nephew) get an interview with Ipswich Town, and eventually his first managerial role at Derby County (quoted in Metro Sport Reporter 2020).

Putting this mixture of media and nationalism into context is to quote Billig's classic text *Banal Nationalism* in which he spells out the relevance of sport coverage to the study of national identity construction in the media: 'All the papers, whatever their politics, have a section in which the flag is waved with regular enthusiasm' (1995, p. 119). He continues:

> As men scan for the results of their favoured team, they read of the deeds of other men doing battle, in the cause of that larger body, the team. And often the team is the nation battling for honour against foreigners. (ibid, p. 124)

This heroic battle is seemingly never won and constitutes a never-ending war of attrition between the opinions, victimhood, and flag waving of the football media and the globalisation of the EPL. These types of comments around who should become the manager of English football teams are not restricted to one specific club. The following quotes, for example, relate to Tottenham Hotspur, Everton, and Leicester City:

i) Former player, pundit and PFM Jamie Redknapp talked of Tim Sherwood's credentials for the Tottenham job in December 2013, saying 'He has played the game at the highest level, understands English football and he knows the club inside out. I don't want to be xenophobic, but it's not just English players we don't give a chance to – it's English coaches as well. Sherwood won't talk tactics, he'll talk football. He's no bluffer, he's a football man and he's exactly what Spurs need' (quoted in Redknapp 2013).
ii) A similar narrative was shaped around David Unsworth and the Everton job, with former Everton player Phil Neville commenting that 'it riles me when I see him described as not having enough experience. Unsworth has done the hard yards as a coach and has done a fantastic job with the Everton Under-23 side' (Quoted in *Football365* 2017b).
iii) The final example is from when Frenchman Claude Puel was made coach of Leicester City in 2017: former Sky Sports presenter Richard Keys simply tweeted, 'RIP British coaching' (2017).

The impact of this rhetoric has had very real consequences. The language of English football has exacerbated the situation by discipling and defining in/out groups. For instance, Joshua Robinson of the *Wall Street Journal* looked at the pre- and post-match press conferences of the American Bob Bradley when he was the manager of Swansea City to examine his choice of phraseology (2016). Robinson found that Bradley had adopted British phrases over their American counterparts to appear less other-worldly, such as 'clean sheet' over 'shutout', 'dressing room' rather than 'locker room', and 'supporters' as opposed to 'fans' (ibid). Bradley's only slip was to refer to a penalty as a 'PK' – and according to Robinson, there was a backlash on social media – and he never once used the term 'soccer' (ibid). Moreover, it is not just what kind of English a manager uses, it is the basic use of any English which is sometimes under focus. When the Italian Walter Mazzarri was coach at Watford, he chose to use a translator in order to avoid mistakes; however, sport journalist John Cross of the *Daily Mirror* painted Mazzarri as a trickster, tweeting 'Walter Mazzarri is an insult to the Premier League. He has been in England for a year and not bothered to learn English. Really poor' (2017). Similar sentiments were expressed when Spaniard Unai Emery oversaw London club Arsenal. For example, the following passage comes from a *Daily Mail* article about the team's on-field struggles at the time:

> Emery's insistence on conducting his press duties in English is admirable. But the Spaniard struggles with the language, which is having an impact on his work.
> The language barrier has caused players to misinterpret instructions in training and has left them confused.

> Sources claim Emery's grasp of English has improved – but it is still not at a point where players can fully understand him.
>
> (Mokebel 2019)

The flip side to this is the English manager who comes across as a victim, ignored by the perceived bigger jobs because of their nationality. This is very much an example of the 'little Englander' mentality used by Maguire (2011, p. 990). Sean Dyche at Burnley has consistently been at the centre of these types of narratives. During one press conference, Dyche was quoted as saying the following:

> Antonio Conte [Italian] came in at Chelsea and he got commended for bringing a hard, fast, new leadership to Chelsea, which involved doing 800 metre runs, 400m runs and 200m runs.
>
> Come to my training and see Sean Dyche doing that and you'd say 'dinosaur, a young English dinosaur manager, hasn't got a clue'.
>
> (quoted in Gaughan 2016)

This thread of being overlooked runs alongside a British/English 'is best' mentality, and a lack of self-awareness appears stark when investigated in greater detail. Take Ray Wilkins's comments about the number of British players at Glasgow Rangers in 2017:

> It's Brits, Brits and Brits again for me, you need more British players in your side not foreigners. Foreign players don't understand the ferocity of Scottish football.
>
> (Quoted in McGarry 2017)

Wilkins himself had been a foreign player while playing in Italy for AC Milan and France for Paris St Germain. Former England manager Glenn Hoddle said something similar about the number of British players at Tottenham, commenting that 'All the other clubs that have been great, they had loads of foreigners, they didn't have enough English people' (quoted on *Football 365* 2017c). When Hoddle was Tottenham manager, he signed 15 players between 2001 and 2003, of whom 9 were neither British nor Irish. Hoddle, like Wilkins, had also been a foreign player when he played for AS Monaco, becoming *Ligue Un*'s Foreign Player of the Year for the 1987–1988 season (ibid). Football media in all these instances is allowing these narratives to be framed by the same people repeatedly. Punditry is the platform for these ideas to flourish. The next example brings together quite a few of these key themes and involves the PFM Sam Allardyce talking on BeIN Sports with the former Sky presenters Richard Keys and Andy Grey:

> I think you are almost deemed as second class because it is your country. … It is a real shame that we are highly educated, highly talented coaches now with nowhere to go. … The Premier League is the foreign league in England now. … When you look across the owners, the managers and the coaches (and) the players, that is exactly what it is now.
>
> (quoted on *ITV News* 2017)

This quote mostly plays on the victim myth, overlooked despite being talented, but Allardyce also scapegoats the level of non-British people at all levels of the EPL. The myths in this statement attempt to harken back to a perceived, yet unspecified, simpler age which is just nostalgically better somehow, and less foreign.Finally, the place of PFMs in football media was amplified over the summer of 2020 when three of the four presenters on *Soccer Saturday* were sacked (PA Media 2020). The event became unedifying on Twitter following the announcement of the sackings with racist abuse and insinuation being levelled at several black pundits, including Micah Richards and Alex Scott, who had nothing to do with the decision but were somehow seen as part of the issue (de Menezes 2020). The way it was handled and the reaction to it became a demonstration of what the programme had come to represent, a mythical white male enclave in a multiracial sport.

Conclusion

The myth of the PFM's continued existence is because it is repeated regularly and illustrates the sense of loss and decline highlighted by Porter (2004). The findings demonstrate that the PFMs managed to create a dominant frame around English nationality and English identity. This myth and overriding narrative are difficult to challenge because of the relative lack of foreign pundits in broadcast media, with the *Soccer Saturday* incident serving as a perfect example of what happens if a broadcaster tries to make a change. Additionally, there is a lack of diversity amongst sports journalists in the written press where PFMs have been previously been employed as columnists. Essentially, myths and assumptions are pushed by those with the loudest voices, and this is aided by the storytelling of the national press. They are representative of Lule's mythmaking where, rather than societal norms, it is English football's perceived characteristics which are defined, defended, and disciplined by those heroic victims, the PFMs. Although these myths appear hegemonic, there is critique of these nationalistic constructs from outlets like the *Guardian* and *Football365*, but they do not have the same kind of platform to redefine the debate. That said, John Nicholson commented in September 2019 that football was changing and that the PFMs were finding it harder and harder to gain employment in football management (2019). The victimhood has dissipated somewhat when the 2019–2020 season saw English managers at Chelsea (Frank Lampard) and Watford (Nigel Pearson), or be promoted with their teams such as Aston Villa (Dean Smith) and Sheffield United (Chris Wilder). A couple of the old guard are still in work during the 2019–2020 season with David Moyes at West Ham United, Roy Hodgson at Crystal Palace, and Steve Bruce at Newcastle United. Nicholson centres his 2019 article on Sam Allardyce and the impact of PFMs' protestations in the football media. He quotes unnamed footballing officials saying that Allardyce's 'small-islander mentality and full of entitlement and bragging' has put off clubs employing English managers (ibid). In other words, the high profile of PFMs for a time resulted in fewer English managers being hired, not more. These attitudes are running against the tide of football's globalisation. Football is a global sport, and Allardyce's little Englanders, like opinions of English heroism and victimisation, are being seen for what they are: myths.

References

Anderson, B. (1983) *Imagined Communities*. New York: Verso.

Bell, D. (2003) "Mythscapes: Memory, mythology, and national identity". *The British Journal of Sociology*. 54 (1), pp. 63–81. Published online: https://doi.org/10.1080/0007131032000045905.

Billig, M. (1995) *Banal Nationalism*. London: Sage.

Black, J. (2016) "Celebrating British multiculturalism, lamenting England/Britain's past". *Nations and Nationalism*. 22 (4), 786–802. Published online: https://doi.org/10.1111/nana.12164.

Bowler, D. (1998) *Winning isn't Everything … : A Biography of Alf Ramsey*. London: Orion.

Boykoff, J., and Laschever, E. (2011) "The tea party movement, framing, and the US. media".*Social Movement Studies*. 10(4), pp. 341–366. Published online: https://doi.org/10.1080/14742837.2011.614104.

Carrington, B. (1998) 'Football's coming home' but whose home? And do we want it?: Nation, football and the politics of exclusion. In A. Brown (Ed.), *Fanatics: Power, identity, and fandom in football* (pp. 121–143). London: Routledge.

Carter, N. (2007) "'Managing the media': The changing relationship between football managers and the media". *Sport in History*. 27 (2), pp. 217–240. Published online: https://doi.org/10.1080/17460260701437045.

Chippendale, P. and C. Horrie (1990) *Stick it up your Punter!: The Uncut Story of the Sun Newspaper*. London: Mandarin.

Critcher, C. (1979). "Football since the war". In J. Clarke, C. Critcher, & R. Johnson (Eds.), *Working Class Culture: Studies in History and Theory* (pp. 161–184). London: Hutchinson.

Critcher, C. (1991) "Putting on the style: Aspects of recent english football" (pp. 67–84), In J. Williams and S. Wagg (eds) *British Football and Social Change: Getting into Europe*. Leicester: Leicester University Press.

Cross, J. (2017) "Walter Mazzarri is an insult to the Premier League. He has been in England for a year and not bothered to learn English. Really poor." *Twitter*. Published 16 May 2017. Online url = https://twitter.com/johncrossmirror/status/864391634334732288?lang=en-gb. Last accessed January 15 2020.

Davies, H. (2015) "How misplaced xenophobia still damages English football". *FourFourTwo*. Published 9 November 2015. Online url = https://www.fourfourtwo.com/features/how-misplaced-xenophobia-still-damages-english-football. Last accessed May 19 2020.

de Menezes, J. (2020) "Ian Wright hits out at 'stinking-mouthed racist' response to Sky Sports pundit sackings". *Independent*. Published 28 August 2020. Online url = https://www.independent.co.uk/sport/football/news/ian-wright-matt-le-tissier-sky-sports-sacked-soccer-saturday-phil-thompson-charlie-nicholas-a9690971.html. Last accessed October 7 2020.

Domeneghetti, R. (2014) *From the Back Page to the Front Room: Football's Journey Through the English Media*. Huddersfield: Ockley Books.

Entman R. (2004) *Projections of Power: Framing News, Public Opinion, and U.S. Foreign Policy*. Chicago: University of Chicago Press.

Entman, R. (1993) "Framing: Toward clarification of a fractured paradigm". *Journal of Communication*. 43 (4), pp. 51–58.

Ewen, N. (2013) "John Terry and the predicament of englishness ambivalence and nostalgia in the premier league era". *Sport in History*. 33 (4), pp. 465–487. Published online: https://doi.org/10.1080/17460263.2013.850268/.

Football365. (2017a) "Mediawatch special: Merson, Thompson, Marco Silva". *Football365*. Published 9 January 2017. Online https://www.football365.com/news/mediawatch-special-merson-thompson-and-marco-silva. Last accessed January 15 2020.

Football365. (2017b) "Mediawatch: The Sun sticks up for 'soft target' Sterling". *Football365*. Published 3 November 2017. Online url = https://www.football365.com/news/mediawatch-the-sun-sticks-up-for-poor-raheem-sterling. Last accessed January 15 2020.

Football365. (2017c) "Mediawatch: Former foreigner complains about foreigners". *Football365*. Published 2 November 2017. Online url = https://www.football365.com/news/mediawatch-former-foreigner-complains-about-foreigners. Last accessed January 15 2020.

Gamson, W.A., and D.S. Meyer. (1996) "The framing of political opportunity." in *Comparative Perspectives on Social Movements* (pp. 275–290), edited by McAdam. D., McCarthy J.D., and Zald M.N. New York/Cambridge: Cambridge University Press.

Grose, R. (1989) *The 'Sun'-sation: The Inside Story of Britain's Best-Selling DailyNewspaper*. London: Angus & Robertson.

Hayward, P. (2013) "Rio Ferdinand could be left to rue his decision to put his chances of reaching Brazil in jeopardy". *Daily Telegraph*. Published 22 March 2013. Online url = https://www.telegraph.co.uk/sport/football/teams/england/9946858/Rio-Ferdinand-could-be-left-to-rue-his-decision-to-put-his-chances-of-reaching-Brazil-in-jeopardy.html. Last accessed January 15 2020.

Gaughan, J. (2016) "I'd be hailed a genius if I was a foreign boss, claims Burnley's Sean Dyche". *Daily Mail*. Published August 10 2016. Online url = https://www.dailymail.co.uk/sport/football/article-3731977/I-d-hailed-foreign-boss-claims-Burnley-manager-Sean-Dyche.html. Last accessed January 15 2020.

Griggs, G., and T. Gibbons. 2014. "'Harry Walks, Fabio Runs': A case study on the current relationship between english national identity soccer and the english press." *International Review for the Sociology of Sport*. 49 (5), pp. 536–549. Published online: https://doi.org/10.1177%2F1012690212463917.

ITV News. (2017) "Allardyce believes home-grown managers are considered second class in 'foreign' Premier League". *ITV News*. Published 27 October 2017. Online url = https://www.itv.com/news/2017-10-27/allardyce-believes-home-grown-managers-are-considered-second-class-in-foreign-premier-league/. Last accessed January 15 2020.

Jones, D. and Rainey, S. (2018) "A football hero England can be proud of: How magnanimous, gentlemanly Harry Kane conjures up memories of Bobby Moore rather than his scandal-tainted predecessors as captain". *Daily Mail*. Published 19 June 2018. Online url = https://www.dailymail.co.uk/news/article-5862651/No-tattoos-polite-patriotic-Harry-Kane-football-hero-England-proud-of.html. Last accessed May 15 2020.

Keys, R. (2017) "RIP British coaching". *Twitter*. Published on 25 October 2017. Online url = https://twitter.com/richardajkeys/status/923266504786767872?lang=en. Last accessed January 15 2020.

Liew, J. (2015) "English football's 'one of our own' chant is a lament for lost times - whatever happened to the home-grown hero?". *Daily Telegraph*. Published 17 March 2015. Online url = https://www.telegraph.co.uk/sport/football/teams/tottenham-hotspur/11478183/English-footballs-one-of-our-own-chant-is-a-lament-for-lost-times-whatever-happened-to-the-home-grown-hero.html. Last accessed May 15 2020.

Lule, J. (2001) *Daily News, Eternal Stories: The Mythological Role of Journalism*. New York: Guilford Press.

Maguire, J. 1999. *Global Sport: Identities, Societies, Civilisations*, Cambridge: Polity Press.

Maguire, J. (2011) Globalisation sport and national identities, *Sport in Society*, 14 (7/8), 978–993.

McGarry, G. (2017) "Rangers Euro exit down to not having enough Brits in their team, says Ray Wilkins". *The Herald*. Published 5 July 2017. Online url = https://www.heraldscotland.com/sport/15391379.rangers-euro-exit-down-to-not-having-enough-brits-in-their-team-says-ray-wilkins/. Last accessed January 15 2020.

Metro Sport Reporter (2020) "Harry Redknapp explains how he got Frank Lampard the Derby job and set him on the path to be Chelsea manager". *Metro*. Published 18 May 2020. Online url = https://metro.co.uk/2020/05/18/harry-redknapp-explains-how-got-frank-lampard-derby-job-set-path-chelsea-manager-12719785/. Last accessed May 19 2020.

Millward, P. (2007) "True cosmopolitanism or notional acceptance of non-national players in English football: Or, why 'bloody foreigners' get blamed when 'things go wrong'". *Sport in Society*. 10(4), pp. 601–622. Published online: https://doi.org/10.1080/17430430701388772.

Mokebel, S. (2019) "Unai Emery is lost in translation at Arsenal with fans disgruntled, players bemused by his tactics and his treatment of Mesut Ozil and a language barrier leaving the shadow of Arsene Wenger looming large". *MailOnline*. Published 4 November 2019. Online url = https://www.dailymail.co.uk/sport/football/article-7649441/Unai-Emery-fighting-save-Arsenal-job-players-left-confused-tactics-language-barrier.html. Last accessed July 14 2020.

Nicholson, J. (2017) 'Second class? Nowhere to go? It's British manager nonsense'. Football365. Published on 31 December 2017. Online url = https://www.football365.com/news/second-class-nowhere-to-go-its-british-manager-nonsense. Last accessed January 19 2021.

Nicholson, J. (2013) "Clever and A 'football man'? Give him a job…". *Football365*. Published on 23 December 2013. Online url = https://web.archive.org/web/20131226014826/http://www.football365.com/john-nicholson/9085960/Clever-And-A-Football-Man-Give-Him-A-Job…. Last accessed January 15 2020.

Nicholson, J. (2019) "The premier league's 'second-class' citizens are on the rise". *Football365*. Published on 30 September 2019. Online url = https://www.football365.com/news/the-premier-leagues-second-class-citizens-are-on-the-rise. Last accessed January 15 2020.

PA Media (2020) "Matt Le Tissier, Charlie Nicholas and Phil Thompson leaving sky sports". *The Guardian*. Published on 26 August 2020. Online url = https://www.theguardian.com/football/2020/aug/26/matt-le-tissier-charlie-nicholas-and-phil-thompson-leaving-sky-sports. Last accessed October 7 2020.

Porter, D. (2004). "'Your boys took one hell of a beating!' English football and British decline c. 1950–80". In D. Porter & A. Smith (Eds.) *Sport and National Identity in the Post-War World* (pp. 31–51). Abingdon & New York: Routledge.

Redknapp, J. (2013) "No reason why Sherwood can't be next Spurs boss, United fans must wonder why Moyes went for Fellaini and not Barkley while Toure is more Beckham than Ronaldo". *Daily Mail*. Published on 22 December 2013. Online url = https://www.dailymail.co.uk/sport/football/article-2528100/JAMIE-REDKNAPP-No-reason-Tim-Sherwood-Tottenham-boss.html. Last accessed January 15 2020.

Redmond, R. (2017) "Paul Merson has made another blunt prediction about Marco Silva". *Joe.co.uk*. Published 31 May 2017. Online url = https://www.joe.co.uk/sport/paul-merson-marco-silva-watford-premier-league-prediction-137015. Last accessed January 15 2020.

Robinson, J. (2016) "An American soccer coach in England learns to speak British". *Wall Street Journal*. December 19 2016. Online url = https://www.wsj.com/articles/an-american-soccer-coach-in-england-learns-to-speak-british-1482163229. Last accessed January 15 2020.

Samuel, M. (2006) "His face may not fit, but McLaren knows that England will be a better team with Venables." *The Times*Published May 24 2006. p. 76.

Smith, R. (2016) *Mister: The Men Who Gave the World the Game*. UK, London: Simon & Schuster.

Tobitt, C. (2018) "National newspaper ABCs: Metro climbs above The Sun's total circulation as Mirror and Telegraph titles post double-digit drops". *Press Gazette*. Published 15 March 2018. Online url = https://www.pressgazette.co.uk/national-newspaper-abcs-metro-climbs-above-the-suns-total-circulation-as-mirror-and-telegraph-titles-post-double-digit-drops/. Last accessed July 13 2020.

Tolson, A. (2016) "'Proper football people': Talking soccer on sky sports news". *Discourse, Context & Media*. 11, pp. 12–18. Published online: https://doi.org/10.1016/j.dcm.2015.12.003/.

Tyers, A. (2017) "Should Leicester City appoint a British manager who 'knows the league' if they want to avoid relegation?". *Daily Telegraph*. Published 27 February 2017. Online url = https://www.telegraph.co.uk/football/2017/02/27/should-leicester-city-appoint-british-manager-knows-league-want/. Last accessed January 15 2020.

Wagg, S. (1986) "Naming the guilty men: Managers and media", in G. Whanneland, A. Tomlinson, eds., *Off the Ball: The Football World Cup*. London: Pluto Press.

Winter, H. (2003) "Head-hunters lost in MBA jungle looking for new chief". *The Daily Telegraph*. Published 4 March 2003. Online url = https://www.telegraph.co.uk/sport/columnists/henrywinter/2397326/Talking-Football-Head-hunters-lost-in-MBA-jungle-looking-for-new-chief.html. Last accessed May 18 2020.

Index

Page numbers followed by "n" refers notes numbers

ableism 63
AC Milan 180
academia 2–4, 11, 22, 29, 32, 39–40, 57, 59, 76, 88–90, 100, 109
Adorno, Theodor 2–3
aesthetics 1, 4, 26, 32–33, 60; spectacle 164; violence 40
affective labour 27, 31, 54
agency 4, 11, 15, 41, 43, 45, 47
aggression 33, 35, 39–42, 44–47, 63–65, 110, 131, 140
Alexander-Arnold, Trent 150
Algonquin peoples 52, 56–57
alienation 110, 118
Allardyce, Sam 170, 178, 180–181
allegory 110, 118
Allison, George 95
Alonso, Xabi 144
anarchism 26, 28–29, 33–34
Anfield 150
Anishinaabe Odawa First Nation 51–52
anomie 39
anthropophony 53–54
anticapitalism 31
anti-communism 134
antifascism 26–29, 31, 34, 35, 126
archiving and databases 92
Ardiles, Osvaldo 15
Argentina 4, 15, 98, 109–112; economic collapse (2001) 109
Arnold, Matthew 3
Arsenal FC 95, 96, 179
art 1–2, 11, 29, 31, 57, 78, 90, 95, 111, 125, 132
AS Monaco 180
association football *vs.* other varieties 90; American football 40, 61, 90; Canadian football 61
Aston Villa 181
athletics 90, 94
Atlético Madrid Femenino 73
austerity 108
Australia 3, 4, 71–84, 90, 99; Australian Women's National Soccer Team ('Matildas') 71; Indigenous Australians 78; National Indigenous Football championship 78; Westfield W-League 71, 75, 78, 79
Austria 93, 126, 176
authenticity 118, 142–145, 160, 162–166, 173, 175–182; 'Proper Football Man' (PFM) 170–171, 174–182
authority 28, 30–31, 111
autonomous zones 27, 42
Ayestaran, Pako 146

Bakhtin, Mikhail 63, 146
Balmforth, David 171
Barthes, Roland 57
basketball 60, 77, 94, 126
Basque region 90
Batley, Ethyle 95
Bayern Munich 27, 144
Beckham, David 76
Belgium 36n1, 93, 131; Heysel Stadium disaster (1985) 132
Bent, Geoff 157, 159
black market 129
blogging 141
bodies 4, 11–22, 26, 33, 40, 41, 45, 48n6, 53, 55, 56, 65, 82, 111, 116, 158; ATP 59; disability 63, 76; embodiment and group identity 12–22
Borota, Peter 125
Borussia Dortmund 27
Bosnia 110

Bourdieu, Pierre 11
boxing 90, 94
Bozsik, József 98
Bradley, Bob 179
Branner, Per-Axel 96
Brazil 3, 4, 39–48
Brentford FC 95, 96
Brexit 87, 102
Brisbane Roar FC (W-League) 75
British Empire 172
British Industrial Revolution 2–3
Bruce, Steve 181
Bundesliga 26, 35
Burkenshaw, Keith 15
Burnley FC 180
Bush, George 111
Butler, Judith 117
Bytown Boys Supporters Club 4, 60–62

Caine, Michael 99
Canada 3, 4, 51–67; history 51–52
Cantona, Eric 5, 108, 113–119; 'kung fu' incident (1995) 113
capitalism 2, 26, 110, 133; 2008 global recession 108; gig economy 118
Cappello, Fabio 176
carnival 146–147
Carragher, Jamie 144
cascading activation 175, 177
Castro, Fidel 109
Cavallo, Domingo 109
celebrity 145, 171
centre/periphery 3, 14
Chadha, Gurinder 76, 99–100
Champions League 64, 150
Chapman, Herbert 128
charity 150
Charlton, bobby 157, 160–161
Chávez, Hugo 109
cheerleading 46
Chelsea 180, 181
child development 109–110
China 76, 163
Christmas 61
class 2–3, 19, 32, 39
Cliftonville FC 87
Coakley, Jay 11
Cold War 172
Coligay 46–47
collective identity 2, 5, 12–22, 34–36, 56, 58, 60–61; belonging 11–22, 35, 36, 57, 58, 117–118, 177; cosmopolitan musical bonding 58, 66; deindividuation 34, 42; identity fusion 22, 39, 42; tribalism 18, 22, 117–118; *see also* crowds
Collins, Jackie 99
colonialism 3, 51, 56
comics 126
commemoration 154–166
communism 18, 98, 126, 128, 132, 134, 135
competition and conflict 40, 41
Conte, Antonio 180
Cooper, Arthur Melbourne 95
counterculture 28–30
cricket 73, 89
criminology 1
Croatia 134
Croise, Hugh 95
crowds 4, 25–26, 28, 30–35, 41, 42, 44, 46, 57, 59, 63–65, 73, 74, 127, 133; neoliberal ambivalence towards 34
Crowe, Russell 77
Cruzeiro Esporte Clube 44
Crystal Palace 94, 113, 181
Cuba 109
Curling, Chris 100–101
cycling 90, 94
Cyprus 36n1
Czech Republic 93
Czechoslovakia 92, 136
Czibor, Zoltán 98

dance 111
dark tourism 158
deindustrialisation 115, 133
Denmark 93
deprivation 132
Derby County 129, 178
Di Stéfano, Alfredo 98
Dickinson, Thorold 95
digital media 5
disease 14, 19–21, 63
documentary 72, 76, 78–81, 97, 108–112, 114
drug abuse 109, 111, 112
Duggan, Amy 77
Dundee United 20
Dyche, Sean 180
Dyke, Greg 177

East Germany (GDR) 89
eBay 163
education 3
Edwards, Duncan 5, 154–167
Edwards, Harry 11
EEC 99

Elvey, Maurice 94
Emery, Unai 179–180
Emmett, EVH 95
England 5, 27, 73, 76, 101, 109, 111, 125–152, 155–159, 170–174, 176, 179–180, 182; 'Englishness' 170–182; 'Little Englander' mentality 174, 180, 181; 1996 World Cup win 172
English Football League 177, 178
English Premier League (EPL) 5, 64, 113, 119, 140, 143, 149, 151, 170–182; broadcasting rights 174; globalisation 140, 178; revenue 140, 174
Ericsson, Sven Goran 176
ethnic conflict 133
ethnicity 27, 56, 76–77, 100, 133
ethnography 1, 16, 29, 44, 52, 60, 80
ethnomusicology 3, 4, 22, 26, 52, 53, 66n4–66n7
European championships 176
European cinema 87–102
European Cup 156
European Union (EU) 99, 102
Eurovision network 128
Evans, Shadeene 78
Everton FC 145–147, 179

Fábio (Fábio Deivson Lopes Maciel) 44
Falklands War/Malvinas War 109
family 166
fandom 1, 4, 5, 18, 20–22, 26–32, 36n1, 39, 108–119, 129, 132, 133, 136n7, 140–167; corporate co-optation 61–62; cultural contradictions 118, 119; cultural production 54–55, 141–151; cultural representation 76; death and bereavement 160, 161, 164; enculturation 35; 'executive fans' 145; fandom experience 146–147; gatekeeping 162–163, 166; hierarchies 154; pilgrimages 158; 'produsage' 144; professionalisation 142–143; psychodynamic investment 108–112, 117–118; representation 143; ritual and tradition 2, 4, 35, 56; transnational 140, 142, 147–151; '*ultras*' 4, 25–36, 39, 53, 133, 149
fantasy 108, 112–119; ambiguity 113
fanzines 5, 132, 141, 144, 151
fascism 16, 17, 97, 101
FC Barcelona 98
FC Barcelona Femení 73
FC United of Manchester 117
fear 32–35, 43, 44, 47; anxiety 173; ecologies of fear 32–33
Ferdinand, Rio 162
Ferhatović, Asim ('Hase') 132
FIFA 61, 72, 75, 76, 109, 111, 127, 129, 148, 149
figure skating 94
film 4–5, 71–119; audiences 80, 91; history 90–102; production 92, 93, 98, 99
film studies 88–91
films 76–78, 80–81, 84, 87, 88, 90, 91, 93–97, 125
Finland 93, 99
Fitzhamon, Lewin 94
FK Partizan 131
flags 133–134
folklore 65
football: commercialisation 26, 29, 36, 117–118, 144; commodification 36, 119, 164; corruption 43; global spread 3; history 2–3, 128–135; management 39, 43, 170–182; as mediator 101–102, 131, 171; metaphor 14–22; origins 173; styles 109, 110, 173
Foucault, Michel 40, 114
Foulkes, Bill 156
Fowler, Robbie 162
France 20, 72, 87, 89, 90, 93, 99, 113, 131, 179, 180
France Ligue Un 180
Franco, Francisco 97, 98, 101
Freud, Sigmund 108, 110, 111, 117
FSV Optik Rathenow 25

G20 summit 2017 30
Galo (Clube Atlético Mineiro) 44
gambling 6, 61, 143
Garland, Judy 15
gender 4, 39–48, 71–84, 99–100, 114–117, 175; female athletes as 'misfits' 81; female athletes sexualised 74; femininity 75, 76, 115; homoeroticism 115, 117; homophobia 4, 26, 31, 42, 44, 47, 48n9; International Day of the Girl 81; media production 83, 95; masculinity 4, 35, 42, 45, 76, 114–118; mentorship 82; misogyny 42, 80; performance 42–45, 117; women footballers in media 72–84; women's football, history 73, 82; women's football, lack of support 71, 72, 81–82

German Football Association 27
Germany 3, 4, 87, 89, 92–94, 97, 101, 131, 148; cinema 97; FC Saint Pauli 4, 25–36; Hamburg 25–36; Munich air disaster 5, 154–167; Nazi regime 97, 101
Gil, Gaucho 110
Giulianotti, Richard 11, 146
Glasgow Celtic (Celtic FC) 16–21, 36n1, 113, 129, 167n2
Glasgow Rangers (Rangers FC) 16–17, 19–21, 22n3, 129, 180
Glentoran FC 87
globalisation 1, 40, 89, 140, 143–144, 149, 170, 173–174, 178, 181–182; 'glocalisation' 127–130; ticket prices 26, 27, 30, 150, 152n2
goalkeepers 44, 55, 63, 87, 94, 97, 131
Goodison Park 150
graffiti 28–30, 150
graves 159–160
Greece 77, 90, 129, 131
Gregg, Harry 156, 160–161
Gremio 46
Grosics, Gyula 98
gymnastics 90, 94

Habsburg Empire 125
Hall, Stuart 2, 26, 32
Hamburg SV 27
health 1, 19–21, 59, 63, 118, 158, 173; injury 158; *see also* bodies
Hebdige, Dick 11, 27, 36
Henderson, Jordan 144
heroes: hero-worship 108–119, 157; journalistic myth 175–177, 182; social construction 156–157, 163–166
heteronormativity 42–3, 45, 47, 117
Hidegkuti, Nándor 98
Hobsbawm, Eric 56
hockey 60, 64, 94
Hoddle, Glenn 180
Hodgson, Roy 144, 176, 178, 181
Hollywood 53, 81, 82, 89, 90, 113, 126
hooliganism 1, 3, 22, 26, 32, 53, 62, 129, 133, 134, 141; performativity 32; spectacle 129
Horkheimer, Max 2–3
Horler, Sydney 95
Hornby, Nick 99
horseracing 74, 90, 93, 94
HŠK Građanski Zagreb 127
Hughes, Mark 178
Hull City AFC 170, 177–178
Hungary 89, 93, 98, 127; Rákosi regime 98
Huston, John 98–99
Hyundai A-League 75

Iceland 93, 99, 172
idealisation 108
identity 65, 76, 154, 170–182; national identity 170, 172–174; *see also* collective identity
imagined community 177
IMF 111
imperialism 3
improvisation 53, 61
infinity 72, 78, 82–83
in-group *vs.* out-group 177, 179
Internet 141–142, 151, 154–157, 164
intertextuality 15, 18, 21
interwar period 127
Ipswich Town 178
Iraq War 40–41
Ireland 16, 17, 56, 90, 93, 100, 102n1, 130, 146–148, 175, 178, 180; Irish Free State 130
Israel 36n1, 76
Italy 3, 77, 93, 98, 99, 109, 129, 130, 136n7, 176, 179, 180

Japan 75
Jesus 110–112
journalism 29, 72–73, 83, 95, 113, 128, 130, 143, 145, 147, 150, 151, 170–182; fake news 165–166; gender imbalance 83; myths/archetypes 175–176; newspapers 94, 96, 98, 126, 128, 171, 176, 177; punditry 175, 177, 180–181
juvenile delinquency 39

Kane, Harry 172, 173
Keleti, Márton 98
Keller, Helen 63
Kerr, Sam 73
kits 129
Klein, Melanie 116
Knowles, Beyoncé 61
Kocsis, Sándor 98
Kubala, Ladislao 98
Kusturica, Emir 110–111, 119

La Liga 64
Lampard, Frank 178, 181

language and rhetoric 125, 148–150, 179; Algonquian languages 52; banter 58, 61, 64, 134; conceptual metaphor 12–21; guilt and blame 171–172; hate speech 16, 63; insults 42–44, 146; jocularity 44–45, 58, 61; language communities 56; linguistics 12–22; modes of communication 13–14; multimodal communication 14, 16–17, 21, 53; scapegoats 175–176, 181; semiotics 11, 13–14; silence 61; swearing/cursing 42–44, 47, 64; 'tricksters' 175–176, 179; victimhood 180–182
latency games 110
Latvia 93
Laverty, Paul 91, 112–113
League of Ireland 18
Leeds United 95, 114, 115, 129
legitimacy 21, 32, 36, 45–47, 161
Leicester city 179
Levinas 72, 78–80
Lévi-Strauss 59
LGBT fandom 46–47
liberalism 34, 36
liminality 109, 110
literature 126
Liverpool FC 5, 20, 129, 134, 141–152; Spirit of Shankly movement 150
Loach, Ken 91, 99, 108, 112–119
Lumière Brothers 87, 90

Macedonia 127
macropolitics 45–46
magazines 128
magical realism 113
Manchester City 15, 20, 87, 95, 101, 102, 163
Manchester United 5, 18, 20, 95, 108, 113–115, 117, 119, 129, 146, 155–166; Busby Babes 5, 18, 154, 157–166; Glazer family takeover (2005) 117
Maradona, Diego 5, 108–112, 118, 119; 'Hand of God' incident (1986) 109, 110
marketing 27, 40, 61, 113, 140
marketisation 61, 113, 119
martial arts 46, 90
Marxism 132
match attendance 73–74, 96, 145
Mazzarri, Walter 179
McLaren, Steve 176–177
media 39, 113, 140
media audiences and reception 83, 171
memory 155; collective 174
Menem, Carlos 109
mental health 59, 67n9, 82, 112
merchandising 27, 30, 129, 140, 143; scarves, caps and t-shirts 129–131, 159, 163
Meredith, Billy 95
Merson, Paul 170, 177–178
micropolitics 45–46
migration 98; forced migration 56; immigration 16, 34, 77, 99, 102; Syrian refugee crisis 34
Minnesota United 63–64
Mitropa Cup 127
modernisation 118
Moore, Bobby 99, 157, 173
morality 3, 17, 18, 27, 32–34, 57, 97, 98, 108, 110, 113, 157, 175; moral panic 3, 32
motor racing 94
Moyes, David 178, 181
multiculturalism 77
music 2–5, 54, 57, 61, 111, 125, 131–132, 134, 135; AC/DC 31; Beatles, The 126; Bieber, Justin 63; Cock Sparrer 134; community formation 60; conga 15; drumming 59; folk-rock 53; gangster rap 53; hip-hop 26, 28, 53; indie 53; Iron Maiden 133; jazz 126; Lennon, John 61; McCartney, Paul 61; meaning 54–55; New Primitivism (Yugoslavia) 132; new wave 53, 131, 134; Oi! 131, 134; pitch 17; pop 2, 131; protest songs 40; punk 26, 27, 29, 31, 33–34, 132, 134, 141; rock 126, 132; Rolling Stones 126; samba 46, 56; techno 28; Ton Stein Scherben 33–34; tonality 21; torture 41–44
myth 5, 170–182

narcissism 5, 108, 110–111, 114–116, 118
nationalism 1, 5, 28, 33, 77, 170–182
nationality 56, 102
neoliberalism 30, 31, 36, 40, 109, 112, 113, 118; precarity 40; privatisation 118; as violence 31
Netherlands 93, 131
Neville, Gary 162
Neville, Phil 179
Newcastle United 19, 21, 129, 181
newsreels 94–96
Nicholson, John 170–171, 181
Nicklin, Frank 171
North American Soccer League 59–60, 65
Northern Ireland 16, 19, 87, 130

Norway 93
nostalgia 5, 27, 171, 173

object relations psychoanalysis 5, 108, 110
Oedipal stages 109–110, 116
Old Trafford 161
Olympic Games 90, 97, 130, 173
Orange Order 16
Ottawa Fury FC 4, 52–67
Ottoman Empire 125
Owen, Michael 162

Paris St Germain 180
parody 45, 77, 114
Pearson, Nigel 181
Pelé 80, 99, 157
pelota 90
performance 46, 65; breaking norms 47, 77, 128, 140; participatory performance 30–31, 33–35, 52–65
phenomenology 12, 52, 53
platforming 55–56
play 109–110
podcasts 5, 141–151, 155
Poland 93
police 4, 25–39, 43, 114, 134, 150–151; police violence 25–26, 28, 31, 33, 35, 43, 150–151
populism 109
Portugal 93, 170, 177
postmodernism 11, 112
post-War period 127
power 3, 5, 17, 28, 31–35, 40, 41, 45, 47, 51, 61, 65, 75, 82, 90, 98, 109, 119, 135, 151, 175; state power 28, 30–33, 35, 114–115, 126–127
Presley, Elvis 116, 117
propaganda 97
propriety/decency 63–64, 159–163
protest 5, 27–28, 31, 35–36, 39, 40, 42, 43
psychoanalysis 5, 108–119; intentionality 55, 65
public discourse 141
Puel, Claude 179
Pulis, Tony 178
Puskás, Ferenc 98
pyrotechnics 26, 28, 30, 32–35, 133

race 41
racism 19, 26, 31, 65, 133, 181
radical fandom 30–31
radio 96, 125–128
Ramsey, Alf 172
Real Madrid CF 98
Redknapp, Harry 176, 178, 179
referees 14, 42–44, 63; unfair decisions 42–43, 47
regional identity 1, 21, 45, 89, 133, 140
reification 145
religion 19, 41, 59, 110–112, 133, 157, 160
resilience 35, 45
resistance 61–62, 111, 118
revolution 45–46
Richards, Micah 181
Riefenstahl, Leni 97
rivalry 39, 41, 43, 45, 47
Romania 93, 127
Ronaldo 80
Ros, Edmundo 15
rugby 40, 44, 89
Russia 93

Sandhausen, S.V. 33
Scandinavia 147
science 59
Scotland 3, 16–17, 19, 36n1, 130
Scott, Alex 181
sectarianism 16–17, 19–20, 133
self/other 4, 11–23, 45, 78–80, 108, 111, 116–118, 174–177
Serbia 93, 127, 134
Sevilla FC 150
Sex Pistols 111
sex work 29
sexism 26, 74, 80, 81
Shankly, Bill 150
Sheffield United 181
Shelbourne FC 18
Sherwood, Tim 171, 179
Silva, Marco 170, 177–178
SK Jugoslavija 129
skiing 90, 94
slavery 18, 56
Slovakia 93
Slovenia 93
Smith, Dean 181
smuggling 129
social breakdown 39
social inequality 132
social media 140, 149, 151, 155, 164; Facebook 149, 154, 161; Twitter 149, 154, 181
social realism 112–113, 115, 117, 118
solidarity 5, 108, 113–115
song and chant 3–4, 11–36, 40–47, 134; physiological response 59; socially situated 14–22; *see also* music

sonic sanctioning 62, 66
sonic weapons 39–47
sonorities 43, 45, 52
South Korea 75
Spain 23n7, 89, 90, 93, 97–99, 101, 150, 179; cinema 97–98
space/spatiality 13–15, 20–21, 40, 41; control 28, 30; gentrification 28–29, 35; place 56–57; sound 41, 61–62; urban space 35, 133
sponsorship 143–144, 162–163
sport and allegory 91–92, 96
sports cinema 88–102
squats 28
SSC Napoli 109
Stalin, Joseph 126
Stallone, Sylvester 99
stance 54–55
stars 5, 108–119, 172, 173
state violence 43
Stein, Jock 113–114
Stemmle, Robert Adolf 97
stock market 113
Stony Monday Riot (group) 4, 51–67; history 60
subculture 5
Sunderland AFC 19, 21, 178
superego 110, 115
surveillance 30–31, 114–115, 118
survival strategies 47
sustainability 59
Swansea City 179
Sweden 3, 93, 96, 131
swimming 94
Switzerland 93, 127, 176
Sydney FC (W-League) 75
Syria 30

team spirit 59
technology 56, 59, 79–80
television 4–5, 14–16, 27, 64, 71, 74–84, 88, 91, 112, 117, 118, 127, 128, 131, 140, 146, 147, 150, 171, 172, 174, 178; match broadcasts 71, 74–76, 96, 118, 127, 147, 174; reality TV 77; television series 72, 76–83
tennis 89, 90
territoriality 42, 61–62, 65
Terry, John 173
Thatcher, Margaret 111
The Anfield Wrap 141–151
Thomas, Mike 161–162, 164–165
Thomson, Phil 170, 177
time 65–66
totality 72, 78–84
Tottenham Hotspur 15, 129, 171, 179, 180
trademark/copyright infringement 129
trauma 41, 44, 114
Trautmann, Bert 87, 100–101
Turkey 30, 93
Tyers, Alan 170–171, 178

UEFA 16, 64, 129, 147
UK 3; Conservative Party 112; film 87–96, 125; 1926 General Strike 112; Hillsborough Disaster (1989) 147, 150; imaginary landscape 88, 96; Jewish community 101; Labour Party 18, 112, 115, 125; National Front 134; popular culture 125–126, 128–129, 131–135; Punjabi Sikh community 99–100; Queen's Diamond Jubilee 173; social inequality 108, 112
Ukraine 93
UN Human Rights commission 43
unemployment 132
UNESCO 51
United Nations 43
Unsworth, David 179
Uruguay 127
US 4, 99, 148; film 87; hegemony 109, 126, 127; National Women's Soccer Team 73; Tea Party Movement 174–175
USSR 92–94, 98, 126; Cominform 126

vandalism 39, 163
Venables, Terry 157, 176–177
Venezuela 109
verticality 14, 17–19
violence 1, 3, 25–36, 39–40, 64–65, 133; constitutive of society 40; enjoyable 36; fighting 25, 32, 39, 46, 57, 98; mediated by sound 42–43, 45; police violence 25–26, 28, 31, 33, 35, 43, 150–151

Wales 93, 130
war 14–18, 21, 39, 41, 43, 53, 97, 99, 101, 109, 126–128, 130, 134, 158, 173, 178; 'shock and awe' 40–41
Watford FC 178, 179, 181
Weber, Max 11
Wembley 130, 172
West Germany (FRG) 92, 101
West Ham United 16, 178, 181
white supremacism 56, 172, 181
Whiteside, Norman 162

Wilder, Chris 181
Wilkins, Ray 180
Williams, Raymond 2, 11
Women's World Cup 61, 71, 72, 76
World Cup 58, 75, 109, 127, 148, 149, 157, 171–173
World War I 127, 158
World War II 97–99, 101, 126, 129, 134, 173
wrestling 57, 90, 95

xenophobia 175–177, 179

youth 109
YouTube 141
Yugoslav Football Association 130
Yugoslavia 5, 92, 93, 125–136; history 125–135; New Primitivism 132